Also available at all good book stores

9781801500630

9781801500067

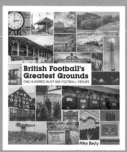

9781785316470

9781801500975

9781801500968

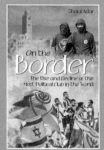

9781801500951

9781801500920

9781801500937

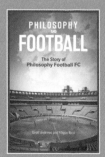

9781801501064

From Kids to

CHAMPIONS

From Kids to

CHAMPIONS

*The History of
the FA Youth Cup*

JONNY BRICK

First published by Pitch Publishing, 2022

Pitch Publishing
9 Donnington Park,
85 Birdham Road,
Chichester,
West Sussex,
PO20 7AJ
www.pitchpublishing.co.uk
info@pitchpublishing.co.uk

A CIP catalogue record is available for this book
from the British Library.

ISBN 978 1 80150 091 3

Typesetting and origination by Pitch Publishing

Printed and bound in India by Replika Press Pvt. Ltd.

Contents

Acknowledgements

WHEN I had the idea for this book in spring 2021, all I had to go on was an online encyclopaedia entry for the competition. Jane Camillin at Pitch gave me the green light and I set about researching the FA Youth Cup.

You can tell it's a Pitch book because the cover was designed by Duncan Olner. I think Duncan's arrangement of the photos makes the book pop off the shelf or the webpage and into your hands. Thanks to Gareth Davis and Graham Hales for spotting some errors in the first draft.

The folk who helped me to tell the story were very generous with their time and knowledge. Merv Payne told me of Millwall's exploits. Rocco Dean did the same with Leeds United, and Neil Heaney took my call from his office and told me all about growing up at Arsenal.

Ian Doyle's 35 years on the Mersey beat helped to contextualise football up in the north-west. Lee Fowler was open and honest, emphasising the importance of the semi-pro game and the bad luck that befell Coventry City at the turn of the century. Thanks also to Tom Everett at the English Football Association for providing a quotation.

Tom Hart gave me a glimpse inside the next generation of Hornets. His team gave a performance against Chelsea that speaks volumes for how he trains them to be the best they can be, even against some top young players in Chelsea shirts. Nigel Gibbs, Mr Watford, filled me in on his life and times, while Rio Campbell brought me up to date with a young player's current perspective.

Personal thanks go to Mum and Dad, without whom I wouldn't be here, and to my brother Richard, who was a strong opponent in garden football, and various editions of *FIFA*.

Without Vanessa Mae, I would probably have procrastinated much more than I did.

Finally, to all the guests who popped into the Football Library in its first two years of existence, I hope that one day we can meet up at a ground near you.

Introduction

OPORTO, 29 May 2021; 41 minutes and 50 seconds into the UEFA Champions League Final.

Chelsea's Mason Mount receives the ball about five yards inside his own half. With the Manchester City defenders choosing to get back into position rather than close Mount down, he takes a touch and lifts his head up.

As the ball leaves his right foot, there are six City players between the ball and the goal. They include John Stones, who has dropped back to play Kai Havertz onside. Timo Werner has run towards the left touchline, which drags Rúben Dias across. Dias, the Football Writers' Association choice for the 2020/21 Player of the Year award in his first season in England, loses a vital nanosecond. Oleksandr Zinchenko is left to mark Havertz but is a yard behind the play when the ball is delivered.

Havertz lets the ball go in front of him and, 25 yards from goal, sees Ederson sprint towards him. All he has to do is touch the ball to Ederson's right. The goalkeeper actually handles the ball, so a red card is certain if the ball sprays to safety. It does not, but something far worse happens.

In the first UEFA Champions League Final in which Havertz and every Chelsea player on the pitch has played (Thiago Silva, a 2020 finalist with Paris Saint-Germain, had gone off five minutes before through injury), the lad born in Aachen, Germany in 1999 rolls the ball into the empty net with his left foot. Mount gets the assist.

There are no further goals in the game.

Reece James dashes over from right-back to celebrate. Both he and Mount were also born in 1999. James captained Chelsea's under-18 side to the FA Youth Cup in 2017/18, a season in which the team scored 85 goals and lost three games across the two stages of the league season.

In the two-legged final, James's team-mates included Tariq Lamptey, Billy Gilmour, Jon Panzo and Conor Gallagher. Gallagher, a used substitute in the first leg and an unused one in the second, spent 2020/21 on loan at West Bromwich Albion but could not keep his side in the Premier League. Lamptey had been doing well at Brighton & Hove Albion (for whom he had signed permanently) before injury. As for Panzo, who was born in 2000, he moved to Monaco in 2018 but, with his path to the first team blocked, signed for Dijon in 2020. They finished rock bottom of Ligue 1 with only four wins.

To return to his old team-mate: the reason Mount missed out on the 2017/18 final was because he was playing in the Eredivisie for Vitesse, Chelsea's feeder club in the Netherlands. In any case, Mount had won the FA Youth Cup twice already, with both the 2015/16 and 2016/17 teams. He played alongside Fikayo Tomori and Tammy Abraham in the former win, and with Callum Hudson-Odoi in the latter.

Tomori was away from Chelsea in spring 2021, having been loaned to AC Milan, who finished second in Serie A; the other two players were both part of the travelling party to Oporto, though only Hudson-Odoi joined Gilmour, James and Mount in the matchday squad. They join the ranks of English talent who have both a UEFA Champions League medal and an FA Youth Cup one.

Collecting runners-up medals for Manchester City in 2017 were Phil Foden and Jadon Sancho, as well as Tom Dele-Bashiru who would sign for Watford in 2019. While the last of these has played for Nigeria at age-group levels, Foden and Sancho have already played key roles as full internationals. They were both born in 2000, nine weeks apart; by their 21st birthdays they had both made over 50 appearances at club level, Sancho making over 130 in three seasons as a first-team player at Borussia Dortmund. The pair helped England secure qualification for the UEFA Euro 2020 tournament, where injury cost Foden an appearance in the final.

Another man in that losing Manchester City side was Brahim Díaz, who would train with his foe Tomori at AC Milan while on loan from Real Madrid, who found him surplus to requirements.

For all the talk about 'Pep's Citizens' or 'Tuchel's Blues', with a modern focus on the system-driven managers who led their teams to the Champions League Final, it was the English players who provided a great hook to begin a story about the FA Youth Cup. Mount and James will cherish the night they won the biggest prize in European football, as will Gilmour, Abraham and Hudson-Odoi. As they received their medals, perhaps they all thought of a youth team coach or family member who had set them on the path to professional triumph and international glory.

Gilmour won that medal before going on to win a full cap for Scotland. He went into Euro 2020 as a member of the first-team squad, perhaps offering some hints and tips about his club team-mates in advance of a group game between England and Scotland. Predictably, he was loaned to Norwich City at the start of the 2021/22 season, where he was embroiled in a tough relegation battle.

Like Sancho, Foden or Mount, Gilmour's story may end with the FIFA World Cup. Foden has already won two Premier League medals and took over David Silva's slot in the squad full of superstars up in east Manchester. Yet a key plot point to his story may well be that FA Youth Cup runners-up medal.

As you find a comfortable seat for this story, here is what you are going to read.

The first chapter heads back to the 1950s and the initial domination of the FA Youth Cup by Manchester United. Chelsea will enjoy their own first flush of success in the 1960s.

In the second chapter, the story moves into the 1970s where a panoply of sides do well, from Sunderland and Tottenham to Aston Villa and Coventry City. I talk to a man who came through the Coventry academy who has lessons on how to develop young talent.

Chapter Three leaps forward to the first few rounds of the 2021/22 FA Youth Cup, as I head to games featuring Barnet and AFC Wimbledon. Discussion of underdogs will take in Millwall, with a fan of the club talking about their 1979 victory with a team of 'Ordinary Boys'.

Watford Football Club is the focus of Chapter Four as we hear from three figures: the club's under-18s coach; a player he coached who has since embarked on a professional career in Swansea; and the man known as 'Mr Watford' whose career has been dedicated to making the most out of his talents and those of younger players.

In Chapter Five, it's time to bring in Manchester City and Leeds United, who both won the Youth Cup in the period before Sky's money changed English football. Two clubs who benefitted from that new money are Manchester United and

Liverpool. They are paired in Chapter Six, in which a journalist from the *Liverpool Echo* details the Scouse kids who became champions, while the heirs to the Busby Babes repeat some famous feats.

Chapter Seven rounds up several clubs who have broken the hegemony of the elite few since 1992: Blackburn Rovers, Middlesbrough and Norwich City. Arsenal are under discussion in Chapter Eight, with useful memories from a player who was part of their 1988 Youth Cup side.

As the tournament welcomes the elite clubs at the third-round stage, two of the subjects in the story set up a tie in the next round, which dominates Chapter Nine.

The story ends with a Youth Cup All-Time XI, based on characters mentioned in the previous 75,000 words, which begin over the page.

Chapter One

The 1950s and the Busby Babes

ANDY AMBLER is the director of professional game relations for the English FA. You may recognise the name because he was CEO of Millwall Football Club when Michael Calvin was writing his extraordinary book, *Family*. Ambler moved eastwards along the River Thames when he became a director at Fulham when Mohamed Al-Fayed was the owner, but was appointed to a position at the FA that was invented just for him.

One staunch critic of the English FA, whose name may have been mentioned in that last paragraph, calls them 'unfit for purpose' with a 'notorious inability to act quickly and decisively'. The scandal surrounding abuse of young players has been followed by one concerning dementia. Could the status of the FA Youth Cup, albeit in an era when club academies are prevalent, act in the credit column?

Andy provided an answer when I asked the FA to praise their competition:

'The FA Youth Cup continues to provide a platform for many of this country's most promising football talents to develop, challenge themselves on a national level and state their case for promotion into both professional and international football.

'While youth football has undergone numerous changes since the competition was introduced in 1952, its status as the most desirable piece of silverware for under-18 teams in England remains 70 years on.

'The country's biggest clubs have achieved success at various stages throughout its history and teams such as the "Class of 92" are just one example of the potential springboard that it offers to this day.

'Only one of over 600 participating clubs from across the English football pyramid can take home the trophy but competing in elite youth knockout football is unparalleled for players of National League System and professional clubs alike.

'Regardless of their subsequent level and achievements, the experiences and memories gained from taking part in the competition will have lasting impacts.

'The talent pathway and youth development are integral to moulding a squad capable of winning international tournaments, and the role that the FA Youth Cup plays cannot be understated.'

Incredibly, the trophy itself, which you can see on this book's cover being held by Mason Mount, was sourced from the Football League, as the FA website illustrates on the page which introduces the competition to curious readers: 'On discovering it in a cupboard, gathering dust, it was handed over.'

The tournament's founding father is named as Sir Joe Richards, whose idea was turned down by the Football League six years before they invented their own domestic trophy. Sir Joe found favour with the FA who 'had the foresight to realise that here was an idea with legs'. This is unsurprising. The FA themselves had begun a Youth Championship in the 1940s, using their role as overseers of the county game rather than the professional leagues. The postwar boom in football led to more youth and reserve teams playing in club colours.

In 1937, just before establishing their junior athletic club, MUJAC, Manchester United played two former trainees in their match against Fulham. Since then, for almost 85 years and across 4,100 first-team matches, every fixture has included an academy graduate, something that impresses Nick Cox. He is the man who, as of the start of the 2021/22 season, is in charge of turning academy prospects into sellable assets or employees – from kids to champions.

'Our fans genuinely want to see local, home-grown players play in our first team,' he told Bill Edgar of *The Times*, himself a United fan. 'If you think back to the culture Sir Matt Busby tried to create, he made the point that people who pay to watch the team at the weekend have been grafting in the factories all week. They're local folk. This is their one release and we have a duty to entertain them and show them we're the same as them, but [who are] just privileged to be the people who are on the pitch. And I think when it's local boys who are on the pitch, that connection becomes even greater and more powerful.'

In the first few months of the 2019/20 season, Edgar notes, 38 out of every 100 minutes were played by an academy graduate, be they Scott McTominay, Jesse Lingard, Marcus Rashford, Paul Pogba (who left the club for Juventus but returned to mixed acclaim), Mason Greenwood, Brandon Williams or Andreas Pereira.

For Cox, a Manchester United person is always someone 'polite, humble, [who has] respect for people … Character is at the centre of everything. It doesn't matter what type of player you are, how skilful you are; character underpins whether you are going to be able to translate your ability when you are under pressure in the first team.'

As with the first lot of Fergie's Fledglings from the late 1980s and the 2011 FA Youth Cup side (Pogba, Lingard, Ravel Morrison, Will Keane et al), the young lads are aware of the Busby Babes. Entire books have chronicled the players or, in Duncan Edwards' case, one particular player. Zidane Iqbal became youth graduate number 246; the son of parents from Pakistan and Iraq, he has declared for the latter's youth teams internationally.

The first tie the Young Reds played in the 2021/22 FA Youth Cup, without Iqbal, took place at Old Trafford against Scunthorpe United, which the home side won 4-2. Fans were enticed to the game, which was also screened on MUTV, without having to pay on the gate, but rain was forecast for the evening and this may have put plenty off.

Just as Real Madrid ran away with the first five European Cups, so Manchester United were kings of the FA Youth Cup. They vanquished Wolverhampton Wanderers in both 1953 and 1954, winning 9-3 and 5-4 on aggregate respectively. The first six minutes of the first leg, held at Old Trafford, included three goals, and United were 3-1 up after a quarter of an hour. They added four goals in the second half and the first Youth Cup was as good as theirs.

The famous names in those sides included David Pegg and Eddie Colman, who both advanced to the first team having captained the youth side. Left-winger Pegg captained the 1954 team even though he was already a starter for the senior side, which won the First Division in 1956 and 1957. He replaced United's Youth Cup winner Wilf McGuinness in the team. Poor Wilf, who did not travel to Belgrade through injury having broken his leg, and avoided the subsequent tragedy in

Munich, famously succeeded Matt Busby as United manager in 1969 and lasted for 18 months.

Colman, meanwhile, scored four of United's seven goals across the two legs of the 1955 Youth Cup Final against a West Bromwich Albion side containing future United player Maurice Setters. Pegg played that game alongside many of the 1954 Youth Cup winners, including Duncan Edwards and Bobby Charlton. Albert Scanlon was also a left-winger who was pushing Pegg for his place in the team.

Chesterfield gave them a closer run in 1956 but could not prevent United achieving four wins in a row. A 3-2 victory at Old Trafford in the first leg was followed by a 1-1 draw. The tight game may have been attributable to the presence in the Chesterfield goal of future England number one Gordon Banks, who played a single season for the Spireites before Leicester City astutely spent £7,000 on him. He was also in goal when the Foxes lost 3-1 in the 1963 FA Cup Final against Manchester United.

In 1957, United won their fifth trophy thanks to a second-leg mullering of West Ham United. Three goals in six minutes, two of which came from Mark Pearson, saw United 6-2 up on aggregate after three-quarters of the tie. Alex Dawson scored twice more in the second half against a West Ham side that included the great John Lyall, the Hammers' version of Matt Busby or Bill Shankly, who enjoyed 15 years as manager and gave his name to the gates at the front of first Upton Park and then the club shop of the London Stadium.

David Gaskell played in that 1957 final and would go on to make his First Division debut later that year. Harry Gregg, who survived the plane crash on the Munich runway that killed many Youth Cup winners including Pegg and Colman, was the number one in the days when there was no goalkeeper (or indeed any other player) on the substitutes' bench. Mark Pearson suffered the same problem, coming in and out of the side for six seasons after he made his senior debut in February 1958.

Famous United youth coach Jimmy Murphy, himself the subject of a biography by Wayne Barton, took on first-team responsibilities while Matt Busby recovered from the crash. He also used 1955 Youth Cup winner Shay Brennan, yet another left-winger who was converted into a defender. He represented United for 13 seasons and was part of a huge contingent from the island of Ireland.

As well as Best, goalkeeper Pat Dunne was first choice for the 1964/65 First Division season, in which Tony Dunne (no relation) was usually the starting left-back. Noel Cantwell was an older squad player who retired after United won the 1966/67 league title, the year before Best and Brennan played in the 1968 European Cup Final. Pat Dunne had been displaced by Alex Stepney and left the club in the same season as Gaskell.

Mark Pearson had been sold to Sheffield Wednesday in 1963, two years after another promoted youngster, right-winger Kenny Morgans, moved back to his hometown team of Swansea City. According to his obituary, Busby had observed his 'prodigious pace and skill on the ball' in a Youth Cup match between United and Swansea. He gave Morgans his debut in December 1957 and took him to Belgrade for that ill-fated European Cup tie. Morgans was in hospital with his manager and Duncan Edwards, the Dudley-born prodigy who was a first-team player at United from the age of 16.

We will never know whether, ten years before United won their first European Cup, the 1958 tournament would have been won by them too. That United side would surely have lain in wait for Real Madrid, just as they had done the previous season when both teams met in the semi-finals of the European Cup in 1957. Alfredo Di Stéfano, Francisco Gento and Raymond Kopa were part of the side who beat United 3-1 in Madrid and drew 2-2 at Old Trafford to set up another final.

Tony Whelan remains a United employee, as the programme advisor for the club's academy. Having written a thesis on the Busby Babes and the club's youth policy in the 1950s, Whelan was a significant contributor to a book called *Growing Up with the Trinity* by Brendon McGuire. The author worshipped George Best, Denis Law and Bobby Charlton, the three kids-to-champions immortalised in bronze for tourists to snap themselves with on a visit to Old Trafford.

Busby's idea of running Manchester United was to have 'decent, dependable men around him', as McGuire writes. Whelan was welcomed into this environment, first as a junior pro in the year the men's team won the First Division in 1967. Back then, the coaches were John Aston and the aforementioned Wilf McGuinness. Their sons, John Jr and Paul respectively, both came through the United Academy too.

Whelan was taught to give the ball to a red shirt and to express himself with no fear of a mistake, in order, he says, to 'bring your talent out in the framework of the team'. The credo was 'Up together, back together'. The lads Whelan meets today are taught to 'protect it, this culture' because they are 'the guardian of that tradition'.

With Champions League knockout qualification secured in December 2021, interim Manchester United manager Ralf Rangnick brought on a couple of lads for their debut. One of them was Tom Heaton, who was first included in a matchday squad for United as third-choice keeper in 2007. Another was Charlie Savage, whose dad Robbie came through the academy in the early 1990s and is pictured on the front of this book.

Whelan says, 'On the field, it's always been about flair, imagination, attacking football, about getting players through the youth system from schoolboy age.' Instantly, Rangnick recognised the importance of the academy and, even if it was a dead rubber, continued the run which may well continue until the last football is kicked.

The hook for Colin Shindler's book *George Best and 21 Others* is that 17 members of the sides who met in the 1964 FA Youth Cup semi-final between the Manchester clubs went on to play for their respective first teams. City had beaten a tough Leeds United side featuring Peter Lorimer and Eddie Gray in the last eight, while United had beaten Barrow, Blackpool, Sheffield United and, in a throwback to those finals of the 1950s, Wolverhampton Wanderers in the quarter-final.

As well as Best, the United team included future Aston Villa mainstay Jimmy Rimmer in goal, wing-half John Fitzpatrick and centre-forward David Sadler. The son of the youth team trainer, John Aston Jr never returned to the club he loved after he was sold on. Bobby Noble captained the side but a car accident curtailed his potential.

For City, full-back Mike Doyle and inside-right Glyn Pardoe made a combined 925 senior appearances. The club were at the time in the Second Division while Busby was building his side which won the First Division and European Cup. In 1968, Manchester was the centre of the football world, with City winning the First Division but failing to be the main story in town. The great city, as Shindler writes, 'was on the way down, struggling to adjust to a post-war, post-industrial world'. The football was a saving grace.

Some 29,000 people attended the semi-final first leg, which was the first game between City and United that season after the former's relegation in 1963. The match at Maine Road pulled more fans than had attended the previous match played by the first team.

No film exists of either game but Shindler's recollections are excellent, even if he argues that 'the camera simply wouldn't be able to communicate the excitement' of the games, which were won 4-1 and 3-1 respectively by United. They took the trophy after beating Swindon Town in the final.

A combined eight players – three at United and five at City – had already represented their first teams. Pardoe played in a game two years prior when he was only 15. Just as incredible to note is that George Best had become a full international for Northern Ireland in between the two legs of the semi-final.

David Sadler recalls that Best would 'much rather play than train, so he was just doing what he loved doing. He played Saturday at 3pm, then on a Monday [the first semi-final leg], then on the Wednesday for Northern Ireland, then on the Thursday in the second leg of the Youth Cup and then on the Saturday again! It was just a given that he would play.'

Soon Best would be playing in front of 50,000 fans at Old Trafford. In 1970, Best would break Glyn Pardoe's leg in a derby match, something often forgotten in the eulogies of the winger, which are full of Best evading tackles rather than making them. Indeed, he was able to avoid four challenges from Mike Doyle, who was out for revenge, in the ten minutes after Pardoe was taken off on a stretcher.

After the Busby Babes came the Chelsea Kids. Many would go on to play for, and even manage, the national team. It is therefore a mystery to me why there is no celebration of these lads outside of the club. Perhaps the marketing department at Manchester United tapped into the Youth Cup far better than that of Chelsea's, which never ensures that the mighty team of the 1960s got their due. A simple reason would probably be the presence of manager Matt Busby and World Cup winner Bobby Charlton, both of whom survived the Munich air disaster but lived with regret for decades afterwards.

But for an absurd second leg in the 1959 final, Chelsea would have won three FA Youth Cups in a row. Credit goes to Wolverhampton Wanderers, who overturned a first-leg 5-1 defeat and won 6-1 at home in the second leg. After coming up against the Busby Babes in two finals, the Young Wolves (Cubs?) had won their first Youth Cup to add to the senior trophies gained in the 1950s, including back-to-back First Division titles in 1957/58 and 1958/59.

Unlike Chelsea or Manchester United, Wolves have not won the league since those glory days. Centre-forward Ted Farmer scored 28 goals in the 1960/61 First Division season as Wolves finished third behind Tottenham Hotspur and Sheffield Wednesday. Unfortunately, a broken leg put paid to Farmer's career and he moved into computer programming.

Chelsea bounced back from their Youth Cup Final defeat, employing talented youngsters such as Peter Bonetti, Bobby Tambling and Terry Venables. In the 1960 final they overcame Preston North End, whose winger Peter Thompson would play for England. That cup run began with victories over West Thurrock, Colchester and the unfortunate Ford United (today known as Redbridge FC), who in their first year of existence were beaten 11-0 in a replay.

Bonetti missed the first leg of the final, having kept two clean sheets in the quarter-final victory over Aston Villa and the two semi-final legs against Bristol City. Fortunately, in the second game, Tambling scored three and Gordon Bolland iced the cake with the other goal in a 4-1 win. Bolland scored in every game but one; sadly, he only played for Chelsea's first team twice. He went on to represent Millwall over 200 times.

Chelsea retained the Youth Cup in 1961, beating Everton in the final. Ron Harris played in every game while Venables was now captain, having also played for the first team. Peter Osgood and Alan Hudson, two of the characters written about by Rob Steen in his excellent book *The Mavericks*, also came through the Blues youth system in the 1960s.

Venables wrote in his 1994 memoir that he signed for Chelsea over West Ham, Arsenal and Tottenham, all four of whom he was training with.

'Stamford Bridge seemed more like a proper football ground should be, and Chelsea always felt more real because the players there were so young', he wrote, adding with historical irony that in the 1960s the pathway to the first team was unimpeded by older players. 'The big time seemed so close there that you could almost reach out and touch it.'

As you may imagine at a time when national service had not yet been abolished, there was a rank-and-file system at Chelsea. Venables was made to sweep the biggest stand at Stamford Bridge by himself, starting at the top and ensuring all rubbish was piled up at the bottom. He was 'covered in sweat and dust' while his team-mates laughed at a player brought down to size. Venables also relates the time he was keen to impress at training and caught up and ran alongside club captain Peter Sillett. The skipper told Venables not to run so fast 'or I'll smash your chest in'.

Although Venables could have been part of the West Ham team alongside Bobby Moore, Martin Peters and Geoff Hurst, he went for Chelsea where he played with many lads he knew from his time at England Schoolboys. Some of them formed part of Drake's Ducklings, named after manager Ted Drake, but as with Manchester United 30 years later this is a misnomer.

Brian Kidd would do the real work on the training ground with the Class of '92. This was done in the 1960s at Chelsea by Dick Foss, a former Chelsea player who as coach who drove the young lads on. 'He had great charisma and an aura of authority' according to Venables, but created 'a relaxed and friendly atmosphere.'

The Ducklings would win games by ten or 12 goals to nil, with lads progressing to the first team as teenagers. The young Blues were the subject of a piece by Chelsea historian Rick Glanvill on the club's website in 2020, which celebrated 80 years since the foundation of the youth policy under the aegis of Willie Birrell, whom Glanvill calls 'one of the club's great unsung heroes'.

Rather than spending vast amounts of money on first-team talent, Birrell wanted to bring in players who were 'young and open to ideas'. Wartime delayed his ambition until 1947, although in 1940 a Chelsea Juniors side containing future England coach Ron Greenwood lined up against Queens Park Rangers. Greenwood thought Birrell was 'an astute businessman [who] believed that a quick mind is as important as quick feet'.

That young side, rather than the ragtag reserves, would represent Chelsea in the London Combination League, in which they would meet Arsenal, West Ham United and Tottenham Hotspur. Those four clubs enjoyed a regular tussle for the title, though their cartel was broken by the triumph of Leicester City in 1958/59.

When it comes to the FA Youth Cup, there were battles between London and Merseyside in the 1960s. Liverpool lost to West Ham in the 1963 final, while Everton pipped Arsenal in 1965. George Scott was, to use the title of his memoir, the 'Lost Shankly Boy' whose book details his time in Liverpool's youth ranks, written with the help of writer and Liverpool fanatic Jeff Goulding. I spoke to Scott in May 2020, a year on from Liverpool's Champions League win.

'I'm sitting here with my loser's medal in front of me,' he said, sighing. 'We should have won it. There's no question about that. Every time I look at it, I feel gutted.

'I went on to play 108 games in the Central League for the reserve team and I was leading goalscorer for three consecutive years and [made] the most appearances by a mile. The problem was, there were no substitutes [in senior matches] and every player was an international and very rarely got injured, so you got very few chances.

'I was 12th man, travelling with the team, but you couldn't get on unless someone got sick.'

Liverpool won the first leg of the 1963 Youth Cup Final 3-1 at Anfield. Scott remembers, 'There were about 25,000 there. They were rebuilding the Anfield Road Stand at the time. We had a really good team [with] Tommy Smith and Bobby Graham. We beat them well but in both games they had a 17-year-old Harry Redknapp and a young lad called John Sissons, a well-known player, who was on the left wing for West Ham. I think he played in the FA Cup Final later on.

'Bill Shankly said to Tommy Smith, "He's too quick. I want him in the 'banned box' [subs' bench] within ten minutes." Tommy obliged and gave him a bit of a kick. As he hobbled off, he was indicating to the bench, "That number four's a psycho!"'

Redknapp wrote in one of his four memoirs that his team-mate Martin Britt 'bashed Smith all over the place'. 'That's not true,' says Scott flatly. 'Britt did break our hearts. He scored four in the second leg and one of them should have been disallowed by referee Jack Taylor. The cross came in from

Redknapp and our goalkeeper Rodney Swindlehurst caught it on the line and Britt bundled him into the net with the ball, a bit like Nat Lofthouse all those years ago [in the 1958 FA Cup Final for Bolton Wanderers]. Shankly was incandescent but that made all the difference.'

It actually squared the tie at 5-5, with a winner coming four minutes from the end. A report on the completely non-biased WHUFC.com notes that a Liverpool handball should have led to an early penalty for the home side. As for Britt's goal, it 'would never be awarded today'.

Both Sissons and Britt had been injured in the semi-finals 'but a combination of their own bravery and the hard work of physiotherapist Bill Jenkins got them both fit for the final. Wretchedly, Britt had to retire at 21 after only 35 games for West Ham and Blackburn Rovers, and never got the kudos awarded to Moore, Peters and Hurst, the three West Ham lads who won the World Cup.

'We let them off the hook in the second leg,' George Scott laments. Having won the first leg '4-1,' he says. There's no way we should have lost it. We only had ourselves to blame and we were really disappointed. No complaints, they won it fair and square. They came back from the dead and won the game. It would have been a nice thing to do to win it for the first time for Liverpool.

'The sad thing for me is that [in] the last minute of the first game, at the Kop end, I had a diving header which hit the underside of the bar and it bounced down on the line and came out. Those few inches is a lead of 4-1,' making it seem to me like the time when Ousmane Dembélé missed a chance to make it 4-0 to Barcelona in the 2019 Champions League semi-final. They lost the tie 4-3 and Scott would watch Liverpool win the competition a few weeks later.

Scott played as an inside-forward in his FA Youth Cup Final, wearing the number eight shirt and playing in front of Tommy Smith. Was Smith expected to advance to the first team?

'I played about 50 games in the reserve team with Tommy. I used to call him my minder! I was quite fast, skilful, quick, nippy, aggressive. I got kicked quite a lot. I was only five foot six, so Tommy used to come over and have a few words, quietly, and used to get me more space,' said Scott.

'He was a fantastic player, a man in a boy's body even from 15. He had the power and aggression and the confidence and he went on to be a club legend, quite deservedly.

'I don't think you could have a Tommy Smith today. He wouldn't survive! The referees and the game now are so controlled by television, 14 or 15 cameras. A hard player would get stuck in and he'd be booked. He would have to temper his game and change. There used to be a few like Tommy in my day, people who used to get stuck in. They were horrible but that was the game.

'We played in mud, floodlights, one camera if [any] at all. It was just as passionate. Crowds were just as big if not bigger.

'Today we've got lightweight boots and a lightweight ball. Every pitch is like Wembley used to be. Wembley was like a bowling green, like the Masters golf; every other pitch, when it got to October or November, the mud was down the middle and the only part of the pitch that was grass was the wings!

'I went to Melwood [Liverpool's training ground and academy] with Peter Moore, the chairman, about three years ago. I was amazed. When I was at Melwood there was one wooden hut and three pitches. One of them was like Wembley, which Shankly had had made for practice matches. You had the shooting boards which was innovative, hitting the ball against the board.

'Today there's plunge pools, a squash court, every modern facility. There's a five-star restaurant serving the most nutritious food, people on computers working out tactics. The whole thing is really top-notch now.'

George Scott's book has a cover with players lined up against a wall, some of them sitting on top of it. 'I remember Shankly told me to "stand up straight, son!" Ian St John was like a ballet dancer. The shirts were crimson, though it's more blue on the cover of the book.

'That photograph was in the foyer at Melwood along with a description of how it was two Franciscan friars, one called Mel and one called Wood, who set it up.'

We spoke just after the 2021 FA Youth Cup Final in which Aston Villa had beaten Liverpool. 'I watched the game and Liverpool were taken apart in the first half,' Scott says. 'The standard, I thought, was very high.'

We will come back to Liverpool and Chelsea, as well as Manchester United, later in the FA Youth Cup story. Turn the page to learn more about Sunderland, Coventry City and Aston Villa, who all had their glory days after England won the 1966 World Cup.

Chapter Two

The 1960s and Assorted Teams

THE STORY of the FA Youth Cup has its lead characters, whom we have just met. Manchester United started the 2021/22 competition in search of their 11th trophy, while Chelsea were trying to get into double figures. But there are many supporting roles in the tale, including a club who won the First Division three times in the 1890s and were the dominant side of their era.

Jonathan Wilson's next book will be on the Charlton brothers from Ashington, a former coal-mining town 15 miles north of Newcastle. Wilson himself is a proud Sunderland fan, although he was born after the emergence of the great side of the 1960s.

They represented the city a few years before Jim Montgomery's double save helped the Mackems win the 92nd FA Cup in 1973.

In the 1966 Youth Cup Final, an Arsenal team that included Pat Rice at right-back beat Sunderland, whose apprentices I suppose we must call the Young Black Kittens. Colin Todd was among the 11 who received runners-up medals, as were Bobby Kerr and Colin Suggett.

Todd, who was born in the mining village of Chester-le-Street, would set aside his love of Newcastle United to sign for a team who had a 'tradition for youth'. He won the First Division at Derby County as a player and gained 27 England caps in the 1970s at centre-back alongside, among others, Dave Watson.

Watson, in turn, was in that FA Cup-winning team alongside Kerr, who may well be captain of any Sunderland XI from across the history of the club. The man who recovered from two broken legs as a young player was the one who lifted the FA Cup and made over 400 appearances for the team, gaining the epithet 'The Little General'. It was a measure of the brilliance of that generation of Scottish talent that Kerr never gained an international cap.

That Sunderland 'Team of all Talents' from the 1890s was filled with Scots such as the captain Hughie 'Lalty' Wilson and goalkeeper John 'Ned' Doig. Pleasingly, there were Scots in the 1967 Youth Cup team too. Billy Hughes was an adopted Black Cat having moved down from Lanarkshire after a Sunderland scout convinced him to sign youth forms with them rather than Glasgow Celtic. Brother John was a Lisbon Lion who was denied by injury a spot in the Celtic team in the 1967 European Cup Final.

Suggett, meanwhile, had been captain of the side that won the 1967 tournament. Also born in Chester-le-Street, he was sold for a club record fee of £100,000 to West Bromwich Albion, who Sunderland beat in the 1969 Youth Cup Final. Thus did Suggett play alongside Asa Hartford and Len Cantello while guiding the next generation of Young Baggies, who will be discussed later in the story. Perhaps Suggett's association with Newcastle United, for whom he played and coached, makes him less beloved than Kerr, but his achievement should be remembered as this was Sunderland's first Youth Cup win.

Two local lads, Richie Pitt and Dennis Tueart, were both part of the 1969 team. Tueart would famously score the winning goal in the 1976 FA Cup Final, his second medal, before joining New York Cosmos in 1978.

Sunderland were not the only team in the north of England with a fine crop of youngsters. In 1968 it was Burnley who took the trophy back to Turf Moor with a 3-2 aggregate win over Coventry City. The team was captained by right-back Mick Docherty, eldest son of Tommy 'The Doc', who managed Manchester United in the 1970s but at the time was at Chelsea. Dad sent young Mick to Burnley for a brief education, where he graduated to the first team. After a very brief few months at Manchester City, he actually signed for Sunderland and, better still, kept them in the First Division in 1981.

Only two of Docherty's Youth Cup-winning team-mates, Dave Thomas and Alan West, joined him in the first-team dressing room with any regularity. Thomas played with Colin Todd for England and helped QPR to a second-place First Division finish in 1975/76, while West became captain of David Pleat's Luton Town.

In 1970, Tottenham Hotspur won the Youth Cup, which is odd because they only seem to win trophies when the year ends in a one. Here's something even odder, a factoid that seasoned football quiz veterans will already know: the goalkeeper who picked up a runners-up medal for Coventry City went on to claim that the Queen was a lizard and to become a tabloid figure of fun.

David Icke moved away from football, but Steve Perryman spent 50 years becoming a footballing treasure and champion, having won his first medal as a kid.

'The interest in me was huge,' Perryman told the Super Hotspur website while promoting his memoir *A Spur Forever*, but Tottenham treated his family well. 'That was down to Bill Nicholson, who had his finger on the pulse of everything that happened at that club. He even visited my house at least twice during the year and he was also writing letters to us … The love for his club just shone through every pore.'

Perryman had already signed professional forms, learning from Jimmy Greaves and Pat Jennings, but the young Spurs also contained schoolboy amateurs who were working a trade. Nonetheless, says Perryman, 'we only lost one game that year, away at Colchester' and he was excused from a north London derby in order to play for the kids under the coach Sid Tickridge.

Tickridge, for his part, had helped Tottenham get promoted to the First Division in 1950 but was edged out of the team by Alf Ramsey, who was part of Arthur Rowe's great side who triumphed in 1951.

Another of those kids, who would become a champion elsewhere, was Graeme Souness, who ironically was kept out of the first team by Perryman himself. 'He was aggressive and could get round the park,' the Scot wrote of Perryman. 'He was in front of me in terms of maturity.'

The 1970 Youth Cup Final was decided over four games, as Souness recalls in his 2017 memoir *Football: My Life, My Passion*.

'We won the first game 1-0 and I scored the goal. Then we went up [to Coventry] and lost 1-0 and I got booked. We tossed a coin for the third game and it was up there. 2-2. I was sent off for throwing a punch at Dennis Mortimer.

'The fourth game was back at White Hart Lane. We won 1-0, I scored the goal again, but the FA said I couldn't get a winner's medal because I'd been sent off in the third game. I got my £12 win bonus but was fined £10 … I never got the medal either.'

Souness was a key part of a 'fabulous' youth team. Main goalscorer Ray Clarke moved from Mansfield Town to Sparta Rotterdam to Ajax having been unable to break into the first team. Bob Almond, meanwhile, relocated to New Zealand as a young man and played in the 1982 World Cup as a centre-back against Souness's Scotland side.

'Homesick' and 'completely at sea in the London scene', Souness absconded to Edinburgh and was suspended for a fortnight. Player power may have existed to move between contracts, but Bosman had not yet rescued unhappy footballers who were supposed to stick to the letter of their contracts. A *Guardian* report at the time noted, 'Spurs have the power under FA Rule 27 to deprive him of his chosen profession for the full year in which they have him under contract.'

The outspoken Scottish MP Tam Dalyell waded into the issue and Danny Blanchflower visited Souness at the family home. The club eventually relented and Souness played once in a UEFA Cup tie before winning trophies galore at Liverpool.

The Young Lilywhites would lift the Youth Cup again in 1974. They did not need a replay to beat Huddersfield Town 2-1 across two legs. Chris Jones, who was born in Jersey and would establish a soccer school, took his youth team experience to the first team, where he was relegated and promoted in consecutive seasons. He trained and played with Ricardo Villa and Osvaldo Ardiles when they joined Spurs in 1978.

In what will become a recurring theme in this story, two players in that 1974 youth side had their passages to the first team blocked. Full-back Micky Stead would move to Southend United before getting The Knowledge and driving a cab in Essex, while Northern Ireland international Noel Brotherston made over 300 appearances for Blackburn Rovers before a fatal heart attack killed him at 38, a week before Rovers won the Premier League in 1995.

Following the Bill Nicholson era, which ended in 1974, Tottenham reached the Youth Cup Final in 1981, winning the second leg 1-0 having lost the first 2-0. West Ham United took the trophy that year. Tony Parks was in goal for Spurs with Mark Bowen and Ian Crook also playing. Bowen became Mark Hughes's lieutenant after a playing career spent mostly at Norwich City, where he was Crook's team-mate too. The senior team managed to win the FA Cup that year – the tradition of success in a year ending in one – thanks to Ricardo Villa's magnificent dribbled goal.

Perhaps Aston Villa should have a 'Year Ends in 2' song. In 1972, they won their first Youth Cup with a 5-2 aggregate win over a Liverpool side featuring Phil Thompson and three men called Tommy. Tommy Maguire was from Northern Ireland and did not progress to the first team, while Tommy Gore was part of the Wigan Athletic era which moved from amateur status to the Football League.

Tommy Tynan might have an even better story. Having won a *Liverpool Echo* talent contest in which he collected 20 tokens in exchange for a trial, which he passed, Tynan ended up as one of Plymouth Argyle's most successful strikers, with 145 goals in seven seasons. Watford famously reached their first FA Cup Final by beating that Plymouth side in the semi-final in 1984.

The former Liverpool apprentice right-back John Gidman was more or less pushed out of his hometown club by Bill Shankly and thus lined up for Villa against many of the lads with whom he had cleaned the boots of first-team players at Anfield. Gidman would go on to make almost 250 appearances in the 1970s before signing for Manchester United, making him one of very few Scousers to play in that red shirt.

The Little brothers, Alan and Brian, had left the north-east to sign youth terms at Villa. Both won the Youth Cup, becoming one of the few siblings to both lift the trophy; Gary Neville has one success, but his brother Phil only has a runners-up medal. Alan Little was sold to Southend United after only three senior appearances but Brian made 300, helping Villa in their promotion push in 1974/75 and dovetailing brilliantly with Andy Gray in the First Division side managed by Ron Saunders.

Brian Little was a one-club man who had to retire early. He was immediately made youth team coach and was at the club when Villa became champions of England in 1981. Their squad was packed with players who had lost to Crystal Palace in the 1978 Youth Cup Final, more on whom later in the story.

In fact, defender Gary Williams and striker Gary Shaw both started the 1982 European Cup Final against Bayern Munich. Colin Gibson was an unused substitute but had been a useful part of the small squad which had won the First Division. Mark Kendall could not displace Jimmy Rimmer in goal, though I wonder if he ever thinks that it could have been him, and not Nigel Spink, who had come off the bench to replace an injured Rimmer and win a European medal to go along with his Youth Cup triumph of 1980.

Noel Blake also has a winner's medal. Born in Jamaica, he was spotted playing locally in non-league and would make his name at Portsmouth with first-team chances limited by the title-winning Villa defence. Birmingham-born Mark Walters did break into the first team as Villa were defending the European Cup in 1982/83. He watched the 1982 final in a bar full of Bayern Munich fans, then a few years later, when English clubs were banned from playing European football, he joined Glasgow Rangers.

In a nice appendix to his career, Walters coached kids under the age of 14 at both Villa and a local school. His aim was to 'instil confidence in the forwards' and he had a hand in the development of future Youth Cup winner Luke Moore.

In his memoir *Wingin' It*, Walters wrote about how he 'never missed a game on TV' and would always try to get into Villa Park even if it meant having to 'sneak in ... we would wait until they opened the gates with around 20 minutes to go and dive in'. He was inspired by Brian Little, calling him 'my favourite. He was a great player and the type I wanted to become: fast and skilful.'

At 15 years of age, Walters was picked for England Schoolboys while he still represented Newtown Unity. He played at Wembley against Wales and was in the group with Paul Rideout, who was later to score the winner in the 1995 FA Cup Final for Everton, and Trevor Steven, a pivotal part of the Everton team of the 1980s. Mark's mum was able to watch her son with the help of the man in charge of developing young players at Aston Villa.

As an aside, it should be noted that Walters writes about the paedophilia which took place at the time. This led to the imprisonment of Ted Langford, who was a Villa scout as well as a manager of a youth team for which Walters played. The treatment of young boys by predatory coaches is beyond the scope of this book although, thanks to the work of journalists like Daniel Taylor, the stories are belatedly being told, with clubs and their employees held to account.

So much football did Walters play – 'around five games a week for different teams' including training with Villa a few times a week – that he developed Schlatters Knee. Having started as a striker, he moved to the flanks because 'it was going to take something special' to displace his future European

Cup-winning team-mates Gary Shaw and Peter Withe. His weakness was heading the ball. 'Let's just say I never quite mastered the art properly,' Walters writes, even though Blake had advised him to keep his eyes open.

Walters came into a workplace buoyed by promotion to the First Division and a League Cup win. Over the summer he had been able to watch the first team do their pre-season drills. He was also given trainers and football kits by the club. Keith Leonard, who had played in that League Cup Final, coached the youngsters alongside Dave Richardson, and Leonard advised young Mark to 'keep it simple and always choose the best option'.

A fellow YTS trainee at Villa was Brian McClair, who was 'a bit of a lone wolf' according to Walters, and the pair of them joined the other apprentices in typical early 1980s tasks such as cleaning the loos. The lads included Paul Birch, who would join Walters in the first XI, and two players who would go on to decent careers in the game: defender David Mail at Hull City and Blackburn Rovers and midfielder Ray Walker at Port Vale, where he made over 350 appearances.

The young Villains had the necessary team spirit to go through the rounds and reach the final of the 1981 FA Youth Cup. They met Manchester City and a 3-1 win at Villa Park set them up well so that a 1-0 loss at Maine Road was moot. Walters writes that he 'realised there was a pathway and that it took time' which gave him 'itchy feet' as he hoped to move up to the reserve team.

A generation after David Icke and company lost to Spurs in 1970, Coventry's kids reached the 2000 Youth Cup Final. It was the other north London side, Arsenal, who won 5-1 on aggregate. Loser's medals went to centre-back and England under-21 international Calum Davenport, who would go on to play for Tottenham, and midfielder Lee Fowler, a Welsh under-21 international whose career makes for a crowded one-page CV.

Fowler played for 27 clubs in his career, starting with Coventry City, where he made his senior debut after the Sky Blues were relegated from the Premier League. Indeed, in the 2009/10 season Fowler played for Kettering Town, Oxford United, Cirencester Town and Halesowen Town before returning to Forest Green Rovers, who had released him in 2009.

Fowler admitted to being an alcoholic in October 2010 and spent a month at the Sporting Chance clinic set up by Tony Adams. 'My drinking got out of control when I was 19,' Fowler said at the time, which meant he had problems while at Coventry.

Fowler was at home childminding on a January morning in between non-league management jobs when he took my call. He told me his alcohol problem was a manifestation of his depression, which became more acute after he dropped down from the top tier of English football.

'Drink was a factor in me doing silly things,' he says. 'It took me 15 months where I didn't drink or take any substances, sorting myself out and doing research. It was the best thing I've ever done.'

After retirement, Fowler moved into management in the semi-professional game, spending a year at Radcliffe. His focus is now on coaching, with those Youth Cup medals forming part of Fowler's past. 'I put everything aside. It's about today, about what you do now. My grandad has got 26 suitcases of medals, programmes, cuttings, sponsorship deals, contracts … They keep everything. It'd be good for the kids to look at when I'm older.

'I give shirts away, medals away. I just don't feel any sentiment towards what I did. I'm proud. Could I have done a lot more? A million per cent. I've messed up loads but we're men. We're built to mess up. I've been there and done it and made the mistakes. You can sit down with a player and empathise with him. It's a positive step forward.

'There's so many rules and protocols in place for the under-18s and under-23s. They're actually wrapped up and being mollycoddled. You can't speak how you want to speak and do certain things that you know is going to help them. What I'd like to do with these young kids is to help them, to guide them. They're more receptive and take information on better.

'When you work in the men's game, they've been there and seen it and don't want to hear what you've got to say in terms of tactics. Young kids are like sponges.'

Fowler was great to talk to, and my ears pricked up when he mentioned that he'd been in regular touch with one of the stars on the cover of this book who is now immersed in non-league football.

'I speak to Sav [Robbie Savage] quite often. He's now at Macclesfield and we've had a few dealings with players. I was in the Wales under-21s, he was in the first team. He was at United but, in my opinion, he was never good enough when you're competing with Scholes, Butt, Giggs.

'What he did do was he knew what he was good at, which he was very good at, which was upsetting people on the pitch.

'People don't give him the credit he deserves for his ability, his free kicks and set plays. He grinded out a very good career with Leicester, Blackburn, Derby, a very good midfielder in the Premier League. His attitude is unbelievable as a player and his boy is exactly the same.'

Peter Crouch, who played for Dulwich Hamlet on his way to an international career, also recently made a film about the lower reaches of English football. 'These people with big platforms, as Savage has at BT Sport, are relevant,' Fowler adds.

'When I spoke to Sav, he has bought into non-league football straight away. It's not the beer drinking, beer bellies. It's very professional and there's lots of money within it. Look at Boreham Wood,' Fowler suggests, also noticing the success of Forest Green Rovers, Sutton United and Harrogate Town, who all spent 2021/22 fighting for promotion from League Two.

All three, it is fun to note, have taken zero elite academy players for their squad, with Harrogate borrowing players from nearby Huddersfield Town and Sunderland. Captain Josh Falkingham and left-back Lewis Page did come through the academies of Leeds United and West Ham United respectively. As happened with Ikechi Anya before he joined Watford, George Thomson got his second chance at the Glenn Hoddle Academy in Spain after being deemed surplus by Nottingham Forest.

'When I was at Wrexham,' Fowler says, 'we played Brentford in the FA Cup. We beat them 1-0. We battered them! There needs to be three up, three down [from League Two and up from the National League], but they won't because of the snobbery of the leagues. Some of these non-league clubs have more money than some League One clubs!'

Fowler played in two Youth Cup finals and was unfortunate to be on the end of tankings from first West Ham in 1999 then Arsenal in 2000. West Ham had to bring down a load of ringers from the first team, without whom Coventry would surely have won their second Youth Cup.

'Definitely. Over the actual season we were better than West Ham. The actual youth team games we used to beat them five- or six-nil. Then came Joe Cole, Michael Carrick,

Adam Newton,' says Fowler. There was also Richard Garcia, the Socceroo whose name is well known to fans of Colchester United and Hull City.

Fowler continues, 'There were a lot of them playing first-team football. When we played Arsenal, we were one of the best teams in Europe. We were regularly beating Liverpool, Manchester United and Chelsa, but Arsenal were a different animal. Too strong for us, too quick for us.'

When asked if he had been born too soon, Fowler is unequivocal. 'Yes. And not even 20 years later. I started being around the first team in around 1999. To be fair to Arsène Wenger he revolutionised English football but I was still in the whirlwind between the old school and the new school.

'When you were playing a kid when I played, it was very much a taboo thing. Very rarely were you allowed to play with the first team. Now, from Premier League to Championship, the average age has dropped down completely. Coventry is renowned for playing young players now, with an average of 21, 22. When I was there, the average age was 31, 32.'

Arsenal's four midfielders in that Youth Cup Final all had decent professional careers. Jerome Thomas and Jermaine Pennant were on the wings, with Steve Sidwell and Moritz Volz in midfield. Both would play for Fulham at different times, and Volz has gone into coaching with the esteemed Red Bull stable. This means that, as RB Leipzig coach, he has been working in recent years with Ademola Lookman and Ibrahima Konaté.

Fowler also played against David Noble, who spent his 40th birthday as a St Albans City player after a Football League career which included spells at Watford under Gianluca Vialli (and alongside Pennant), Bristol City, Rotherham United and Exeter City. Having played youth football for England,

Noble switched allegiances to Scotland but never became a full international.

'With Arsenal,' Fowler says, 'every player was very, very good', while Coventry had 'four or five each year who were good enough to play in the first team'.

He adds, 'Coventry recruited a lot of "foreign" players – Welsh, Scottish, Irish, then Italian and Swedish. We had quite a mixed team under Richard Money. Craig Pead and Gary McSheffrey were the only ones from Coventry, and the captain Thomas Cudworth, who wasn't good enough for first-team football.'

Given that Watford's under-18s from 2021/22 would not all make it as senior pros at the club, in spite of two of them playing in their FA Cup third-round loss to Leicester City, aftercare is crucial when a player is not given a senior contract. I use the phrase 'gilded cages' in conversation with Fowler when we are talking about the Premier League, which was probably something Michael Calvin said in his brilliant work on youth football, *No Hunger In Paradise*.

'I do a lot of work with non-league,' Fowler says. 'I've had many arguments with Football League managers and heads of recruitment. There's a snobbery. You'll know the stat better than me but 98, 99 per cent, of Premier League youngsters will fail. What they should do, from day one, is ingrain themselves so that part of their work experience is to do a couple of months in non-league football.

'These people from the Football League said, "Well why should I do that? If I go there, I have to play." My argument was that it should condition them for a future income. Although they may not be able to play in the Premier League, there is still revenue and still football to be played from the lower leagues down. That's where these kids have got a problem now.'

'You look at mental health. You see these kids being promised the earth. They drop down to non-league and they think the world owes them a favour. The clubs have a due diligence to look after their player welfare.'

The reader will recall what brought on Fowler's own depression and alcoholism. Having already managed Nuneaton Borough and Ilkeston Town, Fowler has first-hand experience of the semi-professional game. This next paragraph contains a heck of a name drop.

'You are looking at the people getting released from Category One and Two [academies]. You can give them that time to develop further along the line because not everyone develops at the same time. You only have to look at my mate Jamie Vardy who went around the houses before he's now, or was, one of the best strikers in Europe. He was making splints, played for Stocksbridge and Halifax Town.

'He joined us at Fleetwood and then went to Leicester City. People wrote him off at Sheffield Wednesday because he was too small and his attitude wasn't great.

'This is where non-league has got a great gap in the market to really recapture players' imaginations to give them time to play. How many players have dropped out of the Premier League into non-league and then all of a sudden the "Next Best Thing" is there? Well, he was at the Premier League club in the first place! He just needed more time.'

Vardy's memoir *From Nowhere, My Story* contains a brilliant chapter on his time at Fleetwood, where he joined 'a team full of good players' who were unbeaten for 27 games across six months. His team-mates included Fowler and Jamie Milligan, who made four substitute appearances for Everton but played 200 games on the Fylde coast in nine seasons. Milligan moved into management with Bamber Bridge, who play at the Sir Tom

Finney Stadium, and set up an academy with Gavin McCann, his old mate from the Everton youth team, who went on to play for England.

'Of all the clubs I've been at, it was like a group of best mates playing together,' Fowler recalls. 'The manager didn't need to do anything. We were all volatile and all bonkers!

'We had 20 captains within that team. You had a good group of winners who knew how to win the National League. We had a team of men. If we needed to have a laugh or a drink or a joke, we would. If we needed to have a fight or an argument to win that game, we would. It's probably the best team that has ever played in non-league.'

Strangely, Vardy's book does not contain details of the future England international threatening to wreck a room, with Lee a witness to it, when Vardy was denied a move to West Ham or West Bromwich Albion. Fleetwood owner Andy Pilley said his star striker would rot on the bench if he didn't help the team get promoted.

This contrasts with how Vardy would have been treated in the dressing room at Leicester, or indeed Sheffield Wednesday, where his contract would have been terminated; non-league, as is obvious, operates at a different level from the Football League.

Fowler moved to Doncaster Rovers. 'Dean Saunders left the day I signed! Andy didn't want me to go but I wanted to be playing week in, week out.'

He had been involved with the Wales side and had been in the squad to face Argentina in 2002. Given that he had been part of a successful Coventry under-18s team, it was a shock to learn that the national team were a laughing stock. They won only once each in 2000 and 2001. 'It was only one or two of us who were actually playing in league football,' Fowler says sadly.

'I was quite lucky that I went into the first team quite early, but we had Gordon Strachan in the youth team [as their coach]. They instilled discipline into us with the jobs. Standards were so high in terms of how you looked, your attitude. These were just things before you stepped on to the training ground. Every pass mattered, anything you did mattered and there was a consequence for not doing what you should be doing.

'When you did go to the first team, they trained you to be ready. You only get one chance and you've got to make an impression. We had Richard Money who was tactically unbelievable. We had George Mackie, who was working for Arsenal until recently, who was a disciplinarian. In the reserves you had Trevor Peake, who had won the FA Cup with Coventry.'

Strachan's two boys, Gavin and Craig, were part of the Coventry set-up. The latter played with Fowler in the 2000 FA Youth Cup Final. Strachan senior was, to Fowler, 'Ruthless. You had to have a bit about you because he's quick-witted, quite aggressive and you have to stand up on your own two feet.

'I lived with Craig in Leamington Spa so I knew his dad. We had a different type of relationship. I knew I was going to be playing in the first team. I was on the bench three times at 15 and 16, but he didn't play me. The likes of John Eustace were ahead of me but I was overtaking them very quickly. I was on a YTS wage and they were probably on eight, ten, 25 grand a week. That's the reason I didn't play.'

In February 1999, Coventry were 3-0 down away at Newcastle United in a game that ended 4-1. Fowler says of his manager, 'Noel Whelan and Gary Breen told him he should have brought me on. He brought on one of the other young kids who hasn't played football since. That's how football works. I just wanted to play but I was a little bit smaller than most people. Nowadays it's not an issue.'

Fowler's team-mates in the 2000 FA Youth Cup Final included defender Richard Spong. He was a Swedish youngster who had a professional career in his home country but was part of a Scandinavian contingent at Coventry which included Tomas Gustafsson and the great goalkeeper Magnus Hedman.

'He was a great lad, Rich,' Fowler says. 'I don't know if you have come across Scandinavian people. They are very laid-back, very chilled out. You go into the room and they'd be naked together! It was natural for them. Rich took to it like a duck to water.

'True story: when Gary McAllister left to go to Liverpool, they put a bid in for me and Rich at £5m and it got turned down. Richard was close but he had a lot of injuries.'

Calum Davenport and Gary McSheffrey both went on to the first team and professional careers which have included coaching. Davenport, like Fowler, has dipped a toe into non-league management, while 'Macca' took over the first-team role at Doncaster Rovers at the age of 38.

'Macca was brilliant. He was called up after the youth team game we played against QPR. He made his debut against Villa as the youngest player to play in the Premier League and scored. When Gary McAllister took over as coach, there were about 20 of us who were surplus to requirements due to wages. We were on quite good wages for young kids.

'Macca went on loan to Luton, and Coventry were willing to sell him for £50,000. McAllister got the sack, Eric Black took over, Macca scores 18 goals that season and six months later he gets a £5m move to Birmingham City in the Premier League. Football is a very opinionated world. Give people time!' Fowler says with a rueful laugh.

As for Davenport, Fowler adds, 'I lived with Cal for two years. We were best mates and we shared quite a lot of good experiences with each other. Ultimately, Cal had a difficult background with his dad. Drink was very much a key denominator in that family, and what happened is well documented. The sister's boyfriend stabbed him in the leg and he had to retire.'

McSheffrey returned to Coventry as a player, which made sense because he 'literally grew up one house away from Highfield Road'. Fowler was not a Coventry-born lad and tells me, 'Once I leave a football club, I detach myself from it straight away. My journey is to keep learning. Once you're a manager, the amount of politics that are above you is ridiculous!

'I've won League One, League Two, the National League twice. Predominantly I played in the National League purely because it's a good standard and the money is bigger than some of these League One and Two clubs.'

All the same, if a player drops down from one of the elite academies, how will they adjust to a world in which a win bonus can pay a bill?

'This is what I'm trying to say to the Football League people. The young player's driving round in a leased Mercedes. He's got all the flash watches on finance. He's living at home.

'Then he drops into non-league where actually the lads are probably on between £50 and £800 per week. That's the top end. The average is £250-£300. When you go in and these kids have got these attitudes, the first thing the manager is going to do is say, "Listen, mate. You're not for me. I don't care where you've been."'

Fowler's Kidderminster Harriers had taken Peterborough United to an FA Cup replay in early 2014 and Posh had a striker 'who is now playing in non-league. The first thing he said to me was, "I'm on three grand a week!" And I was like, "I don't care." I was overweight, we were non-league and we battered them.' Kidderminster lost 1-0 away at Sunderland in the next round, for which Fowler was absent.

Joe Lolley, whose goal had made the difference against Peterborough, had moved to Huddersfield Town. He had a brilliant game against Watford that season and had already become a cult hero up in Yorkshire. He has since played over 100 games for Nottingham Forest, where he has become a fans' favourite there too and is a patron of the homeless charity Framework. Significantly, Lolley had been released by Birmingham City at 16 and rebuilt his career at non-league clubs like Littleton and Kidderminster.

'Let your football ability do the work,' Fowler advises young players. 'You don't need to go out ranting and raving. You'll end up there at some point anyway. Your time comes to a premature end and if you don't look after yourself, you could be like me. I was playing for Scarborough in the Conference at 19, going from four grand a week to £1,500 a week. Your life can change in months.'

With the chimes of a child's toy coming through the call, I ask Fowler if he'd let his children enter the academy system. 'Well I didn't. You see all these kids, five years of age, "he's the next Messi". How?

'My brother [Mark, who had a ten-year career in non-league] was a football player at Crystal Palace so I've seen all the downfalls of what went on. I was turning down Man United, Arsenal, Liverpool, Tottenham. My mum was going mad! All I wanted to do was play with my mates, whether it was rugby, football or baseball. At 15 I needed to make a decision.

'The youth team my brother was in was all residential, nine to five, old school. The way Coventry did it was quite new era: we had Tony Strudwick, who is now at Man United, who was our strength and conditioning coach, so we had the best person around for us to get fitter and stronger. Everything was to a clock on a heart-rate monitor. We were pretty much ahead of the game.

'Other than the finals, I can't remember losing a game. We won a tournament in Italy, in Germany. We were just better. You know when you play 11 v 11 against the first team? We didn't lose!'

As became apparent in England's Euro 2016 game against Iceland, it is fine to be technically gifted but it is what happens when a player is asked to invent a solution, instead of following guidance, that makes good players great.

'I play the game different to most people,' Fowler says. 'I'm more of a street footballer. I was never coached in terms of how to play football. The best players in London – Eberechi Eze and Wilfried Zaha at Palace, Joe Cole before he got conditioned by José Mourinho – these footballers are the way they are because they are street footballers.

'They play with a smile on their face. Once you start getting tactics and disciplined, if you're out of shape you're dropped.

'Where's the next Paul Gascoigne? Phil Foden is the closest thing. He just plays like he's playing with his mates in the street, even though he's at the biggest club in the world.'

It's also a status thing within the game. 'It's all very well and good saying you won a Premier League but you only played ten games. It's about your self-worth as a player. Everyone said to me, "You must be embarrassed," because I had 27 clubs. I said no.

'As a fan, if you're paying my wages, would you pay to see me play or pay to see me sitting on the bench? I'd rather play football every Saturday than watch all my mates do well and win leagues. I'd get to the back end and say I won three titles.

How many games did I play? Four. I didn't contribute to it. That's my view on football: train every day for the end product, which is to play in front of the fans on Saturday.' How much better is it, Fowler asks rhetorically, to play 'real men's football' rather than play for the under-23 team of Manchester United, Arsenal or Chelsea.

Britain left the European Union in 2016, which has stopped African or American players coming to England.

'I deal with agents and you have to be over a certain age; you can't even get trials, without a visa. These clubs can't get the players they were getting before so they are all looking in non-league.

'That's why you're seeing these younger players coming through and playing at the lower levels.' One of them, James Hill, turned 20 on the day Fowler and I spoke, and had been sold by Fleetwood Town to Bournemouth for £4m. At Fleetwood, owner Andy Pilley is 'going down a Crewe-type model: get the young kids in, give them a platform and sell them on'.

The argument for paying more attention to the Youth Cup is that it gives fans, as well as clubs, the chance to spot this talent. Fowler has been playing this game for years, often texting his mate Pilley the names of young Chelsea players.

'Charly Musonda, Izzy Brown, Ruben Loftus-Cheek, John Swift, about six players. These kids were 16, 17 at the time and I'm saying, "Pilley, these kids are unbelievable. They could play in your first team right now at 17!" He wasn't sure.

'Literally two weeks later Musonda went abroad, Brown went to one of those Dutch clubs [Vitesse], Loftus-Cheek went on loan to someone else. Pilley texted me two years later! All they needed was a platform. Tammy Abraham has gone to Roma. These players don't get a chance.

'The loan market is a business now. A 17-year-old Chelsea player is on £20,000 a week. They'll loan him out and sell him at the end of it. They aren't paying anything in wages, then they will sell him for £15m, £20m. They are actually using the players as loans.'

When Fowler was doing his UEFA A Licence, one of his fellow students was Eric Ramsay. A quick look at Eric's LinkedIn profile indicates that he will soon be Doctor Ramsay, as he is due to complete a PhD in Elite Youth Development at Loughborough University. He coached the uni's first team before moving first to Swansea City then Shrewsbury Town. Having gained his Pro Licence in 2019, he moved to Chelsea where he coached the under-23s, shepherding the latest talent on the Cobham conveyor belt in to the men's game.

In 2021 Ramsay was poached by Manchester United to work on set pieces with the men's team, which surely means he has been teaching Cristiano Ronaldo where to put his free kicks. More likely he has been directing Harry Maguire's head to get on the end of a delivery.

Before these two players were born, Crystal Palace became kings of the FA Youth Cup, but it is somewhat disappointing that Vince Hilaire skips over the two triumphs for his Crystal Palace side in the late 1970s. Palace celebrated back-to-back wins in 1977 and 1978, the latter a one-game shoot-out rather than the usual two-legged final. Terry Fenwick scored goals in both triumphs.

Here's some useful Youth Cup trivia for free. Palace were the only team to retain the title after Chelsea in 1960 and 1961 and before Arsenal in 2000 and 2001.

In Hilaire's memoir *Vince*, we learn a lot about why Palace's youngsters were so good: they were set up to be that way. Malcolm Allison's project was to build a first team comprising players who would be the sort of players he needed to win things. Nowadays known as the 'Team of the Eighties', at one time nine pros had come through the youth ranks under the guidance of John Cartwright, a foil to Big Mal's leader who had not been physical enough to make it as a pro at the West Ham 'Academy of Football'.

Hilaire came across from West Ham himself and was blown away by the treatment of the young players. Allison sought to replicate Matt Busby's United side of the 1950s but had to deal with the grumbles of the first team. 'He was putting some of us up in three- or four-star hotels, which wasn't really necessary, but he wanted us looked after,' Hilaire writes.

It was schoolboys vs first team in training, and maverick manager Allison called the latter 'rubbish'. Rather than watch *Match of the Day*, the Palace players were encouraged to buy *World Soccer* magazine, while there were sessions in which they were 'taught to copy great players' technique from around the world'. There were lessons in the shielding prowess of Italian winger Franco Causio, while they bore witness to the brilliance of Ossie Ardiles in a pre-season friendly.

Before new rules limited young players to their local areas, Palace would attract lads from around the country, 'selling Palace to people' while sitting in a local café. When they signed, Hilaire notes, they were 'complimented all the time' and a pro career was a given.

Kenny Sansom became England's left-back for a decade and Hilaire pinpoints why he was a stellar young pro who made his debut for the first team while still a schoolboy, 'The confidence that he had at 16 or 17 was unbelievable. He was upset if someone that he was up against even got a cross in.'

It helped Sansom that he was the furthest ahead in his group, which meant that 'he became even more of a leader' when he was joined in the first-team dressing room by other academy graduates. The unspoken truth about Sansom, one of many footballers who suffered in later life, was that he 'didn't learn how to handle adversity' due to the too much, too soon credo.

The aforementioned Terry Fenwick got special treatment. He was 'very, very shy and got homesick' so Allison 'told him to bring his brother down with him' even though he wasn't much good at all as a player. This was, to Hilaire, 'a ruthless and clever' move. Fenwick stayed in London, playing for QPR and Tottenham. He made 20 appearances for England.

In fact, the whole academy team got special treatment, with no requirement to clean terraces or the dressing room or the boots of the first team. As for education, 'we'd been told that we'd become professional footballers' so nobody took up the option of college.

It was, in any case, the school of hard knocks which provided the education for Cartwright's Kids, Allison's Adolescents (less good). Cartwright was known to take young players to see 'what it was like to really graft' at a local factory. The Young Eagles, for their part, were 'playing against men, and even though they were kicking lumps out of us, we didn't back down'. It was handy that their coach was Ron Harris's brother Allan, who conveyed a 'win-at-all-costs mentality'.

Hilaire also has kind words for Brian Kidd who, like John Cartwright, seeks to 'mould players at that level and the way they think about to game … You couldn't have Alex Ferguson taking a youth team because those kids would probably be broken by the time they were 16.'

While Crystal Palace were impressing in the 1978 FA Youth Cup, Ipswich Town met West Bromwich Albion in the semi-final of that year's FA Cup. This is significant as both teams were among those who triumphed in the Youth Cup in the preceding years.

Run by the Cobbold family, provincial Ipswich were the biggest club in the county of Suffolk. They had won the First Division under Alf Ramsay – five years before he became Sir Alf – in 1962 but were relegated two seasons later after the manager was poached by the national team.

After four seasons in the second tier, Ipswich went back up to the First Division and became a club who rested in the lower half of the table. However, 1972/73 was a dream season as they finished fourth and won the Texaco Cup, which was for teams from the home nations. Better still, the final was against their Norfolk rivals Norwich City.

Their one-club man Mick Mills was a stalwart of the Ipswich team of the 1970s, along with full-back George Burley, defenders Kevin Beattie and Alan Hunter, South African-born midfielder Colin Viljoen, winger and expert cricketer Mick Lambert and forwards Clive Woods and Eric Gates.

Ipswich were Youth Cup winners in both 1973 and 1975. They beat Bristol City 4-1 across two legs in the former and West Ham 5-1 on aggregate in the latter, defeating a Young Irons team which included Alan Curbishley, Terry Hurlock and Alvin Martin.

John Wark started a celebrated career as a medal-winner in that latter cup victory; he re-joined Ipswich twice, first after four seasons as a squad player at Liverpool and then after a solitary season up in Middlesbrough. Wark made his debut against Leeds United, with his side so badly hit by injuries that he started in defence and was made to mark Allan Clarke, with Beattie and Hunter educating him in the dark arts.

Today, Wark still lives in Suffolk and works for Ipswich in corporate hospitality. I imagine you can find his memoir *Wark*

On in the club shop, and I am sure the current owners will have read up on one of the heroes of the Bobby Robson era.

As for West Bromwich Albion, they won the Youth Cup in 1976 against fierce Black Country foes Wolverhampton Wanderers. Goalkeeper Mark Grew became the backup in Ron Atkinson's first-team squad behind Tony Godden, while Baggies star Derek Statham, who was actually born in Wolverhampton, was the left-back. He eventually moved to Southampton after Kenny Dalglish tried to sign him for Liverpool. Statham was named as one of the club's greatest ever players in 2004, alongside the famed likes of Jeff Astle, Don Howe, Laurie Cunningham and Cyrille Regis.

Before we move to the next chapter of the story, it should be said that sometimes a youth team can rescue a club in need of quick finances.

When Wigan Athletic went into administration in 2020, the fire sale of talent contained in the youth team saved the club. Three young lads moved to a club in a higher league: Joe Gelhardt to Leeds United, Antonee Robinson to Fulham and Alfie Devine to Tottenham Hotspur, captaining their 2021/22 tilt at the Youth Cup. Devine famously came on to the pitch for his first-team debut for the FA Cup third round tie at Marine and scored the fifth goal in front of the BBC cameras. Commentators were enthralled by the fact that Spurs' youngest player had also become their youngest goalscorer.

It is a shame that he could not do the same for the club who spent the 2021/22 season near the summit of the third tier of English football. The Wigan squad contained players who had come through the academies of Charlton Athletic (Jordan Cousins), Middlesbrough (Joe Bennett), Inverness Caledonian Thistle (Graeme Shinnie), Portsmouth (Jack Whatmough) and Manchester United (Ben Amos and Will Keane).

Captain Tendayi Darikwa made 150 appearances for Chesterfield while the club yo-yoed between the bottom two tiers, receiving a League Two winner's medal in 2013/14. After being ever-present in their League One season of 2014/15, when he won both Player of the Year and Players' Player of the Season, Darikwa he signed for Burnley but was soon moved to Nottingham Forest. Chesterfield had prudently included a sell-on clause so they could pick up a slice of any transfer fee.

While in Nottingham, where Darikwa was born, he became a full international after declaring for Zimbabwe. By the beginning of 2021 he had lost his place in the Forest team and became a senior player in the Wigan Athletic dressing room.

Darikwa was named Wigan's captain for the start of the 2021/22 season, and stayed loyal to his club by turning down the chance to play in the African Cup of Nations. Two players who did travel from the UK were Jordan Zemura and Admiral Muskwe.

Muskwe was the 2016 Academy Player of the Year at Leicester City but left the Foxes for Luton Town in the summer of 2021. After growing up in south London and studying at Canterbury University, Zemura signed a professional deal with Bournemouth and took the left-back spot vacated by Diego Rico.

With those two players but without Darikwa, Zimbabwe could not advance beyond the AFCON group stage. They were especially unlucky to lose to a last-minute Sadio Mané penalty in their opening match against Senegal. Brendan Galloway, an MK Dons academy graduate who joined Everton and spent the 2021/22 season at Plymouth Argyle, was ruled out of the tournament after dislocating his knee.

Given the rules governing which players can represent the nations of their parents or grandparents, it is entirely possible that a kid currently in an English academy can become an

African Cup of Nations champion. One of them may well have played in the 2021/22 FA Youth Cup, which will be discussed when you turn read on.

Chapter Three

The Early Rounds and the 1970s

DID YOU know that there is a preliminary round to the
FA Youth Cup? Sadly, in light of the challenges posed in a
global pandemic, several teams withdrew from the 2021/22
competition. They included AFC Darwen, Prescot Cables,
Dudley Sports, Yaxley FC, Lewisham Borough (Community)
FC, Raynes Park Vale and Elmore.

Of the matches that went ahead, several were notably
one-sided. Eastbourne Borough crushed Walton Casuals 9-0,
Bilston Town put seven past Malvern Town and AFC Fylde
overcame Avro 6-0.

The first qualifying round in the middle of September
had its fair share of uneven fixtures, with convincing wins for
Morpeth Town (9-1 over Birtley Town), Worthing (8-2 away at
Horsham YMCA) and Gosport Borough (10-0 away at Hamble
Club). Typically, teams which are geographically close together
play one another: Skelmersdale United and Prestwich Heys in
the north-west, Ashford Town and Hendon FC in north-west
London, Dorchester Town and Poole Town on the south coast.

A fortnight afterwards came the second round of qualifying.
While non-league clubs cancelled first-team games due to the

fuel crisis, local youth fixtures were more easily playable. North Shields versus Morpeth Town (6-1) and Tonbridge Angels versus Croydon (6-0) were the pick of the round.

Hemel Hempstead progressed with a 3-1 win against Bedfont Sports Club. Professional clubs such as Grimsby Town, Torquay United, Stockport County, Southend United and Barnet all joined them, as did Boreham Wood whose youth team won at Ashford Town. In a fun local derby, City of Liverpool beat AFC Liverpool 5-3 but, distressingly for their new American owners, Wrexham lost on penalties to AFC Blackpool. Wealdstone were trounced 4-1 at Kings Langley, which must have upset famous fan Gordon the Wealdstone Raider, who will have seen plenty of Young Stones make it to the first team.

The final round before the tournament proper brought together National League sides Barnet and Bromley. Barnet had reached the third round in 2019/20, losing 4-3 to Bournemouth. In front of a small and relatively quiet crowd at The Hive, some of whom had paid £3 but most of whom seemed to be teenage friends of the Barnet side, Bromley won 5-0.

They could have had 15 had their shooting been better and had they held their runs a bit better to avoid being given offside. Two penalties contributed to a hat-trick for Soul Kader, while Lateef Aoaja took his goal well but was booked for trying to win a penalty through simulation.

I was impressed with some of the patient build-up play from the tall Bromley centre-backs, together with the pace of their attacking right full-back. Barnet's play – which wasn't much to write about as they kept lumping it long and wasting their possession – mostly came through their blonde number eight; at one stage he ran 50 yards and shot speculatively, such was his determination to take charge of the game, while he was also denied a penalty at the start of the second half.

Barnet didn't really test Bromley's goalkeeper all night and he kept warm by bellowing, while I caught the Barnet coach telling someone in the crowd he was 'giving it a go'. They had trained in a 3-5-2 formation, apparently, but they didn't have the personnel. I was pleased for the parents of David Osei-Wusu, who spent the first half watching David warm up and saw their son play 40 second-half minutes, although he couldn't get in the game so much. Organisation and planning seem so important even at under-18 level, and it's something I would watch out for throughout the competition.

Thanks to their win at Barnet, Bromley would play Lewes in the first round proper. Joining them were Torquay United, Worthing, Lewes, Grimsby Town, Blyth Spartans, Stockport County, Southend United, Woking, Erith Town (who beat Boreham Wood) and the big winners of the round, Chelmsford City, who won 8-0 against Felixstowe & Walton United.

With the entry of Football League clubs into the competition, the first-round ties which interested me the most were: Carlisle United v Oldham Athletic, won by the visitors on penalties; Accrington Stanley v Wigan Athletic, won by the home side after extra time; Sunderland v Bradford City, won 2-0 by Bradford; Walsall v Port Vale, settled on penalties with victory to the away side; and Erith Town v Portsmouth, which the away side won 1-0. Sadly, Hartlepool United withdrew and gave Bolton Wanderers a walkover.

Oddly, despite Bromley winning 2-1 at Lewes, the tie was ordered to be replayed because 'the game was not played in accordance with the Laws of the Game as these had not been applied by the referee'. The given reason was that sin bins were used but in the Youth Cup they are not yet part of the rules. The replay, which Bromley won 4-2, was played on Friday, 12 November.

Four days later, Bromley won a seven-goal thriller 4-3 away at Forest Green Rovers.

London Lions first-team coach Darren Yarlett offered a 'Wowow!!!!' upon learning that, having beaten Concord Rangers 4-0 at their Rowley Lane home base just off the M1, the under-18s would be travelling to Milton Keynes Dons. 'This side have been together for ten years now and been the most successful youth side at the club … The future looks very bright,' Yarlett said on Twitter of the Jewish youngsters who populated his side.

The first team were, at that time, on a six-match winning run which had propelled them to the top of Division One of the Cherry Red Records Combined Counties Football League, which is step six of non-league, ie. five steps below the National League and seven below League One, where MK Dons play. Lions lost 5-0 and the journey ended at the first round.

AFC Wimbledon's Young Dons were to play at Plough Lane, recently renamed The Cherry Red Records Stadium. The club's spiritual home had been rebuilt by the new fan-owners after, famously, MK Dons had been formed to replace the old Wimbledon. (The magazine *When Saturday Comes* still only asks 91 Football League clubs to preview the new season, calling MK Dons 'Franchise FC'.)

It seemed only fitting to eschew a trip up the train line to Milton Keynes to watch London Lions and instead head down to SW19 to see what pearls lay in Wimbledon's youth ranks.

It was the type of weather England gets when the clocks go back but the sky was clear and dark, allowing the folk living in the new-build flats to watch the game, should they wish to. As I entered the ground, some older kids had been chastised by a teacher who spotted them. 'So you can be on time for the match but not for school!' he chuckled, as if there was nothing unusual about spotting his students out and about.

The bars were open, as were two blocks of seats, and some wizened fans had spotted some former Dons in the crowd as well as coach Mark Robinson.

The sacrificial victims were Woking, who had one player clearly on a different wavelength to the rest of the side but who rather let himself down when he looked, spun and dived to get his marker booked. By that time his side had conceded four goals, one of them a curling net-buster from the edge of the area by a player wearing 67.

The first team had given some young players some action the previous Tuesday in the EFL Trophy and thus half the Dons XI were sporting their squad numbers. Coach Robinson would have been impressed by that number 67, the marvellously monikered Quaine Bartley, a fan favourite who was cheered on by a gaggle of kids in the front row. No wonder Arsenal and Chelsea had scouted him at the end of 2020.

The game had started slowly, with lots of passes from one Dons centre-back to the other. This wasn't the Crazy Gang who lumped it to big John Fashanu in 1988; this was the modern passing game played on the floor. 'BASIC!' was the shout from Dons coach James Oliver-Pearce.

Most of the play went through the wings, and there wasn't much play going to the central midfielders. One of them, shaven-headed Welsh youth international Morgan Williams, hardly had a touch until he scored two goals, one of which went in direct from a corner, which I cannot remember ever having seen happen in three dimensions.

Woking players slipped on the surface to give Dons players precious seconds to make their move, which Crystal Palace's young pros would not have given them the previous Tuesday in the EFL Trophy match. The second half was only interesting because it offered the chance to see which of Williams and Bartley would take home the ball and grab a hat-trick. Neither did. Williams hit the bar and Bartley missed a couple of sitters, and the game finished 7-0. One Wimbledon goal was disallowed because of an offside decision which may have been given out of mercy to Woking. Hilariously, one away fan was giving the assistant referee some chat, which encouraged those kids in the front row, who proved they knew the 'Who Are Ya' chant.

The draw for the second round looked like a set of ties for the men's FA Cup first round: Northampton Town v Stockport County, Bradford City v Oldham Athletic, Accrington Stanley v Bolton Wanderers. Ties in the south included Cheltenham Town v Portsmouth, Stevenage v Sutton United, Reading City v Oxford United and Leyton Orient v Newport County.

Orient would make the match available with commentary on their YouTube channel and the few hundred fans who remembered that kick-off was at 7pm would see a goal at 7.02pm. Two more assured goals followed before half-time, with a fourth just afterwards due to a horrific goalkeeping error. Striker Daniel Nkrumah completed his hat-trick on the hour, weeks after turning pro and making his full debut for the Os.

The game finished 6-1, with Orient dominating every part of the pitch. Chairman Nigel Travis sent a message encouraging fans to turn up for the under-18 league games on Saturday mornings.

The surprise packages of this year's tournament were Corinthian Casuals. They had beaten Montpelier Villa 5-0, Burgess Hill 6-0 and Welling United on penalties in the qualifying rounds before edging Hayes & Yeading 1-0 away. Their reward was a tie against the young pros of League One side Cambridge United at their UBG Stadium. Also known as King George V Stadium, it is located in Tolworth in Surrey, just south of Surbiton. A 5-1 loss, including a goal direct from a corner, saw Cambridge advance, 'a step too far against a very organised side' as the club's social media wrote.

When Saturday Comes ran a piece from Will Magee, headlined 'Smart Casual', in its November 2021 issue, bigging up the Kinetic Foundation which, ironically, allowed players 'to go pro on the back of representing a club proud of their amateur roots'.

The Foundation was set up after the ugly London riots of 2011; co-founder Harry Hudson wanted to change the narrative of kids being 'bad ... anyone who had done anything should be locked up' to one of rising above the barriers created for them. The Foundation offers training sessions, education and vocational courses in their quest to ensure players have a Plan B.

Those who succeed in Plan A, as of the second-round tie, have reached 52. Joe Aribo plays for Rangers and Nigeria's Super Eagles via Staines Town and Charlton, his fellow Nigerian full international Josh Maja was born in Lewisham and moved from Sunderland to Bordeaux in 2019, and Omar Richards moved from cash-strapped Reading to Bayern Munich. The trio were joined as successful alumni by Ralfi Hand, who moved across town to Charlton. The announcement was made with the hashtag #FindYourFuture, with Magee himself pushing readers of his social media feed to 'pick up the latest edition' of *WSC*.

Young Ralfi didn't make consideration for the second-round match, played down at Dartford FC in darkest Kent, Charlton's tie with Wimbledon. Williams and Bartley would find a sterner game against a club whose graduates include one-club man Richard Rufus, England internationals Rob Lee (whose son Elliot was on loan at his dad's old club in the

2020/21 season) and Joe Gomez, a European Cup winner with Liverpool. Of today's crop, Deji Elerewe made his first-team debut against Wimbledon in the League Cup.

Playing in front of first-team coach Mark Robinson, the game looked exciting as I followed along on the Wimbledon Twitter feed, with chances at both ends – 'What a chance! Bartley across goal and it just needed Onabanjo to connect!' – and it went into extra time. Charlton scored twice to take the tie but the Wimbledon lads did not disgrace themselves. Quite incredibly, the team would play less than 24 hours later in another cup tie, and win, perhaps because the boy Morgan Williams had been withdrawn midway through the second half of the Charlton game.

Both club websites carried match reports. Charlton recognised that Wimbledon's 'attacking threat was posed by Bartley' and praised 'Abdi Ali's heroics' as Charlton pushed for a goal. The Wimbledon report also mentioned his 'brilliant tackle' as well as the team's 'spirit and determination'. They gave 'absolutely everything ... a display that offered real promise for the future of our club'. There was also a mention for Bartley's 'strength and ability' and how in the second half Dons 'grabbed the game by the scruff of the neck', trying to stop 'tricky left winger' Tyreece Campbell, who set up the first Charlton goal.

There was a familiar surname among Charlton's ranks, as young Harvey Kedwell had gone into the family business following his dad, Dons hero Danny. Wimbledon were denied a penalty in the first half ('the referee thought otherwise') and in the second half of extra time ('he seemed to be hacked down in the area'). The Charlton match report did not mention this incident, strangely.

Although they famously won the 1988 FA Cup, Wimbledon have never won the Youth Cup nor even reached the final. This may be because they only entered the Football League in 1977 and are close in location to Chelsea and Fulham, who hoover up young talent in south-west London.

There have, however, been some surprise winners upsetting the natural state of English football, including another London team with a passionate fanbase.

Rather than trot out the whole story of the 'Ordinary Boys' who helped Millwall win the Youth Cup in 1979, I'd much rather direct your attention to Merv Payne's book on the team. Merv – it feels improper to call him by his surname – has been chronicling the history of Millwall in a series of books, five of which are already in print. For those unaware of the greatest book on the club, Michael Calvin spent the 2009/10 season embedded with the promotion-winning side and chronicled it in his book *Family*.

Merv's work contextualises the ups and downs of a club who are the pride of Bermondsey, south-east London. We spoke on a wet Tuesday morning, with Merv talking from his adopted home in Stockport. He tells me that in his newspaper days he used to be criticised for writing too much copy, something that will never happen when he is in control of the word count.

Merv's book was the victim of a Covid-19 cancellation in March 2020. 'The club always hold a Dockers' Day, the community awareness day for the older generation of fans. The focus in 2020 was, by coincidence, the Class of '79,' he says.

'The players were all going to be there and we arranged for the fans to meet them all and get some books signed. That was the Saturday after we went into lockdown. We never got to do it.'

As befits a man whose first book is called *Because My Dad Does*, Merv has been a Millwall fan since the age of seven.

'If it wasn't for Millwall I probably would not have had any proper relationship with my dad at all. There was literally nothing else. My dad was very old school, up at the crack of dawn even when he was out of work in the 1970s. He was a man of routine and didn't believe in activities with your kids and bonding.

'Saturday would come around and part of his routine was going to Millwall. If I wanted a relationship with him, I had to jump on that. He was quite reluctant to take me as that was his treat. He took me along and I was absolutely hooked. I think he loved that. He didn't get involved watching me when I played, which was quite common among fathers of that era.'

The chain continues with Merv's own son. 'I'm taking him to Blackburn v Millwall and I'm looking at spending not far off 100 quid for a day where we'll probably get beat and get soaking wet!'

Merv bought his first season ticket for £30 in 1985. It was funded by a few weeks' pocket money and gave him a chance to watch football at what is now called the Old Den. 'It was a whole culture that a lot of kids have been denied now,' Merv says, although clubs are very good at keeping kids' season tickets relatively cheap or offer 'Kids for a Quid' days across the season to hook them while they are young.

'It's more than just a football club for me. For too many people today it's just football, it's all about success and money. The *FIFA* [video game] generation. We've gone past the point of no return.'

Merv admits that there is 'an unsavoury element at the club. But people do not understand the efforts the people go to. They do stuff in the community and they make the players go out to local schools and give talks about racial equality.

'They did it in the 1980s. The guy in charge was Gary Stempel, who was an international coach at Panama. He was a glorified social worker at the time and his remit was to get out to the schools, build links and do coaching courses. I was 13, 14 at the time and I went to one.

'If Gary heard anything he didn't like or if a kid had a go at another kid, he would stop the match and talk it through, "That's not what we do." At the end of the coaching sessions all of the kids would get a free ticket for Saturday's match!

'The area is diverse. There's always a lot of racial tension on both sides. You're never going to win the argument and I don't get into it on Twitter. Until you go down there and see what the football club do behind the scenes, it's black and white to the media perception.

'I once asked my editor-in-chief why he was treating Millwall so differently. "You're an easy target," he said. Journalists are lazy. If they can get some neat and sensationalist copy easily, then they will. They can sell newspapers or now get clicks.'

Back in 1977, the BBC's *Panorama* show had broadcast a report on the hooliganism blighting the English game. Millwall manager Gordon Jago was so upset that he resigned, moving to the United States where he made a living. He was 89 at the start of 2022 and is still held in high esteem in SE16.

'He was heavily influenced by America,' Merv says. 'He wanted everywhere to be family friendly, which did clash with the fans in that respect. He was possibly 20 years ahead of his time. There was no place in the English game for it. It was such a coup to get him.

'You cannot underestimate the damage *Panorama* did. It was when this culture of organisation started getting oxygen and publicity. The club was stitched up. They were absolutely gutted. There was a lot of community soundbites they wanted to show.

'The BBC can argue that a couple of months later we played Ipswich in the FA Cup and there was a huge riot. Even my dad stayed away the trouble against Ipswich Town. It put a lot of people off. Crowds were woeful.

'I interviewed the chairman of the club in the 1990s. Millwall had finished tenth in the First Division. In the summer of 1989, he was trying to get sponsorship. There had not been an incident of trouble for a good few years, but all he got back from various companies was the *Panorama* programme thrown in his face. It feels like we will never shake that off, that there was a complete culture of violence.

'There's a famous quote by Reg Burr, another of our chairmen, where he said we were "a convenient coat peg upon which to hang all of society's ills". It sounds melodramatic but it's true. We were a useful scapegoat: if they make an example of Millwall and kick them out the league, nobody will miss them. Football's problems are still there, though.'

Such is the context for what happened in 1979. In the season where the men's team dropped into the third tier, the Young Lions upset the odds and proved there was romance in the under-18 tournaments just as there was in the top tier of the game. Brian Clough's Nottingham Forest were champions of Europe, which may have filled newspaper columns that spring, but Millwall's triumph should not be overlooked. They beat Forest's youth team in the quarter-finals and, after all, as Merv reminds us, 'They got held to a draw at home and went to Forest expecting to get well beaten. They came out with a 1-0 win. They were a very confident bunch and they weren't humbled by it.'

There was, Merv tells me, something impressive about the pull of Millwall, not just for players but for coaches as well. Tom Walley, whom we will soon meet properly in this story, coached at Millwall after leaving Watford in 1990, while striker Alan McKenna moved down from Glasgow Rangers. Based in Dulwich, he was shown the ropes by some Millwall fans who insisted they take the new boy out for dinner.

'For some reason, Millwall could assemble an array of polished coaches,' Merv tells me. 'The Argentinean guy, Oscar Fulloné Arce, was the architect of that '79 team. His surname was pronounced "Arthur" to avoid embarrassment, I think!

'The players all talk about his influence as the overriding element for their success. The guy was decades ahead of his time in his techniques. Most coaches back then would send you running for hours on end. Oscar wanted them to play with the ball. It was all about being comfortable with the ball. He wouldn't dream up training-ground exercises. He made some free-kick walls out of dustbins, which wasn't going on at the time.

'The players really responded to it. He coached player by player. A lot of defenders would say to me that Oscar had told them just because they were defenders they couldn't play football! His reputation got out and he ended up going to coach at Sheffield United.'

Arce, who died in 2017, was in Yorkshire in 1978 when the Blades attempted to bring in Diego Maradona. While young Diego was starting on the path to secular sainthood, there were plenty of London-born kids who would also become champions.

'It was a real hotspot of local talent,' Merv says. 'All the footballing talent seemed to be in the south-east of the country. It's a shame because that kind of culture I think has gone forever. Now, if you get a good young player coming out of Camberwell or Peckham, he'll be at Manchester City within days.

'Maybe 30 years ago Jadon Sancho would have come through the ranks at Millwall or Crystal Palace. We've had £1m, £2m off City for 15-year-old kids. You never see them again, but we're quite happy and we'll take the money, especially as the club lost £30m over the pandemic and we're only just keeping our heads above water.'

In 2021 a BT Sport documentary called *South of the River* showed off the jewels who had emerged from south London. Hosted by Peckham-born Rio Ferdinand, the programme laid bare the importance of football in keeping young men off the streets, especially given the knife-crime epidemic which has so sickened the area recently. The focus, naturally, was on players like Michail Antonio and Eberechi Eze who would be easily recognised by the viewer, but that lineage stretches back to the late 1970s, a time when both Millwall and Palace, as we have already seen, were full of astonishing young players who grew up in that stretch of London.

'It was this amazing wealth of talent,' remembers Merv. 'There's always very working-class areas where kids would constantly have a ball at their feet. Rio Ferdinand says his days were filled with street football and there were concrete cages you were playing in. These areas are so densely populated and there are 14 clubs, with a diverse culture which massively helps.

'Back in the mid-1970s Millwall picked [black players] Trevor Lee and Phil Walker up from non-league and they were massive fan favourites. Ian Wright was on Millwall's books at one point, and the Wallace brothers [Danny, Ron and Ray] were moved out of the area for their own good by their mother. The community produced so many brilliant footballers from all ethnic backgrounds.

'Bob Pearson, the chief scout, was instrumental. He just wanted good footballers. He would drive miles and miles to find them, especially if they had been messed about by Arsenal and Chelsea.'

Pearson worked in 'a corridor to the west of Slough right up into Essex'. It was from Berkshire that he picked up Dean Horrix, who had two spells at Millwall and died in a car crash in 1990. According to Merv, Pearson would tell the players, 'If you sign for us and put the work in, you could be in the first team.'

'That's what happened to that team of 1979,' Merv adds. 'While they were getting to the final of the Youth Cup they were trying to help the senior team avoid relegation to the Third Division. Dave Mehmet, our midfielder, was playing Southern Junior Cup football on Saturday, an FA Youth Cup tie on Tuesday and a Second Division match the next Saturday.

'It would be frowned upon now. When I spoke to him, he says he didn't care. He just wanted to play football. He loved it! It didn't do them any good, though.'

We saw how young George Best had a similarly hectic schedule back in the mid-1960s, something that would cease for good with the FA's intervention in the Premier League era. Yet in 1979, with a team of 'Ordinary Boys', Millwall had a side that matched their local rivals. Vince Hilaire, whom we met a short time ago, told Merv that only the Young Lions could match the Young Eagles.

'The two clubs competed for local talent and they both paid for a lot of players to come out of a team called Belmont. Hilaire could easily have played for Millwall,' says Merv.

'As a young footballer you didn't have to commit to a club. Now you are obligated to from the age of six. Then they were training with West Ham on a Monday, Chelsea on a Wednesday, Arsenal on a Friday. It was quite informal and you just went along and trained. But they knew that, no matter how good they were, the chances of them making the first team was quite slim.'

Thus did the south London lads compete with and against each other on Sundays. Indeed, Merv tells me, Billy Gilbert, who won those two Youth Cups with Palace and played over 200 games for them, was actually a Millwall fan.

Hilaire meanwhile went to Crystal Palace and young Irish winger Kevin O'Callaghan played for Millwall. As tends to happen in football, they were thrown together at Portsmouth in the mid-1980s. Both men repeated Bob Pearson's words about being thrown into the senior team if you were good enough, in conversation with Merv, who found out a titbit about Cally from Vince.

'He had the reputation of being a bit grumpy. Vince said he wanted things just right and he's the loudest tutter! You could hear him tut from across the pitch.

'At Millwall he never missed a penalty, straight down the middle usually. He got the nickname "Cool Cally". I asked him if he'd ever missed one and he said he missed the first one he took for Portsmouth.

'O'Callaghan was one of the stars but he wasn't head and shoulders above the rest. He wasn't the go-to man. He was the one that coped and would have coped better with the transition to the first team.

'He scored the only goal in my first ever match and he was gone eight weeks later. For a left-winger in the Third Division, to be on six goals after 12 games was a pretty good total. All the successful Millwall teams have been with wingers. That sort of play gets the crowd going.'

When O'Callaghan returned to Millwall in 1987, having helped Portsmouth gain promotion, he did exactly the same thing with his old club. After all sorts of internal strife, George

Graham had assessed the club and, as he would do at Arsenal, turned the tanker around.

Says Merv, 'George Petchey was a good manager at the time [1980] but a new chairman came in who brought in Peter Anderson. He was an absolute disaster. It was all about spending big money on old established players, like Sam Allardyce and Willie Carr. They hardly played a game between them. All the youth players were mothballed because Anderson had no faith in them and the club almost went down to the Fourth Division in 1983.

'John Docherty came in after Graham went to Arsenal [in 1986]. The fans were livid and they thought it was a terrible appointment. But his attitude was the same as the late '70s. He recognised how important it was that the fans related to the players. He was mad keen – well, through necessity because the club had no money – to bring through young players.

'Graham had given Teddy Sheringham his debut in one of his last games of the season but Teddy had been released. Graham found him a bit too full of himself! Docherty was looking at what he could play with and he had no bloody players!

'So he kept a hold of Sheringham, who scored a hat-trick in I think his sixth game that season, and played him alongside another striker called Michael Marks. They were both 18, 19. He brought other young players in, plucking Jimmy Carter from QPR. Tony Cascarino came in too.

'Reg Burr and the board could see that Docherty's mindset was just right for the club and they came up with money for him to invest. Docherty made sure the players he bought understood the club so by '87 the club had gone full circle. That mentality, that culture of the late '70s from building a band of brothers, was back, and both Cally and Phil Coleman were in that squad.

'There were players who all came through the youth team and were instrumental in finally getting us promoted to the First Division: goalkeeper Brian Horne, defenders Alan McLeary and Keith Stevens. O'Callaghan scored the goal that actually won us promotion!

'It was an eight-year delayed reaction and proof that they were on the right path in 1979. If they had stayed true to it and had a bit of faith in it, the success may well have come sooner.'

The 1979 Youth Cup winners included in their ranks some very strong characters. Captain Paul Roberts was a year below everyone else. Merv said of Roberts, 'He's a cabbie now. He's such a big larger-than-life, confident character. He said they had 11 captains and that, "We all talked and we were all passionate."

'They didn't need much encouragement from the coach. That was David Payne, who was a former Crystal Palace player and a mild-mannered sort of guy. He was in the fortunate position when he turned up. There wasn't much for him to do aside from keep them all together and keep them fit. The squad motivated themselves.

'Palace had a good strong first-team squad that was doing well in the Third Division, then the Second Division. It's a lot easier to bring a youth player into a happy, successful team than it is into a struggling one. Palace were able to nurture them among old pros like George Graham, and to play little bit parts and cameos and learn.'

Had O'Callaghan not signed for Ipswich Town for £250,000, he would have been a pivotal cog in the Millwall first team. But there was no guarantee he would have stayed.

'The damage was done even before the Youth Cup Final win,' Merv said. 'It was a knock-on effect from the *Panorama* programme. Jago was gone and there was a lot of faith lost in the club. They were in a state of decay and it was remarkable that the club could thrive at youth level when as a business it was sinking fast, losing money hand over fist.

'We were one of the few clubs from outside the top flight who won the Youth Cup but didn't go on to have success. Palace were the "Team of the Eighties" but for whatever reason it didn't work out for Millwall. They were trying to keep the club in the Second Division with these kids in the first team instead of knowing their place. At the time it was fun but looking back, our development was hampered by that pressure.'

Wayne Rooney, James Milner and Trent Alexander-Arnold were first-team regulars in their teens, but back in the late 1970s the pitches were far muddier and the rules let opponents get away with tackles from behind.

Merv says, 'A few of the lads mentioned being put in the reserves, which were brutal. They were basically for first-team players out of favour or coming back from injury. Phil Coleman mentioned Teddy Maybank who was at Brighton. He was an absolute monster of a player who just went out to hurt you. It did toughen them up but they had a bit too much of that.'

These young men, who had escaped life on the docks or in the factories, were superstars around that part of London. 'They didn't consider themselves special. They just wanted to play football and at Millwall here was a club which gave them a chance to play at the highest level as established professionals. The same was true at Crystal Palace,' Merv adds.

'Dave Mehmet grew up on the local estate. He went to school with [future Millwall player] Pat Van Den Hauwe, who said he was the most skilful footballer he had ever seen.'

In the spirit of those lads of 1979, Millwall won their second Youth Cup in 1991, against Sheffield Wednesday, with a team including captain Mark Beard (son of coach Mick), Andy Roberts, Sean Devine and Lee Walker. It wasn't a fluke and the club were really planting seeds in their academy. In 1992, Millwall reached the Youth Cup semi-final against Manchester United.

'I'd just got married,' says Merv, 'and I went with my new father- and brother-in-law to the first leg of the semi-final at Old Trafford. They were both avid United fans.

'On the coach up the Millwall players had got bored and had shaved each other's heads! My father-in-law looked at me and said, "What a bloody pub team this will be!" But we beat them, we won there but we lost the second leg 2-0.' How different this story, and what followed, could have been if the Class of '92 had not come back to win that semi-final.

What of the Young Lions? Andy Roberts was a first-team midfielder for four years before moving around the M25 to first Crystal Palace and then Wimbledon. 'We used him as a makeweight to sign two bang-average Palace midfielders but there was a lot more going on in that transfer,' mutters Merv.

Sean Devine went on to Barnet, Wycombe Wanderers and Exeter City, although injury prevented him from signing for West Ham United and having a career in the elite levels of the game. He was, however, part of the group at Exeter who got a goalless draw in the 2005 FA Cup third round against Manchester United.

Lee Walker, meanwhile, scored in the 1991 final and signed for Sing Tao SC in Hong Kong where he fought with the manager and was, he said in an interview, 'escorted from the 31st floor of a building by five security guards'. He returned to England and played for Wealdstone in the Isthmian League, playing a role in the 1997 Division Three title-winning team.

Jon Goodman was signed from Bromley, Merv tells me, as a 'part-time fitness coach, so he was very good at looking after himself'. After 100 games for Millwall, he too moved across town to Wimbledon. He had no problems taking over as the academy manager of Milton Keynes Dons in 2019, working under Russell Martin initially. Goodman told the club website that Martin wanted to use academy products, 'It creates a pressure on us which we should thrive upon to help deliver that … to enable him to have homegrown talent.'

Roberts did enjoy a second spell at Millwall between 2002 and 2004, where he was part of the group who reached the 2004 FA Cup Final against Manchester United and lost 3-0.

Curtis Weston, who was 17, came on at the end of the game to set the record as the youngest player to appear in an FA Cup Final. 'Big things were expected of him,' Merv says, 'but it never happened. We could talk for hours about the likes of Cherno Samba but that's another story!'

Many of United side for that final in Cardiff were themselves academy products. Gary Neville, Wes Brown, Darren Fletcher, Ryan Giggs and Paul Scholes all started, while Nicky Butt was brought off the bench to make his final appearance for the club.

'History repeated itself in a way,' adds Merv, who has written two books about Millwall in the 1990s. 'We had Mick McCarthy as manager and he was more reluctant to use the youth players. He filled the squad with experience and the team never really fulfilled its potential. We sold on a lot of that 1991 Youth Cup squad to Wimbledon to finance more overpriced journeymen.'

Ditto in 1994. Despite Millwall winning 3-2 in the first leg of the final, Arsenal scored three goals without reply in the second leg to take another Youth Cup. By 1995, three of that team had been sold: Geoff Pitcher went to Watford; Jermaine Wright never played for Millwall but had a decent professional career with Ipswich Town, Southampton and Leeds United; Mark Kennedy was even more successful, representing the Republic of Ireland 34 times but unfortunately missing the 2002 World Cup through injury.

By that summer in Japan and South Korea, Kennedy was at Wolverhampton Wanderers. He had already played first-team football for five clubs (Millwall, Liverpool, QPR, Wimbledon and Manchester City) and would play for three more (Crystal Palace, Cardiff City and Ipswich). When Kennedy moved to Wimbledon in 1998, he trained with Andy Roberts and two other Lions-turned-Dons.

One was Kenny Cunningham, from the side that won the 1991 Youth Cup. The other was Ben Thatcher, who went on to become a squad player at Tottenham Hotspur, Leicester City, Charlton Athletic and Manchester City. Thatcher had been up against Arsenal starlets like Double winner Stephen Hughes and QPR stalwart Matthew Rose, who was captain of that 1994 Youth Cup-winning side but could not get past the famous back four.

After retirement from playing, Rose moved into finance. He told the *Yorkshire Post*, 'I had to take time off football … My brain was fried!' Yet one day he realised the bug was still there and he gained his coaching badges and helped keep Barnsley in the Championship in 2019/20 as Gerhard Struber's number two.

If you ask Merv whether a team like Barnsley or MK Dons would do well in the FA Youth Cup in the 2020s, he would tell you not to lay down any money, 'I doubt very much you'll see the like of it again when a team from outside the top clubs will be able to achieve [a Youth Cup win].'

THE EARLY ROUNDS AND THE 1970S

Old hands returned to Millwall to try to turn other kids into first-team players. 'O'Callaghan and Mehmet both ended up working for the academy in the late 1990s and produced that team who came close to getting into the Premier League in 2002. The last golden era at Millwall in terms of youth was that team: Paul Ifill, Tim Cahill, Steven Reid,' says Merv.

'Once Kenny Jackett came in, when we were bottom of the third tier, he felt that the £1m a year spent on academy status was wasted because of how long it took for those players coming through to benefit the first team, and the chances of that happening.

'He favoured spending that money on loan deals for players like Andros Townsend and Harry Kane, which was great but those players don't hang around so you are left with gaps to fill.

'Both Mehmet and O'Callaghan were very critical of the move by the club to go away from full academy status. It took ten years to build up that status, to nurture the players from a young age to being ready to play for the first team. Mehmet said that by doing that, the club was going to fall behind and it would take at least ten years to get it back.'

Without wishing to spoil the ending of Michal Calvin's book *Family*, which is so good that it has already been mentioned three times, Millwall won promotion back to the second tier a few years after Jackett came in. His decision was vindicated.

Following the exploits of Millwall in 1979, two notable runners-up broke through the hegemony of big clubs in the 1980s.

Coventry City, who we met earlier in this story in one of their three losing Youth Cup finals, needed 210 minutes to beat Charlton Athletic; Steve Livingstone had already played for the first team when his goal in extra time of the second leg took the 1987 Youth Cup to south-east London. He was sold in 1990 to Blackburn Rovers where he must have learned some tricks from Mike Newell and David Speedie whom he understudied. Livingstone was then sold to Chelsea to make way for Alan Shearer and would become a mainstay of Grimsby Town's team of the 1990s.

That Charlton team contained the chant-friendly Paul Bacon, future Bury and Plymouth Argyle striker Ronnie Mauge and Lewisham-born Carl Leaburn, whose wife is the player liaison officer at the club. Leaburn and Scott Minto, who played for Benfica either side of spells with Chelsea and West Ham United, both made plenty of appearances for Charlton. One of their team-mates was Tommy Caton, who may have sympathised with their loss in the final from his days at Manchester City.

In a season in which the men's team dropped down to the fourth tier, Doncaster Rovers were Youth Cup runners-up to Arsenal in 1988. The final was over after a 5-0 demolition in the first leg but Doncaster did achieve a creditable draw in the second leg. The team featured some local lads, including midfielders Steve Gaughan and Mark Rankine. Gaughan would play for his hometown club over 50 times before being part of the Chesterfield team who reached the FA Cup semi-finals in 1997.

Rankine, meanwhile, had been released by Manchester United before signing YTS forms and had already played in the Doncaster first team as a 17-year-old. He signed for Wolves in 1992, then Preston North End in 1996 where he played briefly alongside Kevin Kilbane and, for four seasons, under the management of David Moyes.

Also in that losing Youth Cup team were future QPR and Fulham star Rufus Brevett, who was born in Derby, and defender Paul Raven, whose success in the Doncaster first team brought him a move to West Bromwich Albion as a teenager, where he also played briefly alongside Kilbane. (Six degrees of Kevin Kilbane would make a good football parlour game, and as discussed in the last chapter, Lee Fowler would be an equally decent figure.)

It is interesting that, unlike Millwall, Charlton are pushing for their academy to have Category One status. Owner Thomas Sandgaard told the *South London Press* in November 2021, 'I am very ambitious. I make sure things come to fruition.'

Charlton were celebrating 75 years since their only FA Cup triumph in 1947. Their 2021/22 squad contained Southwark-born Diallang Jaiyesimi, who started his career at Dulwich Hamlet's Aspire Academy, defender Deji Elewere, midfielder Albert 'Albie' Morgan and striker Mason Burstow.

All four of them had been on the radar of club captain turned manager Johnnie Jackson, who came through Tottenham's academy and made over 275 appearances for the Addicks over eight seasons, having been signed to replace Jonjo Shelvey in 2010. The bald- and hot-headed midfielder earned a move to Liverpool after two fine seasons at Charlton, where he trained alongside fellow academy graduate Harry Arter, who has also had a career at the elite level.

Jackson spent three months on loan at Watford during the 2004/05 season, which is as good a segue as I can manage to link this chapter and the next.

Chapter Four

The 1980s and the Golden Boys

AS THE FA's official page on the FA Youth Cup states, the tournament 'became, perhaps, a little devalued through the 1980s as, with more substitutes allowed in senior football, youngsters were often moved through the ranks a little quicker'. Who, do you think, waved through that rule change?

In 2019, the FA Cup Final was contested between two contrasting sides. One was a plucky underdog based a 15km run away from the national stadium, while the other was based at the stadium built for the Manchester Commonwealth Games, which had been gifted to City to turn into the jewel of the Etihad campus. It is beyond the scope of this book to delve into the politics of the Abu Dhabi-led takeover of Manchester City, but your knowledge on the club's success in the last 15 years will be enriched by consulting David Conn's book *Richer Than God*.

When you are richer than Croesus, you can afford not to start the FA Cup Final with your most creative player, as City did without Kevin de Bruyne. In fact, the Manchester City substitutes' bench when they scored six goals without reply to win another trophy included a sole academy graduate in the matchday squad, as Phil Foden was absent. Ari Muric, the 2m-tall reserve goalkeeper, was signed from Grasshoppers Zurich in 2015 and, after his scholarship, turned pro with City two years later.

This was a world away from the local lads who had played the 1964 semi-final or even the boys of 1986. Interestingly, there were three Manchester United graduates in the Watford squad that day. Usual first-choice goalkeeper Ben Foster was an unused substitute, while Tom Cleverley came on in the second half to play in front of Craig Cathcart. The man whose two goals helped Watford make the final, Gerard Deulofeu, was a starlet of the Barcelona academy at La Masia. It was a synthesis of foreign talent and British experience honed at Carrington, Manchester United's own academy.

As we shall see later on in the story with both Blackburn Rovers and Chelsea, it didn't hurt the Hornets to have someone bankroll the club. Reggie Dwight, as he was known on the Watford terraces back when his uncle Roy was playing, is due to play two gigs in the summer of 2022 as part of his Goodbye Yellow Brick Road tour.

As club owner, Elton John would delight in being one of the lads. He even confessed in his memoir *Me* that Graham Taylor helped guide him away from temptation. You may have spotted the brief seven-second allusion to his hobby in the movie *Rocketman*, albeit a hobby that involved the investment of plenty of cash accumulated from his record and concert ticket sales.

Just as Jack Walker needed Kenny Dalglish, and Roman Abramovich needed José Mourinho, it was Elton's money which pushed Watford up the divisions as much as Taylor's managerial expertise. At £70,000 a year, the academy was not cheap to run but it brought through a fine crop of Hornets, to mix the metaphor.

The YTS lads were coached by the legendary Tom Walley. He wrote in the programme to the 1982 Youth Cup Final second leg that, when it comes to young players, he looks for 'character and skill' and how 'winning and losing can be of equal benefit … it's part of the learning process'. Walley wants to see a 'hungry attitude' in his players with 'complete commitment and the will to win'. All the same, success in the Youth Cup is 'an added bonus and nothing more. My job is to groom players who, hopefully, will turn out for the first team'.

Humorously, with hindsight, though not at the time with hooliganism making the headlines, Walley writes that 'the days of big money transfers have almost certainly gone' and so clubs should pay attention to the youth policy while they 'keep a close eye on the pennies'. Players in 2022 are bought and sold for billions of pennies.

The 1982 final was contested between Watford and Manchester United, who were managed by the equally legendary Eric Harrison. He brought through the lads who became champions of Europe in 1999 and, when he died in 2019, plenty of them had paid him a visit to try and jog a memory beset by dementia. Watford won 3-2 at Old Trafford against a team which included Norman Whiteside (who would shortly be off to the World Cup with Northern Ireland) and Mark Hughes, who was yet to make his first-team debut. Tommy Docherty's son Peter was also in the XI.

Two days after the Watford senior team gained promotion to the top tier of England football, the Young Hornets won the cup after extra time in a thrilling second leg in front of 8,000 fans. Having defeated Southampton, Middlesbrough and Wolverhampton Wanderers along the way, they had passed the ultimate test.

The side included Neil Price, who would start in the 1984 FA Cup Final, and Jimmy Gilligan, who scored the Youth Cup-winning goal. In his book *Enjoy The Game*, the definitive story of Watford's rise through the divisions, Lionel Birnie writes that Walley 'turned boys into men ... He did it in a way that meant the players grew to love and respect him ... Many have kept in touch to this day.' We will meet one of them later in this chapter.

Having joined Watford as a player in 1967, Walley was part of the first great side who, under the management of Ken Furphy, reached the FA Cup semi-final in 1970. After he left the club and returned, he was given the youth coach role after Graham Taylor came in and realised Walley's knees were knackered. His first great decision was to retain Luther Blissett and Ross Jenkins, who became the mainstays of Taylor's great team.

This, annoyingly, meant that Gilligan couldn't get a game, even after Walley had beaten Chelsea to sign him as a 'gangling 13-year-old'. Walley did not have the same luck with Paul Merson, whose parents were given a new washing machine by Arsenal. Gilligan and the other lads would be told to run part of the way back from training to Vicarage Road.

'He was tougher than a sergeant major' is what Gilligan himself says of Tom Walley, who would also ring the lads' homes on Friday night 'to make sure they were in bed by 10pm ... He's the hardest man I've met in my life. He ruled with fear at times but he loved us and he wanted the best for us.'

Gilligan had been given a first-team debut in 1981 but, with his path further blocked by the presence of Gerry Armstrong, he didn't get many games in the first team and went on to have a decent career with five years in Wales. Probably because he's English, Gilligan is one of very few players to have represented both Cardiff City and Swansea City.

After retirement he returned to the youth set-up at Watford before spending time at MK Dons and Nottingham Forest. Gilligan then worked for three years at the Nike Football Academy and gained his UEFA Pro Licence in 2019, studying alongside Steven Gerrard, who himself worked with Liverpool's kids before his time as manager at Glasgow Rangers and Aston Villa.

In a weird pairing which football sometimes throws up, Gilligan has returned to Watford to work with a player whom he coached in the 1990s. In conversation with Watford's in-house show *Inside The Hive* in December 2021, Gilligan and Richard Johnson told of their hope that an academy product would break into the first team.

'It's the person first, then the player' was Gilligan's credo, while Johnson was 'under no illusions to what we're trying to do'.

The guys were speaking the week before the first FA Youth Cup tie of the season at Cardiff City. Luckily, fans could watch a stream on the club website and check out the young lads who played 'in wet and windy conditions' according to the Hornets' Twitter feed.

Watford came from behind to win 2-1 with goals from Shaqai 'Shaq' Forde and Adian Manning, who scored in the final minutes to prevent the game going into extra time. It was pleasing that both scorers were 'one of our own' having come up through the age ranks.

Also in the XI were defender Hamzat Balogun, who had joined from Manchester United, and a Hackney-born striker of Nigerian descent in Tobi Adeyemo. Captain Will Hall had been loaned to Kings Langley earlier in the season but, as the rules of the competition state, he was eligible to play for his parent club in the Youth Cup. The Watford matchday squad also contained the Lisbie twins: Kyreece played the whole game while Kyrell was left on the bench.

The man in charge of the twins could remember which one was which 'only by the boots! If they change boots for the day I'd be really struggling, they're that identical. Kyreece plays on the right, Kyrell plays on the left. They work really hard and they push each other.'

I caught up with Tom Hart him during his lunch hour on the day that several first-team players tested positive for Covid-19. This caused the postponement of two crucial fixtures against Burnley and Crystal Palace.

Although Youth Cup ties have in recent years been played at the grounds of St Albans City or Wingate & Finchley, the club secured Vicarage Road for the fourth-round tie, where Hart would pit his wits against his old friend Ed Brand's Chelsea side. This, admittedly, sounds like a pairing you'd get in *Football Manager 2032*.

'I did my UEFA B Licence with Ed about 11 years ago,' Hart says, 'so it's quite a nice story that we're going to be up against each other. I know the players are looking forward to really testing themselves against a massive academy.

'It can't be bad going to sign international players and putting them together but we've seen a little bit of an upset. There's normally a couple of clubs that do well that are a bit of a surprise package. If you've got high ambitions to progress in the game, you want to test yourself against those types of players. I do, as a coach, so we won't fear them. We'll be prepared.'

In any case, Cardiff had tested Watford in what Hart says was a 'tough, tough game. They were off the back of six wins in a row, conceding one! Their under-23s had won 11 games in a row and they get players in their first team. That will give the boys massive confidence.'

When it comes to assessing an opponent, I ask Hart what they prepare themselves for. 'What they are like in possession, certain patterns of play they work on,' he says. 'What they are like out of possession, on transition both attacking and defensively. Key players we might have to keep an eye on or certain weaknesses we might exploit to our strength.'

The Youth Cup, he continues, 'Is the biggest competition for a youth player. We don't always get the boys together in our games programme, because there are often under-16s in the under-18s. We've got boys out on loan who all come back to be available for these games.

'Ryan Andrews and Shaq Forde have both been up in the 23s … They all want to play in the Youth Cup. They all know what doors it can open. The 23s coaches are really accommodating and we try and do as much preparation as we can with them, managing their training load. It's enough for them to gel together again.'

It makes Hart more akin to an international manager than a club manager. He works with the under-23s coaches Omer Riza and Richard Shaw, who 'have a smaller squad than us' and often take players from the under-18s. Ryan Cassidy, recuperating from injury, spent 2021/22 undergoing rehabilitation at Watford, guiding the young players with the experience of a former youth team captain as a 'senior figure' providing advice to Forde and other attackers.

The youngsters train on the same site as the senior team, with academy players joining up with the first team and often appearing on the substitutes' bench due to the various first-team injury crises. 'We're just waiting for someone to play consistently and break through,' Hart says. The likes of Joseph Hungbo are out on loan to clubs around Scotland to gain invaluable experience in the men's game.

Hart was at Stevenage, which was a Category Three academy, where he helped Ben Wilmot rise through the age ranks to make his senior debut at 17. Unfortunately for Watford, having played for Udinese and Swansea City on loan, Wilmot chose to join Stoke City and play regularly in their first team.

'I've known Ben since he was 13 when he came on trial from grassroots football,' Hart remembers. 'I worked with him for the next two years. He turned down a scholarship because he wanted to stay at school and do A-levels but the academy manager sat down with him and his mum and dad and persuaded him to stay on because of his potential.

'He was training with the first team and I remember Darren Sarll, the manager, asking his first team if he should play him and they said, "You HAVE to play him. He's the best player."

'I remember hundreds of scouts being at the games watching Ben. He didn't put a foot wrong. It was like he'd played there for years, with a mentality of a 27-year-old. You tell him something once and he'd add that to his game straight away. It was an elite mentality, which has been his biggest strength, and his journey has been unbelievable. Good luck to him.'

As a first-year pro at Stevenage, Wilmot scored the consolation goal when his side lost 10-1 – Hart says they 'took a big bashing', without mentioning the score – in the third round of the 2016/17 Youth Cup against a Tottenham side featuring future first-team candidates Kazaiah Sterling and Japhet Tanganga.

Hertfordshire-based Broxbourne Borough, who were playing in step five of non-league that season, were the story of that year's competition, though. They came through the three qualifying rounds and were given a bye (along with Metropolitan Police) to the second round. They then overcame Boreham Wood, Chester and Yeovil Town before coming up against Aston Villa in a match covered by both the *Hertfordshire Mercury* and the *Daily Mail*.

Villa's captain that day, Jake Doyle-Hayes, went on to play in three EFL Cup matches before spending a season at Cheltenham Town. On his release during the Covid pandemic he moved up to Scotland, first to St Mirren and then to Hibernian, where he became a first-team regular in the 2021/22 season. Harvey Knibbs, who scored four of the seven goals against Broxbourne, moved to Cambridge United and started wide on the right at Newcastle United in one of the FA Cup's mightiest upsets in January 2022. Villa went on to lose against Manchester City in the last eight of the Youth Cup.

In the fifth round of the 2012/13 tournament, a Spurs team including Harry Winks, Nabil Bentaleb and Josh Onomah lost 8-4 to the Baby Whites of Bolton Wanderers: Tottenham Hotspur 4 Bolton Wanderers 8 (eight), to use the correct typography. Spurs' academy manager John McDermott said, 'At 4-6 down and having scored two quick goals with 15 minutes to go, we thought we could claw something back.'

Hat-tricks came from both Tom Walker and Tom Youngs, who I hope each got a match ball to take home. The former Tom was part of the Bolton side who played in the Championship between 2015 and 2016 and has since done a tour of the north-west. Bury FC, Stockport County, FC United of Manchester, Salford City, AFC Fylde and Altrincham are on Walker's CV, as are two caps for the England C team which calls up players from non-league football. Bolton, by the way, were knocked out by Nottingham Forest in the quarter-final.

In 2014, Spurs were knocked out of the FA Youth Cup in the fourth round by eventual runners-up Fulham after a Patrick Roberts hat-trick. Moussa Dembélé won his team a thrilling semi-final, which was 4-4 after 180 minutes, by completing his own treble. In 2015, Spurs reached the semi-final themselves and were knocked out by Chelsea 5-4 on aggregate after leading the tie 3-0 after 130 minutes. Chelsea scored five inside half an hour to reach yet another final, and in 2021/22 it was Watford's turn to try and tame the lion.

Like Chelsea and indeed all elite clubs, as well as most who sit just underneath the elite, Spurs have a Category One academy. In fact, Watford were the only Premier League club in the 2021/22 season ('other than Brentford who have their own B-team model' Hart notes) to have a Category Two academy rather than Category One. 'It shows how tough it is for us to produce Premier League players on Cat Two resources. We have Cat One academies in the Championship,' Hart says.

Players might have the talent but 'fall short in terms of their work ethic, their honesty, their attitude … They can have all the skill of Jadon Sancho but all those other values as well are so important. In our recruitment process Watford look at that first before looking at the player's ability,' adds Hart.

'It's going to start changing in terms of culture and environment so those values of Tom Walley and Graham Taylor, that are always mentioned, will start to be seen a lot more. Watford will be a force to be reckoned with in local professional football.'

In 2018/19, Watford reached the Youth Cup semi-finals. They put together a great run by beating Birmingham City (who had a very young Jude Bellingham watched by 'hundreds of scouts'), Southampton and Ipswich Town, all at home. In the last eight, they went up to the King Power Stadium to beat Leicester City, whose captain Luke Thomas is now part of the first-team squad. 'The rounds before [the quarter-final] just built the momentum,' Hart remembers.

Alas, Liverpool triumphed 2-1 in the one-legged semi-final at Anfield with a team that included the two Williamses, Rhys and Neco. 'For whatever reason, we didn't have to opportunity to go back to Vicarage Road ... We had a chance to make it 2-2 which would have made it very interesting for the second leg!'

Watford's side included Ryan Cassidy, who scored their goal, and the prodigious Sonny Blu Lo-Everton, who has since signed professional terms with the club and is enjoying a season in Somerset with Yeovil Town. He thus follows the path set out by Irishman Cassidy, who went up first to Accrington and then, in January 2022, over the Irish Sea to Bohemians, where he came in a package deal with fellow graduate JJ McKiernan.

I ask Hart how many first-year and second-year scholars were in the team that played at Anfield and he counts them off. Among several trialists signed to cover for injured players, there were plenty of lads who hadn't yet won a two-year scholarship. One was George Langston, who 'played every minute of every round as an under-16 player' and followed his dad Matthew as a Watford pro, having been let go at age 12 from the Spurs academy.

Among those under-16s was Rio Campbell, who left Watford by mutual agreement after his scholarship to sign as a professional footballer with Swansea City. He was given the squad number 51 for the 2021/22 season and plays as either a winger or an attacking midfielder.

Campbell spoke to me from his bachelor pad in Swansea on a Sunday, his day off. I began by asking him if getting paid for doing something he would do for free was starting to feel like a job now that it's paying the bills.

'You have days where you have to get up and it's sometimes a struggle to get out of bed. Your body is screaming for a rest,' he admits. 'When it's something that you love to do, you start kicking the ball and all of that goes away. The easy part is going on the pitch and showing what you can do.

'I'm working on everything in general. Sharpness, always staying sharp. I have a lot of ability already so anything that adds on to it. I'm maintaining fitness, staying strong, keeping up with gym and doing extra when needed. Then there's talking to experienced players or coaches, anyone I need to get information from ... to get to that next level and make sure I am on top of things.'

Campbell grew up in east London but as a nine-year-old joined Barnet, which meant he had to be accompanied all the way up the Jubilee Line to Canons Park in the north-west of the capital. 'It's fun playing football at that age. When you're young, all you're thinking about is, "Can I play for a football club?" It doesn't matter which one. It was a new experience at Barnet so I was ready to take on information, play football and enjoy it.

'My dad, anytime he got off from his job, would take me in the car. When he had work during the week, my mum would take me on the train. My brother or his friends would do that too. Everyone who was close to me played a part in assisting me to get to training.

'My mum would say positive things. When I got on the ball on the wing taking on a player, she'd say, "Rio, do your thing!" Even before the game she'd give me words of encouragement.'

He trained with Charlton Athletic but the financial constraints at the club meant he could not sign there for an age group. Someone at the club called Martin Munday referred him on to Tottenham. Now at Manchester United, Munday was a scout and development coach at Spurs while Campbell was training in Enfield alongside Nile John and Dane Scarlett, who both gained scholarships and have already played for the Spurs first team.

Campbell was at Spurs between the ages of 11 and 14, when 11-a-side matches were introduced at under-13 level. It was there that he learned about the FA Youth Cup. Then, in 2017, Campbell moved to Chelsea.

'I could only get better there,' he says. 'It definitely benefitted me. I went there between 14 and 16, so I was still in school. We trained quite a lot, two or three times a week, with a match on the Saturday.

'What the coaches do is they give you ideas and ways to be successful as a winger and get the best end product. When you are on the pitch it's up to you to take charge and find the solutions at the time on the pitch.'

He was convinced to move to Watford at 16, where he signed a scholarship. 'There was a lot of options. Teams ring you – I don't know how they get my mum's number! But I went for a trial, played a game with the under-18s and thought Watford was the best place for me. It was the right move at the time and I enjoyed it. It's a brilliant club and they taught me a lot of things.'

Campbell was aware of his new team-mate Dan Phillips who, incidentally, also moved to Watford after a few years at Chelsea. After making a senior appearance in 2020, Phillips became a full international for Trinidad and Tobago in March 2021. He then moved on loan to Gillingham for the 2021/22 season to gain the sort of senior football that was denied to him at Watford.

At Anfield, Campbell came on to the field against Liverpool in the Youth Cup semi-final. 'That experience was one of the highlights of my football career,' he says, his voice amping up. 'I was 16, playing up [the age groups]. I was waiting, I was itching! There was even a point where I didn't think I'd get on. Just being at the stadium, it was "Wow!"

'When Tom told me I was coming on for the last ten minutes, I thought, "This is my chance." I went on the pitch and I started enjoying it. I just took in the moment really.'

It was soon time for Campbell to choose his first professional club. After he left Watford 'by mutual agreement, I wasn't signing on and I chose to leave', Campbell opted for Swansea City. 'It's the kind of place where you want to get to know it better,' he says of the fine Welsh city. 'It's quiet, not too rowdy and it's by the sea.'

Does he get recognised as Rio Campbell, Swansea City player? 'I'm not sure, you know. Maybe they do but they don't want to come up to me. I stay out the way.

'Everyone in Swansea comes to you and says, "Hello, how are you?" In London, people just go about their business.'

Campbell was called up to train with the first team twice when Steve Cooper was manager. 'I appreciated that, to get the chance. I was 18. The intensity was good and it was a good environment to be in, with the top of the club. You just want to do your best and the manager just wanted us to express ourselves.

'There's a lot of different types of characters here. We're taught to get to know other people and how it is in their country. You adapt and pick up new things just as they are from you.'

His current team-mates at Swansea include at least five Premier League academy graduates who joined the Welsh club after they could not progress to their first team following their two-year scholarship. Having been developed as a youth player in a top academy, talent filters down to the Championship and the lower professional divisions. Perhaps one day they will make their old employers regret the decision to release them, especially if they sell them on and forget to include a buy-back clause in the deal.

Yan Dhanda joined the Swans in 2018 after his path to the Liverpool first team had been blocked by the signings of Fabinho and Naby Keita. He would also have had to get past Adam Lallana, Curtis Jones and Sheyi Ojo just to reach a competitive squad who would finish the season as winners of the UEFA Champions League.

Dhanda spearheaded the rise of former elite academy players going to Wales and the West Country. Midfielder Liam Walsh, for instance, came through at Everton but was signed by Bristol City. With his path interrupted there too, Coventry City took him on loan in the 2019/20 season and Swansea must have been impressed enough to bring him into the club over the summer of 2021 without paying a fee.

After four years at Glasgow Celtic following his release from Manchester City, Olivier Ntcham was persuaded to join Swansea. He had two seasons of first-team football as a young pro with Genoa in Italy and represented France in the 2019 UEFA European Under-21 Championship, coming on as a sub to play against Manchester City starlet Phil Foden.

The game was decided by a last-minute Aaron Wan-Bissaka own goal. Born in Croydon, the defender had quickly made a name for himself at Crystal Palace with some impressive blocking and tackling, which prompted Manchester United to pay an astonishing amount of money to deprive Palace of another magnificent graduate in the tradition of Malcolm Allison's boys of the late 1970s.

While Wan-Bissaka deals with the daily soap opera of Old Trafford life, Swansea centre-back Joel Latibeaudiere is another graduate of Manchester City's Etihad Campus to end up in

Wales. Four years younger than Ntcham, he joined Dhanda in 2020, enticed by the presence of manager Steve Cooper. Cooper decided that Bersant Celina, another former Manchester City player who declared for Kosovo after it became a nation who could compete in international competitions, was better off playing elsewhere.

Swansea also took Freddie Woodman, Marc Guéhi and Morgan Gibbs-White on loan from Newcastle United, Chelsea and Wolverhampton Wanderers respectively; Cooper had managed all three of them in his time as England under-17s manager. After failing to gain promotion to the Premier League, Cooper left Swansea in September 2021, a year after Rio Campbell had come in.

Campbell was joined by Michael Obafemi, who had trained at Watford as a young teenager before heading first to Leyton Orient and then to Southampton, where he was in and around the first-team set-up for three seasons. Young Ben Cabango spent the 2021/22 season wearing the number five shirt for the club, having become a full international for Wales at the start of the previous season.

As an aside, Swansea were FAW Welsh Youth Cup finalists every year between 2008 and 2019. Except in 2009, they won each time to hold a Chelsea-like grip on the trophy.

Three of those wins have come against rivals Cardiff City, the most recent being on penalties in 2018 when Cabango was in the starting XI. Goalkeeper Steven Benda and striker Liam Cullen played alongside him. Benda was understudy to Ben Hamer in 2021/22 before being loaned out to Peterborough United, while Cullen made 37 first-team appearances before Lincoln City borrowed him in January 2022.

The new Swansea manager Russell Martin, recruited from MK Dons to replace Cooper, seems to have realised that locally raised assets are important for the future of the club. Thus, players who cannot play regularly at Swansea must get football elsewhere. Rio Campbell is still developing and spent the first half of the season with the under-23s, who try to mirror how the first team are set up. 'You never know when it might be your time so you always have to make sure you are in the best form as possible,' Campbell says.

What would success be like? 'You might do stuff, you might win this and that,' Campbell adds philosophically. 'Football is the beautiful game and we all started playing it because we were enjoying it, not for the money. If we can do that and make a living off it, what more can you ask for?

'When you enjoy it more, that's when more success starts happening and you start winning more. You get your rewards for enjoying it and working hard at your craft.'

Is he, I ask, interested in coaching? 'I honestly haven't thought that far ahead. I wouldn't want to be a main coach but maybe for kids in my area, not directly with the clubs, but I could do something that helps them get into the clubs,' Campbell says, making me think of the Aspire Academy run by Dulwich Hamlet or the Kinetic Foundation who provide players for amateur side Corinthians Casuals.

Before Ghana international Jordan Ayew left Swansea for Crystal Palace, Campbell had a brief chat with him. 'We weren't even talking about football. It was a good vibe.' Would he declare for Ghana? 'We'll have to see.'

Campbell was released by Watford so no fee was involved in the transfer but the club have recently sold players on who have been developed in the academy, as Tom Hart tells me. Tomas Galvez was born in St Albans and joined Watford at 11, before Manchester City offer him a scholarship and dangled the promise of a locker at the Etihad Campus in front of him.

Training with some top international talent may ease Galvez's path to become a full international for Finland, for whom he has declared.

James Debayo and Romari Forde went to Leeds and Arsenal respectively, which is proof that Watford are, to Hart, 'getting a lot of attention about our young players, especially in the 12–16 phase. Whether they stay with us and we help them develop, or we move them on and they have a career elsewhere, we've done our part that way.'

Hart is thus echoing what his bosses told *Inside The Hive*. Richard Johnson admits that with 'the way football has gone, it's a difficult task' for players to transition from young pros to seniors, adding, 'Being a Category Two academy, our games programme isn't as strong as it should be to progress kids to that level.'

Asked how he sells the club to young lads, Jimmy Gilligan notes how, in his day, Watford used to cover the county of Hertfordshire. With Arsenal next door, the challenge is more stern, but lots of private academies offer players who are 'fresher' and liable to succeed in a new academy environment.

Is Hart's style similar to that of Tom Walley? He does hear stories from Jimmy Gilligan and Omar Riza, who played for him at Arsenal. 'They call him the Walleyman and tell stories about the tough love you need at that age,' Hart says.

'Times have changed! Finding ways of disciplining the players and giving them that education but within the guidelines, treating people with respect and installing the values we have at the club. It's a key time and a key age group and they need that discipline.'

Adrian Mariappa was one of 60 graduates emerging from the partnership between the club and the local Harefield Academy, which became a development centre for young talent.

Players trained for two hours a day, with competitive matches and fitness schedules, while working towards academic or professional qualifications.

Speaking to the BBC in 2010, the then first-team coach Malky Mackay boasted that 'they get three times as much football as any other academy', while Nick Cox revealed that 'the club has put ten per cent of its annual turnover' into the project. Remember how Elton John gave £70,000 per year to operate the academy? To quote Tom Hart, 'Times have changed.'

The partnership is no longer active because Watford are instead able to develop players under the guidance of coaches like Tom Hart at London Colney, Watford's home base.

Fans will be familiar with the likes of Gavin Massey, Sean Murray and Adam Thompson, who all appeared for the first team in the years directly before the new investment. Mariappa was the most successful of those affiliated to Harefield: his career included promotions, international appearances for Jamaica and an FA Cup loser's medal, as he was in the matchday squad against Manchester City in 2019. Having played for Reading, Crystal Palace and Bristol City, he moved to Australia's Macarthur FC where he joined former Watford team-mate Jordon Mutch.

It remains a shame that, since Murray and Tommie Hoban played regularly at the start of the Pozzo family era, no youth graduate has had a steady run in the team except when Mariappa himself starred in the second season when Watford were back in the Premier League in 2016/17.

After the 1982 Youth Cup win, the Walleyman brought through another bumper crop of hornets. A Watford side containing both David and Dean Holdsworth upfront came up against Newcastle United in the 1985 Youth Cup Final. After a 0-0 draw in the first leg, and having gone behind at

THE 1980S AND THE GOLDEN BOYS

Vicarage Road, Newcastle scored four times to win the match and the cup. It was the first time they had won the competition since 1962 and they have not won it since.

It was the first medal for young Paul Gascoigne, who scored the third goal of the second leg after dribbling across three defenders and shooting past Sean Griffith, who made two poor errors for two of the goals. Griffith became a coach at several clubs in the south of England, including, away from the senior game, Arsenal Fan TV FC.

At the very end of Elton John's involvement with the club, Watford won the Youth Cup for a second time in 1989, against Manchester City, whose side included Martyn Margetson, Gerald Taggart (as the programme printed), Neil Lennon and Ashley Ward. Future City goalkeeper David James and Bristol-born Lilleshall graduate Jason Drysdale at left-back helped overcome City after extra time in the second leg. Lilleshall, the national centre of excellence, also helped develop Jason Solomon and Rod Thomas; the latter had been coached by John Barnes and Nigel Callaghan in training sessions run by the club in Watford.

As a measure of how tough the tournament was for Thomas and his team, the second leg of the final was the 11th game they had played across six rounds. They needed two replays against Leyton Orient in the second round and replays against both QPR in the third and Portsmouth in the fourth. In his programme notes before the 1989 final's second leg, Tom Walley wrote again of how he wants to see 'that will to win … [that] attitude can help develop an also-ran into a thoroughbred'.

I hope Tom Hart and other Watford coaches can turn some of these kids into champions, although Walley's words makes me think that *From Also-Rans into Thoroughbreds* would have been a good title for this story.

I got in touch with one of those men who became a champion of young players and was part of the Watford squad that achieved successive promotions in the late 1990s. Nigel Gibbs, henceforth 'Nigel' (though not 'Sir Nigel' as he is affectionately nicknamed), spent 2021/22 as an academy coach at Tottenham Hotspur. We spoke in the week that he was helping to prepare the under-18s for their fourth-round tie against West Bromwich Albion. It was the same week in which the seniors had beaten Leicester City with two injury-time goals.

Though the Youth Cup game would be played on the Friday night, Nigel was instead heading to Vicarage Road, where he would sit in the Upper Graham Taylor Stand watching his old side play Norwich City in a relegation nine-pointer. Fans were encouraged to show a scarf for Graham Taylor but three second-half goals from the away side ruined the occasion. Watford fired yet another manager three days later. Taylor's first era at Watford lasted 12 years; the Pozzo family have hired and fired 14 managers in fewer than ten seasons. That Tom Hart quote about how times have changed comes to mind.

It is now 40 years since Nigel and company won the youth competition and most of the gang are still together after all these years. 'Tom Walley lives round the corner from me,' Nigel says. 'I've seen quite a few of those players over the last few years. It'd be nice to catch up with some of them.

'My medal is in my little trophy cabinet in the front room. It was a fantastic achievement. It's not an easy thing to do.'

Nigel waxes lyrical about Walley. 'His coaching, the environment he created, the demands he put on the players … He was the biggest instigator of players coming through and having careers.'

What about Jimmy Gilligan's story about running back to the Vic from a training session? Nigel chuckles. 'There weren't so many cars around when I was apprentice and it was a bit safer to run back to the training ground! It's all about developing the person as much as the fitness side of it.'

When I mention that Spurs are yet to win the Youth Cup in a year starting with a two, I ask Nigel if it's an important trophy to the club's chairman Daniel Levy.

'You'd have to ask him! Certainly for the academy, the most important thing is readying players for the first team. It's been very successful: Oliver Skipp, Japhet Tanganga, Harry Winks and of course Harry Kane. If you speak to any youth player, in any year, it's a massive thing to win the FA Youth Cup. It's the equivalent of the FA Cup for the under-18 teams. From my experience as well, it's magical. It's massive for them.'

Kane famously hires a personal chef to look after his caloric intake, something which must set an example to younger players at the club.

Nigel says, 'We say to them all the time, "If you want to get over there and into that first-team squad, you have to be the total professional, a 24-hour one." When you're at home, you're resting and eating right and doing the things that make you become a top player.'

Just ask Gary Neville, who went to bed early and ended up being the Nigel Gibbs of Old Trafford. At Watford, Graham Taylor placed importance on leaving a legacy and giving your best. Nigel, like his Welsh team-mates Kenny Jackett and Rob Page, takes that advice to heart. 'The pathway is to work hard every day to be the best you can. If the opportunity comes to go into the under-23s or the first team, you have got to take it.'

Nigel was a first-team player at Watford for so long he was granted two testimonials. He thus shepherded many fellow

Hornets from kids to champions while he was still playing. Given that his dad, Dennis, worked alongside Tom Walley as a youth coach – indeed, he was the physio for the 1982 Youth Cup victory – young Nigel would help out in the academy while he was a first-team player.

'I was playing on the Saturday and going twice a week in the evenings to work with them and show them what a first-team player looked like. The principles, the basics and the morals were the same. You've got to have technique and be physically fit. But you have got to have the right mentality. There's going to be ups and downs, but you have got to keep working, pushing yourself.

'That is difficult for young players because they want to get there quick. They want that "Speedy Boarding"! It doesn't work like that.

'You have to keep doing it day in, day out. There are no shortcuts. Until you put them in there [the first team], you never know. You've got to be able to handle it on a big stage. Many a good player has had a fantastic chance but they don't continue to develop as you thought they would.'

Nigel himself was thrown into the first team in a UEFA Cup game then dropped back to the youth team because Graham Taylor had three other right-backs to pick ahead of him. When I surmise that he might have gone to those away ties as a fan, he reminds me that as a club employee he would probably have been working, either in the reserves or in the apprentice side.

'You didn't really carry big squads in those days,' he adds, 'and I was still learning my trade. I'd done reasonably well in the youth team but we had a lot of injuries. Quite a lot of young players – Neil Price, Jimmy Gilligan, Worrell Sterling – all played in that UEFA Cup run.

'Was I ready? I don't know, but I played the home and away leg and the manager was pleased with me. We got a taste of it but we had to keep working and keep those feet on the ground. You hadn't done anything yet!

'Before I signed as an apprentice I went home and away. A group of us used to jump on the Abbey Flyer at Park Street to go to Watford Junction and on to the game.

'I went to school in St Albans until I was 16 and then I signed as an apprentice. I had seen the rise of the club, starting from 1977/78. I was a schoolboy playing twice a week and in school holidays. That was my youth. Elton was a big supporter who would go to as many games as he possibly could.

'Under the age of 12, it's too young to be in an academy. You should be playing other sports, living your life and enjoying playing with your friends. It won't happen. Everybody is trying to get the young players and develop them. Between the ages of eight and 16, when they sign their scholarship, is a long time where you need a lot of commitment from the parents.

'Do they get more contact time with the coaches and with other players against better opposition? Yes, but in my opinion I am not sure that's the right route. The most important thing is developing the player. You want a safe environment but you want them to enjoy what they do.

'I've worked in academies three or four times, so I have had snapshots of it. There's a lot of benefits to it, in terms of facilities, the standard of coaching and support staff has improved. Otherwise I've worked at first-team level.

'You have to carry a big squad because of the games programme, which I think dilutes the quality. You take players that you know are not quite going to be good enough, but you need to fulfil the fixtures. The good players come through.'

As with Gilligan and Johnson at Watford, former Spurs players return as coaches, such as Troy Archibald-Henville, while Matt Wells was a scholar who, when we spoke, was assistant to Scott Parker at AFC Bournemouth. 'Matt was a scholar who went away and learned how to be a sports scientist.

'We develop players for life after football or instead of football. You might not have the talent to be a player but you will have the mentality to be successful in life in whatever you do. Not everyone can be in Tottenham's first team or get football in the league.'

Nigel was part of the senior staff when Ryan Mason took charge for the 2021 EFL Cup Final in his first game as manager, as caretaker after the departure of José Mourinho. What advice could Nigel give the rookie gaffer?

'Be yourself. I think he was well prepared. He'd been coaching for a few seasons. He's a very bright person and he felt confident enough to do it. If he needed any advice or support, I was there for him. Not only do you have to handle the coaching and team selection but the press as well.'

While Nigel was coaching young lads at Spurs in 2021, Elton John was topping the UK charts again. It's a shame Watford could not reach the heady heights of those UEFA Cup days, and instead spent another season deep in a battle to retain Premier League status. Reforming the Watford academy, Nigel says, 'won't be an overnight success' but the team is full of kids who have gone into the family business.

Striker Shaq Forde's dad Fabian came through the Watford academy around the time the club had financial issues in the early 2000s, while the father of right-back Ryan Andrews is 'electric' striker Wayne who was at Vicarage Road when Nigel was still playing, having broken into the team when Watford were a third-tier side in 1996/97. Unfortunately, Wayne broke his ankle and lost his place in the team, another victim of injury at precisely the wrong time.

Nigel, meanwhile, eventually handed over the right-back slot to Lloyd Doyley, one of those lads whose development he had been part of. 'I wasn't sure where I was going to fit in. It took a while for me to get into the team. I played right-back and Dave Bardsley played right-wing.

'It wasn't a smooth ride. Des Lyttle came in, Neil Cox came in, but I got back into the team. There's always battles.

'I saw a lot of me in Lloyd: dogged, very good one-v-one, hard-working, a good team-mate, very trustworthy.'

Today, many young players who represent Watford have been brought in from abroad thanks to the global scouting network which brought so much talent to Udinese before the Pozzo family bought Watford in 2012. Players like Ismaïla Sarr, João Pedro and Matěj Vydra have taken the pegs in the first-team dressing room away from local young talent.

Forty years ago, John Barnes and Luther Blissett represented Watford and England, such was their prowess and also the trust placed in them by Graham Taylor. I ask Nigel whether he would have made it to the first team had he come through the academy during the Pozzo era.

'If I was good enough, I'd have been in the team! You don't become a regular in a Premier League team until you are older now. It is so competitive and the quality is very, very high.

'We'd all like young players to come through the academies into the first team but you have to help your manager win. I'd love to see another Lloyd Doyley, Kenny Jackett, John Barnes. We all would. Hopefully with Jimmy and Richard in place now, if they get the backing they can start to produce the players. It won't happen overnight. It could take three to five years because of the cycle of players.

'You also need to have the opportunity. You can't be given it just out of sentiment. The Pozzos have bought some very good young players and sold them on. The most important thing for them is staying in the Premier League season after season and, alongside that, they can develop young players who are good enough to get into the team. We all as Watford fans want to see a local lad come in and do well, singing, "You're one of our own."

'Lloyd and Adrian Mariappa were the last couple who had long careers. It's very difficult to break through, even at Tottenham.'

Troy Parrott spent the 2021/22 season on loan at MK Dons, which prompts Nigel to tell me just how internecine the youth football world is.

'I worked with [MK Dons academy director] Jon Goodman. He was fitness coach at Reading and came up with us at Leeds. He was also a coach at Spurs prior to going to MK Dons.'

Young Dane Scarlett, meanwhile, has come a long way from learning how to play 11-a-side football alongside Rio Campbell. 'He's a very talented boy, very good mentality. He had a bad injury prior to his scholarship but he's earned the opportunity to be up in the first team. He's in and around the squad,' says Nigel. Just as Phil Foden learned from David Silva how to be a graceful creative midfielder, so Scarlett has Harry Kane teaching him how to bend the ball and attack it.

When he was at Reading, Nigel helped bring through Jem Karacan, Hal Robson-Kanu and Gylfi Sigurðsson. Alex McCarthy made his journey from a kid under Nigel's tutelage to an England international. Nigel won the FA Premier Reserve League with Reading having done so at Watford, where he was the first coach to lead a side to the title when their first team were outside the top division. Doyley and Ashley Young were in that team, which started the winger on his path to Premier League medals and a place in the England squad for the 2018 World Cup.

'He's got an interesting story,' Nigel says. 'He never got taken on as an apprentice. He stayed on at school because the club weren't sure whether he would be good enough. Halfway through that first year he'd been training twice a week, coming in during the day around his college work and Watford signed him. Then he got a pro deal and I took him for his first year as a pro and worked with him. Ray Lewington gave him his debut when he was 18.

'You knew that his character would be good enough. His mentality and his attitude was incredible. He was so determined and single-minded. He had the ability to go past people, ride tackles. He was versatile. He had the attributes to become a top player but you never know how far he's going to go. He earned the opportunity to get in front of a manager and be selected along the way.'

As we were talking, it occurred to me that only one player had worn the number 18 shirt for Manchester United before Ashley Young, who took it from Paul Scholes and passed it on to Bruno Fernandes. Indeed, Young was United's captain for the first few months of the 2019/20 season. I was at Vicarage Road when he scored two goals against his old club in November 2017 as Manchester United won 4-2. During the game, three graduates of their own academy played: Paul Pogba and Jesse Lingard started, while Marcus Rashford came off the bench. Scott McTominay was an unused sub.

With the presence of Adrian Mariappa at the back for the home side, Watford had as many of their own graduates as United did; they even fielded a former United player in Tom Cleverley, who had originally gone out on loan in 2009/10 to play first-team football at Watford. He was so impressive that he was named Player of the Year. Like Young, he graduated to the national side and represented Team GB at the London Olympics in 2012. It was no surprise that Cleverley moved back to Hertfordshire after he found his path blocked by the many attacking midfielders signed by Everton, where he moved to after leaving Old Trafford, in 2016/17. They included his old United team-mate Wayne Rooney.

It may be that Cleverley follows Rooney into coaching. Nigel Gibbs holds a UEFA Pro Licence which places less emphasis on youth development. At least it did when Nigel gained his certificate in 2005. FA Youth Awards exist for those who coach under-18s.

As we learned earlier, Watford lost the 1985 FA Youth Cup Final against Newcastle United. Nigel was familiar with the lynchpin of that team, Paul Gascoigne, because they represented England under-21s together. Could there ever be a player in the modern game, perhaps whom Nigel has coached at Spurs, of Gazza's type?

'He was a one-off. I was a couple of years older but he was unbelievable. His ability to go past people, his skills and finishing … I hadn't seen anyone like him. Phil Foden and, with his dribbling, Jack Grealish, are similar.'

The one that got away from Watford was Gifton Noel-Williams, whose career was wrecked by injury. 'I use Gifton as an example of doing the basics, some of the more mundane stuff,' says Nigel of his former team-mate. 'He was a late developer and he had to fill out physically. Whenever you do warm-up drills, he would be maximum on it. I'm boring you with this but again, it's about his determination and mentality. He was always out practicing his free kicks and deliveries.

'It's no accident. You've got to have the talent but also that steely determination to push yourself, to always be better. Gifton started on the left wing before he got into the central area.'

Gifton is back at Vicarage Road and in January 2022, was entrusted with the Watford women's side who were having a tough season in the second tier.

Given that Robbie Savage's face is on the cover of this book, I posed a hypothetical question to Nigel. Savage is a key part of the reborn Macclesfield FC. Because he came through at Manchester United under Eric Harrison, perhaps Savage would want to construct firm foundations at the club with a strong academy.

Macclesfield's website notes that kids can train with the team's senior squad while playing competitive matches, and use the club gym, all the while working towards a professional BTEC qualification with 19 units. These include Applied Coaching Skills, Sports Psychology, Functional Sports Massage and Nutrition for Physical Performance. This may in turn lead to an apprenticeship, finding work abroad or going off to university.

Nigel has spent a lifetime in the game, so if Savage headhunted him and could match his Spurs salary, what would he do to ensure young lads in the area come to Macclesfield rather than any number of clubs based in the north-west?

'Certainly you have to have an infrastructure in place and develop a good environment with good coaches,' he says, with 'holistic support and opportunities and pathways. That is what you can sell to them, guarantee them. Then it's up to them. You've got have someone who is committed. If he's not happy then it's really difficult to progress.

'The majority of the players I was brought up with at Watford really enjoyed going into training. I could have gone elsewhere but I liked the coach. I wanted to work for him and he gave me a lot of confidence.'

I would hope that the young men at Spurs would enjoy working for Nigel Gibbs, who remains one of the most loved players in the history of Watford FC. The next chapter begins with a mention of one of Manchester City's homegrown heroes.

Chapter Five

Trying to Break Through: Manchester City and Leeds United

IN HIS memoir, *I'm Not Really Here*, Manchester City academy graduate Paul Lake reckons that the bonuses he won as part of the 1986 Youth Cup winning side added up to £56. He treated himself to some trainers, the latest NOW CD – *NOW 8*, featuring the hits of 1986 such as 'Notorious', 'Word Up' and 'Walk This Way' – 'and a Terry's chocolate Orange for my parents'. Though the £25 win bonus helped (it would have been half of that if they had lost), 'All the money in the world couldn't have bought that cup-winning feeling.'

The Class of '86 are the subject of *Teenage Kicks*, written by City fanzine writers Phill Gatenby and Andrew Waldon. They beat a Manchester United team that included captain Steve Gardner, who retired at the age of 26 after making over 100 appearances for Burnley, then in the fourth tier. Gary Walsh and Lee Martin went on to play for the United first XI, Walsh most famously against Barcelona in a 4-0 Champions League defeat, Martin as first-choice left-back in the 1989/90 season when he scored the goal which won United the FA Cup. Denis Irwin's arrival and Ryan Giggs's stardom displaced Martin, though he will always be bought drinks by fans who were at Wembley in 1990.

As you would expect from an area in which thousands of jumpers were thrown down as goalposts, plenty of kids in the eastern part of Manchester have graduated from apprentices to pros, from kids to champions, in City's history. The late 1960s had Glyn Pardoe, Neil Young, Alan Oakes and Tommy Booth; the 1976 League Cup winners included Joe Corrigan and Willie Donachie, while Paul Power was the captain of the 1981 FA Cup Final team which included seven academy graduates.

Those same kids had lost both the 1979 and 1980 FA Youth Cup finals. Here is the honour roll: Clive Wilson (whose given name is Euclid Aklana Wilson), Steve Kinsey, Alex Williams and Tommy Caton played in both finals, while Nicky Reid, Steve MacKenzie and Dave Bennett all went on to play at Wembley in 1981. Perhaps they keep their three loser's medals on their shelves, which were a consolation in the days when City were always the bridesmaids.

In 1986, writes Andrew Waldon, Manchester did not have the tram running through it and the Hacienda nightclub 'was empty most nights' with indie music still the preserve of John Peel's radio show and not the Top 40. United had been overtaken by Liverpool as the most consistent champions in the land, while City had been relegated from the top tier in 1983. Chairman Peter Swales had to balance the books and stop signing expensive talent such as Trevor Francis and Steve Daley. At a game against Notts County, fans held up the start of the second half as they tried to pull down fences and storm the pitch, annoyed that City were 3-0 down and possibly wrecking their promotion hopes. They went up anyway.

Along with the Lancashire County Youth Cup, which City won four times in a row in the 1980s, the FA Youth

Cup allowed youngsters to shine. One of them was Andy Hinchcliffe, a future full England international who had already spent eight months out of football with a back injury and in a steel corset.

Paul Moulden had already played for the first team in a cup tie in November 1985 ('I was pleased with the five or six touches I had') the day before a Youth Cup game. He was in the family business, following his dad into the game and using his nous to score 289 goals in 40 games as a young teenager playing for Bolton Lads Club. This was despite breaking his leg when he was only nine years old. Having been offered trials at four other clubs he signed for City after feeling 'right at home' at Maine Road.

As a show of faith, coach Tony Book used the same line-up for every game in that year's 1985/86 tournament. City beat Tranmere Rovers 7-1 in the first round the day after David White turned professional on his 18th birthday, then saw off Blackburn Rovers by the same scoreline.

They then had to deal with a tough pitch and snowfall at Blackpool and won with the only goal of the game, from Ian Scott in front of Swales. Around 1,300 people watched their fourth-round victory over Leicester City, which included 'five distinct chances' in the opening seven minutes.

After the game, Book told the team to stamp down the divots so that the first team had a decent playing surface for their game two days later. Book's approach was typically old school, according to the authors of *Teenage Kicks*, '[His] style often would not have been out of place on a drill field rather than a football pitch.' This was to give them 'a proper professional attitude'. Ian Scott praised how Book 'kept us in line and kept our feet on the ground', while Steve Macauley said, 'If any of the lads had pissed him off during the week, sure enough they would be on the wrong end of one of his infamous scissor tackles!'

Book's job, as with every young coach, was to 'make men out of us and sculpt our personalities to that of a professional footballer'. As a lieutenant, he had Glyn Pardoe, a local hero who was always ready to play good cop and help guide the young lads to success.

Paul Lake scored within a minute to start a 3-0 win down at Fulham in the last eight. To emphasise that it was the mid-1980s, the goal came after a contested drop ball. Because the first team were playing at Chelsea, the game was held three days after it should have been held, so it became a double-header for fans down from east Manchester.

In fact, Steve Crompton says, it was the first time the youth team played in London at all, because it was always easier, and cheaper, to travel to Midland-based clubs or others in the north.

Youth team captain Steve Redmond, who was born in Liverpool, played in a 2-2 men's Manchester derby before the Youth Cup Final. The next day, the Full Members' Cup Final was played at Wembley between City and Chelsea, which the Londoners won 5-4 after being 5-1 ahead. Some of the young lads travelled with the men's team to contest a five-a-side match between YTS lads across the width of the pitch. Ominously, City won 2-1.

City then went on to defeat an Arsenal side in the semi-final of the Youth Cup. Their team included Michael Thomas, who had already played for the seniors, and Paul Merson, who would do so later that year. City lost the first leg 1-0 but overcame the Young Gunners in the second leg, which fans could pay '150p for adults and 100p for juniors'. After 120 minutes, and with Arsenal's away goal not counting, the game went into penalties and City advanced thanks to the heroics of goalkeeper

Crompton, who at one point mimicked Bruce Grobbelaar's 'jelly legs' from Liverpool's 1984 European Cup Final penalty shoot-out victory over Roma.

United's path to the final included wins at Burnley, Chesterfield and Notts County, then a home victory against Sheffield United in the last eight and a 3-1 aggregate success against Coventry City.

The first leg of the 1986 Youth Cup Final was a 1-1 draw in front of over 7,500 fans at Old Trafford, with the match report quoted in the book full of praise for 'the splendid goalkeeping of Gary Walsh'. David White complained of having 'a nightmare … I was physically tired and mentally drained' because they'd only played Arsenal two days before, giving United fresher legs.

Redmond, for his part, had played two games for the men's team as well as the semi-finals in the lead-up to the final, giving him a total of seven matches in 17 days (and four in seven) and a grand total of 61 games across the season. This would, of course, be impossible today, but Redmond 'wasn't complaining', so he joins a club containing George Best and Dave Mehmet.

Over 18,000 fans – officially it was 18,000 but many players reckon it was far more – showed up on a Mancunian Tuesday night. Throughout the first half, the many thousands of United fans would make their way around the pitch into the North Stand, which had not been intended for use. They would be distraught by full-time with Boyd and Mouldon scoring the goals as City won 2-0 and took the FA Youth Cup.

The match report noted that City 'had strength to go with their style' and Ian Brightwell especially played 'with the innocence of youth … and a sure-footedness in everything he did'. Brightwell's parents were Olympic athletes; City fans and pub quiz veterans will know his mum

Ann Packer won the 800m gold for Great Britain at the Tokyo Olympics in 1964.

Astonishingly, Andy Thackeray was denied a medal as he had not played in the second leg; he was released that summer and played over 100 times each for Wrexham, Rochdale and Nuneaton Borough, and was given a watch by the club in lieu of a tankard.

Ian Scott would echo the words of many Youth Cup winners, 'It was the greatest feeling to have won … with a group of lads that you had been with since 15 years old and worked with and played with every day for the past two years.' Paul Moulden, meanwhile, was unhappy that his side had stopped at two, because 'on paper we were worth four or five goals better than them'.

Moulden stayed at City for three more seasons, breaking his leg in 1987, before touring clubs including Bournemouth, Oldham Athletic, Birmingham City and Molde in Norway.

Moulden, Hinchcliffe and Redmond went off to China with the England youth team while the men's season was still going on. In 1986, country went before club.

Having been given a bye from the first round as holders, City's 1986/87 Youth Cup side was made up of Paul Lake (who made his debut for the men's team that season) and a new batch of youngsters. They overcame Wigan in the second round on a Saturday morning replay after the first meeting had been played in a storm having been postponed twice.

Then came victories against Newcastle United and Liverpool, who fielded Craig Hignett and Steve Staunton, followed by Leeds United in the quarter-finals. An 'inept display' in the first leg of the semi-final against Coventry City was neutralised by a win in the second leg but, oddly, there was no shoot-out after 120 minutes. Instead, the teams played a third game which Coventry won. A few weeks later, Manchester City lost their place in the First Division and there was a clear-out among the first team. Many of the Class of '86 contributed to promotion pushes; promotion was achieved at the second attempt.

In a game against Brighton in 1988, the Magnificent Seven – Brightwell, Hinchcliffe, Lake, Redmond, White, Moulden and Scott – played together from the start. In 1989, the first five of these played in what was known as The Maine Road Massacre, when City beat Manchester United 5-1. Hinchcliffe scored the fifth with a rare header.

As the rest of the Class of '86 were sold on, and as Lake underwent 15 operations to save his career, only Brightwell remained around the first-team squad. He eventually became captain in 1996. He had served under ten managers (plus three caretakers) and made his last appearance at Reading in February 1997. City were relegated to the third tier in May.

Happily for City, in the 2000s another golden crop emerged. Nedum Onuoha, Ched Evans, Ben Mee, Kieran Trippier, Daniel Sturridge and Micah Richards all became first-team pros at City or elsewhere, but Michael Johnson was the standout, 'the next Steven Gerrard, a future England captain' according to team-mate Kelvin Etuhu in a later interview with *The Athletic*.

In 2007 came the Thai takeover and Etuhu slid away from the first team and had a short spell in prison. Indeed, he watched the 2011 FA Cup Final, won by a Yaya Touré goal at Wembley, from there. Richards and Sturridge thrived, he says, because they 'had good father figures and influences in their lives'; Sturridge is a devout Christian.

After retirement, Onuoha started a media career which included a podcast, *Kickback with Nedum*, which resulted in a book deal. His conversation with Sturridge included some chat about their academy days – 'You used to run 10,000 channels!' – and the group who came up from the youth ranks. 'I felt at home straight away,' said Sturridge. 'We all had such a great relationship because we all grew up together.' Stephen Ireland was 'on my wavelength … I'd make a run and I'd expect the ball to be where I'd go'.

Ireland ('the main man' according to Onuoha) played for the City first team over 170 times, having come over at 15 to play for the younger age groups. In a chat with his dressing-room chum Onuoha, he described City in the early 2000s as an 'old school club with an old school mentality … It took a lot of hard work, especially mentally'. Wages and fashion and social media were not a concern when he was 17. 'Everyone [was] playing head tennis or two-touch … It makes me emotional how happy it was.'

The other jewel of the Platt Lane academy era was Michael Johnson, whose career was cut short by a spate of horrible injuries. As a teenager he moved from club to club (Leeds, Crewe, both Merseyside sides, Feyenoord) before signing youth terms at City at 16. Onuoha caught up with him for the podcast, in which Johnson said he was 'trying to be a normal guy', looking after the tenants in his properties and eschewing the media.

Micah Richards, whose absence led to Johnson being named captain in the Youth Cup Final in 2006, revealed in his chat with Onuoha that he enjoyed training with Nicolas Anelka and playing alongside Richard Dunne. Young Richards had moved back from midfield for a Youth Cup game due to a team-mate's injury and Stuart Pearce, the first-team gaffer, applauded his performance as one of the best centre-back displays he had seen in a Youth Cup match. Richards was quickly called up to the first team due to more injuries, including to Onuoha. 'You just needed that little bit of luck. If you did okay, you'd get a chance,' Richards said.

In the days when City's first team had trouble scoring at home, the youngsters 'didn't really have a style of play. We just had good coaches who got the best out of what they had.' They trained in the middle of Moss Side – 'the Wild West!' chuckled Onuoha. 'It added to the character of the play.

'We'd jog through the streets! It toughened us up, getting us ready. They looked for physicality first, then looked at technicality.'

The side that won the 2008 FA Youth Cup, captained by current Burnley skipper Ben Mee, contained a mix of local and international talent, including Slovakian pair Vladimir Weiss and Robert Mak. Weiss's career has taken him to Italy, Greece, Spain and Qatar, and he finally returned to his home nation in 2020 to play for Slovan Bratislava. Mak has likewise travelled widely, from Germany to Greece to Russia to Turkey to Hungary.

Both have been regulars for their country but never got to show their talent for City's senior team, aside from Weiss getting on for the last 20 minutes of the 2008/09 Premier League season and playing in playing in four cup ties the next. Bolton Wanderers and Rangers fans may remember him for his loan spells as City tried to prepare their talent for first-team football.

In fact, that seemed to be the formula for City's 2008 team who couldn't break through: defender Ryan McGivern had six separate loan spells in a five-year period before signing for Hibernian in 2013; Andrew Tutte, from Huyton in Liverpool, got experience at Yeovil Town and Rochdale before signing for the latter and becoming part of Bury's mid-2010s side; having been kept out of the Swindon Town team by Charlie Austin while on loan there, striker David Ball was also at Rochdale, though he is most associated with his five years at Fleetwood Town. He has ended up in New Zealand playing A-League football.

Even future England international Kieran Trippier, who signed for Newcastle United in January 2022 after two and a half years with Atlético Madrid, spent a year with Barnsley and one at Burnley before signing for the latter in 2012, where he came in a package deal with Mee. At least the latter got to play a game for City, something Trippier failed to do, though both have been back to the Etihad several times in their career. Ironically a positive Covid test meant that Mee was absent in a 2-0 loss in October 2021.

Trippier's Youth Cup Final was soured when he was injured and had to be substituted at the very end of the second game of their 4-2 aggregate win over Chelsea. Mee scored the first goal in the 3-1 home victory, with Weiss and Ball completing the set at the Etihad in front of 20,000 fans. Daniel Sturridge had scored City's goal in the first leg.

Onuoha talked about his own time in the City academy on the official Manchester City club podcast. He used to try to get players' autographs at Platt Lane, in the days before the new Etihad Campus sucked in the world's best young players. He sat in the Kippax at Maine Road whenever he wasn't a ball boy, 'gravel destroying my kneecaps'. While he worked at one Youth Cup match, Onuoha marvelled at Shaun Wright-Phillips. He was given confidence by someone who had 'made it … knowing you're not too far behind that' in the youth team.

When Onuoha was asked about his coaches, Jim Cassell's name came up, as did those of youth coaches Frankie Bunn and Alex Gibson and reserve coach Asa Hartford. With over 25 players brought through, including Stephen Ireland and Kasper

Schmeichel from the same group, 'The Academy went from getting beaten regularly to losing two games in three years.

'We came in full-time. These were tough, tough guys but it grounded us. I enjoyed it. We were all in this together, all the time. Those guys prepare you for what is to come.' The club became a conveyor belt for 'tough, committed hard workers', adds Onuoha. 'We were a big group of Mancunians. They were handing me beatings when I played for my Sunday League team!'

Keen readers of this story will remember south London in the 1970s, where future Millwall and Crystal Palace players would come up against each other in their teenage years. Onuoha continues the tale of his own professional career.

'Out of nowhere I was on the bench for City versus Chelsea. City won, I was in college [and I] got a win bonus that was more than I'd received anywhere in my life,' he remembered, following it up with a League Cup tie against Arsenal. 'I still had to do my A2 in Business the next year' while still being an academy player. Onuoha was named Young Player of the Year and played more times for the first team as a teenager.

His team-mate Kasper Schmeichel comes across as a masochist in his chat with Nedum – 'Everything could go wrong if I messed up' – but the pair talked about life in the academy. Schmeichel trained with the first team before he did so with the academy ('I ended up doing shooting with Anelka!') and would meet up with the young lads on Saturdays and in school holidays. 'When I meet one of the boys from back then, I'm straight back to how it was,' he says warmly.

Schmeichel played for the under-18s, looking up to the club's number one David James – who was on the losing side to Kasper's dad in the FA Cup Final of 1996 – before Joe Hart was brought in from Shrewsbury Town. In fact, Schmeichel played on the same pitch as Hart when he was on loan at Bury and there's plenty of mutual 'respect and friendship that surpassed football. Whoever got the spot would probably keep it.'

We will see how Manchester City get on in the 2021/22 Youth Cup later in the book.

Coincidentally, in one of this story's more clunky segues, Leeds United a) once employed Kasper Schmeichel and b) were Manchester United's main rivals in 1993. Oliver Kay and Phil Hay teamed up to write a piece for *The Athletic* in February 2020 to remember the 1993 FA Youth Cup Final in what must have been trailed as the War of the Roses.

One commentator 'below the line' reckoned that teams who 'win at the youth level through physicality and bullying smaller more technical players ... fall by the wayside when the technical players grow and just being aggressive isn't enough any more'.

Another reckoned that Jamie Forrester's overhead kick for Leeds 'still remains one of my favourite goals I have ever seen live'. A fan who watched the final on Sky Sports saw how 'the crowd just kept filling and filling during the game', which had its start delayed because of it. They watched a team triumph through, say the authors (although probably leaning on Leeds fan Hay's words), 'A superhuman effort by a group of young players who were determined to bring their much-vaunted rivals down a peg or two. Those Leeds youngsters were at the peak of their powers that night.'

While Manchester United were triumphant in the 1992 Youth Cup, Oldham Athletic had disposed of Leeds that year, the year in which the Yorkshire side famously pipped their rivals as the last champions of the old First Division. Manager Howard Wilkinson wanted to add to the quota of academy graduates, which included David Batty and Gary Speed, in his first team.

As with Glyn Pardoe at Manchester City, a local hero was in charge of the youngsters. Paul Hart had been poached from Nottingham Forest and he 'demanded discipline' according to Mark Tinkler, who could play in the centre of defence or in midfield. Interestingly, one apprentice was the famous Forrester, who chose to continue his development at the Auxerre academy which was 'way ahead of its time'. Happily for Leeds, homesickness forced his return as well as that of ex-United kid Kevin Sharp.

Sharp played with Tinkler and Noel Whelan at youth level for England, which helped form their friendship. They both got to know the lads from United, such as Paul Scholes, Chris Casper and Gary Neville, and England under-18s won the 1993 European Championship, held at home, with a squad containing those six players. Robbie Fowler was up front. Again, it was the era of Lilleshall and a national performance centre, which helped the clubs, rather than what happens in the modern era, in which club academies bring through talent which in turn helps the national team.

On their journey to Youth Cup triumph, Leeds overcame Stoke City, Queens Park Rangers and Sheffield United, then went through 4-3 on aggregate against Norwich City in the semi-final, having won the first leg 4-1. Wilkinson made good on his promise and used several of the young lads in the first team, who were involved in European competition and the three domestic trophies.

Famously, Leeds's defence had enormous trouble adjusting to the outlawing of the pass back to the goalkeeper and they avoided relegation to what was then the First Division by just two points. More famously still, they sold Eric Cantona to their rivals, who directly inspired the work ethic of the young lads at Manchester United.

In front of nearly 31,000 people, the first leg of the 1993 Youth Cup Final took place at Old Trafford where the home team conceded two goals. 'They weren't ready for it at all,' remembered Noel Whelan, who scored the second Leeds goal.

Phil Neville came into the side for the second leg. 'I've played Champions League games away to Fenerbahçe and [Glasgow] Rangers and places like that,' he later said of the occasion. 'The atmosphere at Elland Road that night was right up there in terms of feeling that noise and intensity and hatred. It's one of those moments in my career where I look back and think, "Wow."'

As for what happened on the pitch, said Neville, 'Leeds bullied us in terms of physicality and game knowledge. Noel Whelan and Jamie Forrester up front were fantastic for them … It was a learning experience.' The latter scored the aforementioned acrobatic goal ten minutes into the second leg. 'I never scored another one like that,' Forrester said. 'It's a special kind of goal for any player to score. To do it in front of 31,000 against Man United, live on Sky, that was even more special.'

While United's team had more talent, Kevin Sharp said, 'We showed more desire than they did and they had two or three weaker positions where we exploited them.' The team followed their coach's demands to be physical, as Hart noted, 'I don't think the Manchester United boys had seen anything like it. At one point, two or three of them were down on their knees. We were just too strong for them.'

It is sad to note that those Leeds lads could not become club legends as Hart had been. None of them played for England or had a foothold on the first team. Here's Sharp to put forward the case for the players,

'It felt like we were fighting against the manager. We did really well in the reserves and we were all making a few first-

In the 1950s, Manchester United won the first five FA Youth Cups. The line-up against Red Star Belgrade was full of Busby Babes including Duncan Edwards (far left) and Bobby Charlton (fifth from left).

The Chelsea senior side of 1963 contained some members of the back-to-back Youth Cup winners, including Terry Venables, Bobby Tambling and Peter Bonetti.

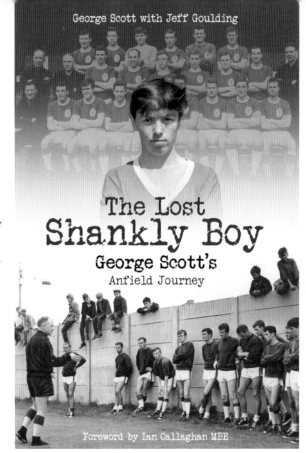

George Scott's book
The Lost Shankly
Boy *is a fine chronicle
of the first years of the
modern Liverpool FC.
Scott and his team-
mates lost the 1964
FA Youth Cup Final.*

*Harry Redknapp
was part of the West
Ham team which
beat Liverpool in
that 1964 final. He
made his first-team
debut the following
year.*

In 1973, Sunderland won the FA Cup with a team which benefitted from the presence of several Youth Cup winners including captain Bobby Kerr.

Steve Perryman won the 1970 FA Youth Cup with Tottenham Hotspur and went on to make over 850 senior appearances as a one-club man.

Watford chairman Elton John is surrounded by the 1982/83 squad. He had seen his apprentices, including Nigel Gibbs and Jimmy Gilligan, win the FA Youth Cup that spring.

After consecutive FA Youth Cup Final defeats in 1979 and 1980, Manchester City finally won the trophy in 1986. Their team included (from left to right) Ian Brightwell, Andy Hinchcliffe and Paul Lake. The three of them played in a 5-1 win against Manchester United in 1989.

Jamie Forrester's goal helped Leeds United win the 1993 FA Youth Cup. Few players from that side were able to break into the first team, much to Forrester's regret.

Liverpool academy director Steve Heighway holds the Youth Cup trophy in 2006 after his side beat Manchester City. Having been a European Cup winner himself, Heighway helped kids like Steven Gerrard and Jamie Carragher develop into champions.

Two products of east London academies are in action here. Millwall graduate Jermaine Wright chases after West Ham United's Michael Carrick, who was part of the 1999 Youth Cup-winning side.

Lee Fowler was part of two Youth Cup runners-up at Coventry City. Now coaching at non-league level, he played for the Wales under-21 team against Sascha Riether and Germany in 2005.

Neil Heaney won the 1988 Youth Cup with Arsenal and enjoyed a professional career with Southampton and Darlington. He was part of the Darlo side that lost the Third Division play-off final in 2000 against Peterborough United.

Rio Campbell came through the Watford academy and played in the 2019 Youth Cup semi-final against Liverpool. In 2020 he signed for Swansea City.

The future of Chelsea FC remains in good hands with players like Harvey Vale, who had made his senior debut the month before scoring the winning goal in the Youth Cup fourth round against Watford. Hornets captain Will Hall (right) did his best to stifle the opposition that night.

team appearances and it felt like we were going to be a part of the first-team squad moving forward.

'But then the manager brought in a lot of older players, like Nigel Worthington, Carlton Palmer and Brian Deane ... Howard Wilkinson did really well for Leeds and is rightly respected for that but I don't think he was big a fan of the youth players.'

Giving the case for the defence, Hart respectfully disagrees, saying that Wilkinson's ten-year plan was 'to make sure that by the end of the 1990s, we were regularly feeding the first team with players from the academy. We did achieve that.'

Witness the next crop, who are written about in Rocco Dean's new book *The O'Leary Years*. 'In 1993, we hadn't built the Thorp Arch academy,' Rocco tells me. 'Wilkinson took over in 1988 and his plan was to build this state-of-the-art training complex and concentrate on bringing youth through. The youth players would all actually live there. Bielsa was doing similar at Newell's in Argentina,' he adds, making it no surprise that Bielsa is keen to work with a small senior squad and fill the gaps with youth products.

'Wilkinson brought in Paul Hart and they had a good team at the time,' Rocco says. 'Sadly I didn't go to the Youth Cup Final, though I had a season ticket at the time. I watched it on TV.'

Forrester was the star of the team. 'He'd already made his debut in the first team. We played Blackburn and beat them 5-2 at Elland Road. Gordon Strachan scored a hat-trick and I'm sure Forrester set up one of the goals. The following season he didn't really get a look in,' said Rocco.

Forrester regrets his poor attitude after winning the Youth Cup which was 'probably the worst thing that could have happened to me at 18 ... My attitude wasn't right when I was at Leeds. I got a bit carried away. People were talking about me, recognising me. I lost my focus a bit.'

'That's a bit of a cop-out,' said Rocco. 'The expectations might have been raised but if you're good enough to succeed at Leeds then you're going to have to deal with high expectations anyway. I don't really buy into that to be honest. It shows a mental weakness.

'Leeds finished fifth but we weren't a good team. Carlton Palmer, David White, Brian Deane: they were mid-range Premier League players sprinkled with class who managed to get Leeds back into Europe. But would we have seen the team explode into life if we'd thrown the young players in together?

'I don't know whether Wilkinson regrets that. They did all get their chance but they didn't take it.'

Rocco's words seem to be echoed in the *Athletic* article by Noel Whelan, who got more chances than the others and played 50 times for Leeds.

'If you get to put the first-team shirt on, there's your opportunity. You've got to take it. We got games but you're playing at the very highest level, the Premier League. After here, how many of them went and played at Championship level? Not many. Sometimes, it just doesn't work out.'

Hart agreed with Whelan. 'A number of those lads did play in the Premier League for the club,' he said. 'But even though they were tremendous players, it was possibly a step too far for some of them at that particular time. That's said with no disrespect and it's the nature of the beast. Many of them found football careers elsewhere and that's really what it's all about.'

In 1997, Leeds regained the Youth Cup with a 3-1 aggregate win over Crystal Palace. Harry Kewell and Paul Robinson were part of that side, along with a young Alan Smith, while future senior Eagles Clinton Morrison and Hayden Mullins were on the losing side. Did Rocco get the feeling that O'Leary was promoting youth himself?

'In 1997 everybody knew how special the team was. They won the youth league by an absolute canter and scored something like 124 goals and conceded 17!

'There was a big clamour for George Graham to put them in the team. He promoted Harry Kewell but not anybody else. The reason Paul Hart left Leeds was because Graham wasn't giving the youth players, particularly Woodgate, a chance in the team. Ian Harte had already broken through but he was in and out the team.'

O'Leary, however, did it instantly. Rocco continues, 'In his first match he played Graham's team and they were rubbish. They lost 1-0 at home to Leicester City. Then in the second match, he threw in Stephen McPhail and Woodgate, who were both 18, and they looked like the best players straight away.

'He was forced to bring in Paul Robinson because Nigel Martyn got injured at Old Trafford and Robinson looked great. He ended up playing the first half of the Champions League season. He had an incredible game against Barcelona at Elland Road.

'Two weeks later we played Liverpool and Alan Smith was thrown on for his debut. I didn't know who Smith was – I even knew the youth players! – and he scored with his first touch. There were constantly five or six products in the team and we finished fourth.'

Rio Ferdinand's addition helped; indeed, only West Ham, who developed Ferdinand, rivalled Leeds in converting kids to pros. 'Nowadays it just wouldn't happen but there were so many really, really good young players. It's a shame that it doesn't seem to happen nowadays,' says Rocco.

Except at Leeds, one might counter. Injuries to Luke Ayling and Patrick Bamford, who won Youth Cup medals with Arsenal and Chelsea respectively, have led to opportunities for Jamie Shackleton and Joe Gelhardt to play for the senior team.

Rocco adds, 'Fans are panicking about the size of the squad but we've got 18 players. It gives the youth players a chance. I don't think Gelhardt would have come to Leeds if Bielsa didn't have his philosophy, or that the pathway to the first team was there. If Leeds had two players for every position and a massive squad, maybe not.'

Leeds have signed young players from abroad. Pascal Struijk was signed from Ajax's youth team in 2018 having been competing with Sven Botman in the age groups. 'A lot of people think he's our best player now,' says Rocco. Struijk's fellow Dutchman Crysencio Summerville was poached from Feyenoord before he could even make a first-team appearance for them. 'They've got Jack Harrison, Daniel James and Raphinha and they wanted someone young to be given the chance to develop into a top player.

'That makes complete sense to me. For a club like Leeds we're going to need players to come through,' Rocco says, even at the cost of removing fan favourite Hélder Costa from the squad. When Manchester City signed Jack Harrison, he was moved to New York City FC rather than train with Manchester City's kids; without a first-team pathway because of England internationals Phil Foden and Jack Grealish in front of him, Harrison decided to join Leeds permanently.

Kevin Sharp, meanwhile, represents Kalvin Phillips, the hometown hero and captain. Rocco would love Phillips to remain at the club, as Jamie Carragher and Gary Neville did at Liverpool and Manchester United respectively in the final gasps of the one-club man era.

'But I can't see it,' Rocco sighs. 'At some stage he'll want to play in the Champions League and he'll deserve it. Maybe Leeds will get there but I can't see them doing it fast enough.'

In the late 1990s, Phillips would surely have trained at Lilleshall but the closure of the central school meant that there are now centres around the country at various clubs.

'It's spread around a few of the richest clubs. You can't really criticise young players for going to these clubs even if they know they're not going to make it there. They're getting the best education and they're filtering down from there,' says Rocco.

'I don't like it. It's completely old-fashioned but I'd like to see these young players coming up through the leagues, being owned and sold by the smaller the clubs, rather than filtering their way down, but that's just my romanticism.'

Unless he's with the first team, manager and cult hero Marcelo Bielsa goes to every single under-23 game. 'Even if it's just recorded, he watches every game,' Rocco marvels. 'It'll be interesting to see if we got to the [Youth Cup] semi-finals and if he would sacrifice having them in the first-team squad that week.'

As a finale in the *Athletic* piece, Forrester says that the following season, the kids had moved up to the reserves and United 'gave us an absolute thrashing'. Everyone knows what happened next.

Chapter Six

The 1990s: Manchester United and Liverpool

IN MAY 2021, a typical 18-year-old would sit examinations assessed by their teachers, hoping that the grades would allow entry into university.

The kids at Liverpool and Aston Villa are atypical. Those at the latter had led the club to the final of the FA Youth Cup for the first time since 2002 and thus in their own lifetime. The likes of Louie Barry and Carney Chukwuemeka are part of a gilded generation who have begun to benefit from a new training ground opened by famous fan and English FA president, the Duke of Cambridge.

As for the Liverpool scholars, they had seen the senior team become first European champions then English champions. In 2019, the class immediately above them defeated Manchester City, captained by Eric García, on penalties. That Liverpool team, as we discovered in the last chapter, included two players called Williams, Neco and Rhys, who would be on the pitch at the end of the senior team's 4-2 win at Old Trafford in May 2021.

In a sad indictment of the modern game, the most fuss about that FA Youth Cup-winning side concerned Bobby Duncan, the number nine who had forced a move from Manchester City to the Reds and then from the Reds to Fiorentina. Duncan later blamed his agent for that 'unnecessary' transfer to Italy and told his social media followers that he was 'without doubt a better player and a stronger person ... it is time for my football to do the talking'.

Duncan joined Derby County early in the 2020/21 season, starting their defeat by Chorley in an FA Cup third-round tie when the first team had to self-isolate. Can he fulfil the potential he showed during that FA Youth Cup run, especially now that he has changed agents and is training with the first team who are coached by Wayne Rooney?

In his 2019 book *How To Grow Old*, comedian and former semi-pro footballer John Bishop talks about following Liverpool. Of course he is a fan of the new breed of footballer who pitches up at Anfield, yet he is slightly sad that no spectator 'went to school with them, or went out with their sister, or played against them for the school team'.

With the rise of the Williamses and the promotion of many scholars to the first team, perhaps Alex Inglethorpe can offer the case for the defence.

He is a former Watford striker who played over 100 times for Leyton Orient. He briefly managed Exeter City and was in the away dugout when the non-league team prevented a Manchester United side including Cristiano Ronaldo, Paul Scholes and Wes Brown from scoring in an FA Cup third-round meeting at Old Trafford in 2005.

Inglethorpe was a Tottenham coach during the Harry Redknapp era and has now been at Liverpool for a decade, first as reserve-team coach, then as under-21 team manager and now academy director. He made national news when he chose to cap the weekly salaries of the young players in 2016; he coupled this with a reduction in personnel, cutting the numbers from 240 to 170.

A £40,000-per-annum limit for a first-year pro was set down, which means humble pros like Trent Alexander-Arnold, Neco Williams and Curtis Jones were not tempted to experience the same pitfalls of other teenage talents at other academies. 'You should build a career and gratification should be deferred,' said Inglethorpe.

As well as working with Steve Heighway, who is a sort of academy worker without portfolio – he was 'Head of Steve Heighway', Inglethorpe once joked – he naturally has the backing of the first-team gaffer, Jürgen Klopp. 'He [Klopp] takes a very healthy interest in what we do and the best compliment I can pay him is he knows the players' names. We've had to earn that trust, who have to carry the name of the academy,' says Inglethorpe.

'If they're to get their one audition, I don't want them to fail. We're not a charity,' he continues, realising that there needs to be a return on all the investment by, at the moment, Fenway Sports Group. 'I love reading the names the day after the game,' Inglethorpe added in an interview with the *Training Ground Guru* podcast, 'and I'm proud they're in the job that they love and we're a part of them doing that, where we gave them some values.'

Michael Owen scored a hat-trick against Manchester United in the 1996 FA Youth Cup quarter-final. His first came after a 50-yard run through the United defence but United came back to lead 2-1, with Michael Twiss scoring the second. After Owen equalised with a penalty that prefigured the cool spot-kick against Argentina in the 1998 World Cup shoot-out, in which the world would come to know what Liverpool fans had known for several months, his winner in the quarter-final showed his bravery: he won a 50-50 challenge with United goalkeeper Nick Culkin and came away with the ball, then managed to evade two defenders with a shot which won the game. Culkin, for his part, played for the United first team for a matter of seconds against Arsenal. Some 1.4m viewers have seen the footage on United's Facebook channel.

Owen added five goals across the two legs of the semi-final, which the Young Reds won 7-5 against Crystal Palace. However, he was unable to play in the first leg of the final against West Ham United because he was playing for England's under-16s. Happily, with the team taking a 2-1 lead into the second leg, he helped Liverpool win their first FA Youth Cup at the expense of another lot of fine West Ham apprentices. They included his future international team-mates Rio Ferdinand and Frank Lampard, who scored with a typical thunderbolt from the edge of the penalty area in the opening minute of the game.

Equally typically, Owen equalised with a header then got an assist of sorts when his second-half shot came off the post and back to Mark Quinn, which put Liverpool 4-1 up in the tie. While Owen had a celebrated career in the game, Quinn's career involved managing warehouses in Cheshire before a decade at JD Sports as an operations manager.

Another future England team-mate of Owen's was Jamie Carragher. In his memoir *Carra*, Carragher admitted that the team 'fumbled through much of the competition'. He actually calls the under-18 side 'a team of scallies … a gang of street urchins'. Selection issues meant that Carragher moved from midfield to defence, having famously started as a striker, for the Youth Cup Final. 'We were on £250 a week,' he said, a figure which trebled after the win after a meeting with manager Roy Evans.

Right-back Lee Prior was good at procuring second-hand gear, while winger Jamie Cassidy suffered injuries and his progress stalled. Ditto David Thompson aka 'Birkenhead-the-Ball'. Gérard Houllier 'couldn't understand the ultra-Scouse sensibilities' of a lad who broke through to the first team before moving to Coventry and Blackburn, gaining caps at under-21 level for England. Thompson now works in Gibraltar.

Having begun as 'kids, unknowns with everything to prove', Carragher and Owen ended the season on the cusp of their full debuts for the men's side. 'This triumph was the platform for much more,' Carragher wrote. As for 'Mo', Owen was 'an animal' whose tackling matched his eye for goal. 'I'd never seen a striker tackle like him,' Carra purred, as Owen's tackle on the United goalkeeper in the quarter-final showed. That spirit may have led to the injuries Owen suffered, which took the ferocity out of his game.

Their coach was Steve Heighway, mentioned above, who had been recruited by his former team-mate Kenny Dalglish to bring through more academy products. Around £10m was spent on the academy building, taking the youngsters away from the first team, and the pressure on Heighway drove him out of the club even as Liverpool's young players won the Youth Cup again two years in a row in 2005/06 and 2006/07.

A decade after he had won his first medal, Carragher watched one of those finals with Steven Gerrard. He was 'partly proud and partly saddened' upon realising that some of these players would never win anything again as Liverpool players, 'None of those players must have felt confident this would be anything but the highlight of their careers in red.'

The concept of the one-club man, even in 2007, was on the way out, 'as if we have erected our own barriers' between under-18 and senior levels. There was, when Carragher's book was published in 2008, 'a nationwide epidemic' of players who couldn't demonstrate their quality, 'progress no further and slide into obscurity'. At the time, his team-mates were Spaniards such as Luis García and Xabi Alonso, who had been brought in by Rafael Benitez, which created fissures with Heighway.

It happened under Houllier too, when young Stephen Wright was deemed too immature and was replaced by new signing Abel Xavier. Ditto Dominic Matteo, replaced by Christian Ziege, and Danny Guthrie, who showed early promise. In fact, with the conveyer belt of foreign teenage talent also blocking the progress of local lads to the first team, Carragher himself grew 'angrier' at how Heighway (who 'added ten per cent' to his own game) was being treated. Rather than talking to the kind of local journalist whom we shall shortly meet, Carragher had to bury his criticisms of the club in the middle of his memoir.

'We're behaving like Pied Pipers, enticing children to England with the promise of wealth,' he wrote, joking that, soon, scouts would be present 'hanging around maternity wards' in Spain or Paris. It speaks volumes that Carragher's own son James signed a scholarship at Wigan Athletic at the age of 16, having come through the age groups at Liverpool. Having been the captain of a successful under-18s group, James made his professional debut in an EFL Cup game in August 2021.

I wonder what would happen if Jamie had to analyse his son's performance in a game aired on Sky Sports. He would probably stand aside and let Gary Neville offer a diplomatic assessment.

As mentioned earlier, Alex Inglethorpe and Jürgen Klopp are in lockstep, with none of the difficulties from the Benitez era. In 2021, Curtis Jones and Trent Alexander-Arnold played in the 5-0 victory at Old Trafford along with world-class talent. The current under-18 squad contains local and international talent, as it did 15 years ago, including German starlet Melkamu Frauendorf, Frenchman Billy Koumetio, and Matteo Ritaccio, born in New York to Italian parents. Also present is the cult hero Oakley Cannonier, the ball boy who famously chucked the ball to Alexander-Arnold to take the quick corner and clinch the 4-0 win against Barcelona in the UEFA Champions League semi-final in 2019, which came two weeks after Liverpool's Youth Cup win.

For the 2021/22 competition, Liverpool were drawn at home to Burnley, the 1968 Youth Cup champions, in the fourth round. Ian Doyle is the man who has covered the Young Reds for the *Liverpool Echo* since his time reporting on Everton in the 1990s. On the day we spoke, Covid had scuppered plans for both that week's Carabao Cup semi-final and, a day later, the Youth Cup match.

The morning press conference with assistant manager Pep Lijnders had been cancelled and Ian made me aware of an 'interesting' development to be released at 9.30am: Lijnders had tested positive for Covid. Soon after, Ian's diary was wiped out entirely, aside from having to post the odd update for the *Liverpool Echo* website. I took a call from an 0151 number that 'won't cost us anything' because it was a staff phone number!

Having looked at the Liverpool FC page of an online encyclopaedia, I noticed that their roll call of trophies does not include their Youth Cup triumphs. Even though the senior team did not achieve it, some of those who were part of the team that won the 1977 European Cup or 2001 FA Cup did start their journeys as kids at the club.

'I can see where you're coming from,' Ian says. 'The EFL Cup is taking on aspects of the Youth Cup, isn't it, just because it's used to blood so many youngsters and see what they're like in a senior competition. There's certainly an argument to say that it's more important than all the domestic leagues purely because it's competitive all the way through.

'The under-23s are halfway through the season then it comes to January and loads of them will either go on loan or leave, so all the under-18s step up. Unless you've got loads of players like City and United, that Premier League North is quite difficult to win. The under-18s then pick up the under-16s but the Youth Cup is the one competition they can get back together again and play.'

As an aside, that league was a three-way race between Liverpool and the two Manchester clubs. By virtue of winning 19 and losing only one of the 24 games, City took the 2020/21 league by a single point. In a surprise development, it was Blackburn Rovers who topped the division at the end of January 2022, with City second and Liverpool third.

Ian says that the players celebrate a Youth Cup win and so do the coaches. 'The coaches put a lot of work in and they like the fact they have helped develop these youngsters who have gone on and won something.

'It's a reflection on them as well. People sometimes forget that it's not just the players who learn but it's the coaches. Liverpool have coaches like Neil Critchley, who came through the 18s and 23s. Lijnders was at academy level and stepped up to the first team.'

Steve Cooper, who as we saw worked with Rio Campbell at Swansea City, was a youth coach at Liverpool before going on to win the World Cup as manager of England under-17s.

'Let's be honest,' Ian says. 'For quite a lot of the young players that'll be the best thing they ever win [the FA Youth Cup] because so few players of that level get to the first team. Stephen Darby played in a Champions League against

Fiorentina, he had a bit of a tough time. It was the tail end of the Benitez era when he was trying players out. By then the youth side of it was getting sidetracked because Benitez was involved in this big argument with the owners so that kind of lost its way.'

Ian contrasts the present era under the ownership of Fenway Sports Group with the cowboys who were in charge during the 2000s: 'FSG have addressed that stuff. They've made some good appointments so there is that conveyor belt for coaches and players. If the coaches are doing well, the players are doing well.'

Klopp's experience promoting from within at Borussia Dortmund has been useful too. I would label Dortmund a 'departure lounge' club because Jadon Sancho was, and Erling Haaland is, never going to be in Germany for long.

'Liverpool had this policy under Benitez where he brought in a lot of youngsters, put them in the under-21s as it was back then, in the hope that one of them would get into the first team and one or two would be worth a bit of money to sell. That would justify buying the rest of them and then he could move on to the next lot,' says Ian.

'I think Liverpool have come to the end of a cycle: Harry Wilson, Sheyi Ojo, Rhian Brewster, Ki-Jana Hoever. Yasser Larouci played a few first-team games. Those players have gone through the system and mostly were sold at profit, though Larouci ran his contract down. They're not just quite ready to do it or they are in the first team already, like Caoimhin Kelleher or Curtis Jones.

'There was a lad called Abdi Sharif. He won the Youth Cup actually in 2019, but the following summer, he did his cruciate about the same time Paul Glatzel did. Glatzel made a recovery and went on loan to Tranmere but the last I heard Sharif ended his contract and didn't get a new one. He was fairly decent. It looked like he had a future but he got injured at the wrong time. It's not just him, it's a few players that happens to.'

Sharif's Twitter page has a big picture of him in what I would call the familiar 'contract signing pose' staring out at the viewer. His thumbnail is a photo of him kissing the FA Youth Cup trophy, which I haven't really mentioned so far in the book. As you can see on the cover, the cup is the size of a typical human face, with ribbons flowing from it down to a platform that makes the entire trophy about 45cm in length.

'But at the moment, you've got James Balagizi, Matuesz Musialowski. A lot of players from the under-18s have stepped up to the under-23s. Tyler Morton hadn't even played for the under-23s 18 months ago and he's come in,' Doyle continues.

'He's been a little bit fortunate but he's been given a chance to be fortunate. In the summer Klopp said he wanted to have the kids come and train with us. When they had a shortfall of numbers, he remembered him and Morton played against Norwich, then Porto, Real Madrid and Tottenham!'

When Liverpool played AC Milan at the San Siro in the final group game of the 2021/22 Champions League, they had already advanced to the knockout rounds. Chelsea had sold their Youth Cup winner Fikayo Tomori for £25m. Tomori opened the scoring for Milan, and the pure profit from both Tomori and Tammy Abraham, whom Roma signed for £34m, was used to re-sign Romelu Lukaku.

Morton, Neco Williams and Nathaniel Phillips all started the game, while Joe Gomez, Max Woltman and Conor Bradley all came on to see out the 2-1 win. The latter two players were born in 2003, the year in which Milan striker Zlatan Ibrahimović, who turned 40 earlier in the 2021/22 season, was playing for Ajax in the Champions League.

'There's a couple of staff who are at the club whose job is to recruit from that age and look after them,' Ian says. 'The decision is made whether to keep them on. These players have come straight through the system. Some of them might not play another game but that's what you get from going to a place like Liverpool.'

Thus can Woltman and Bradley always say that they shared a dressing room with Mo Salah and Alisson, as did the unused substitutes Elijah Dixon-Bonner, James Norris and Harvey Davies. In fact, for the FA Cup third-round match at Anfield against Shrewsbury Town, Kaide Gordon, Woltman, Dixon-Bonner and Bradley (deputising for a Covid-stricken Trent Alexander-Arnold) started.

These lads would have been playing that Youth Cup tie against Burnley two days beforehand, so the postponement of the game had inadvertently made life easier for the manager. He still had four first-team players on the pitch (Fabinho, Andy Robertson, Ibrahima Konaté and Virgil van Dijk) when the players walked out to 'You'll Never Walk Alone'. The other seven starters were homegrown players, fulfilling a dream or still living it in the case of Jones, Kelleher and Morton. Young Balagizi watched on from the substitutes' bench.

'That's the best thing for them,' reckons Ian. 'Klopp understands that they are all assets and you can bring them through. I think it was the first week Klopp was there, it might have been the first afternoon, he was spotted watching an under-18s or under-16s game at the academy. Rhian Brewster was playing and so straight away Klopp wondered who that was. Brewster ended up playing for Liverpool.'

The second-year scholars at the club in 2021/22 were born in 2003 and 2004, which means they will have no memory of the 2006 and 2007 teams lifting the Youth Cup. Are the lads even aware that it happened? Ian thinks so.

'I'm not even sure there's many or any of the staff from that time still there. Inside the academy they will see pictures of when they won it. They will know the history. They will have been told it if they haven't gone out of their way to see it. They know the importance of the Youth Cup.'

Certainly it is something for their footballing CV that makes them stand out from the crowd when they finish their scholarship and, like Yan Dandha at Swansea, become a free agent whom other clubs can sign. In the previous generation, Gérard Houllier was assisted by 1972 Youth Cup winner Phil Thompson, which would have kept the lineage of the Boot Room era going, although ironically Houllier's appointment brought that run of coaches descended from Shankly to a close.

Ian goes on, 'I had just started reporting on Liverpool then. Carragher and Gerrard had come through. One of the first things Houllier did was to give Gerrard more chances. Houllier had a strong connection with the city from having lived here so he'd probably have watched Thompson play. It's not like a complete foreigner coming in like Benitez or Klopp, who had no previous link to Liverpool. Houllier understood what was going on.

'The local presence is important for every club, especially now. They can pinpoint these local lads who want to come through because they will always have that extra edge. They might not be as good in terms of talent but Tyler Morton is a local lad. If you can cope with the expectation of being a local player, because they always get more criticism than most of the other players, you are halfway there.'

Brendan Rodgers, meanwhile, had been one of those coaches who did well at youth level before taking senior teams like Reading and Swansea City. (He was also at Watford for 15 minutes, famously preaching 'integrity' before leaving days later.)

'They had Andre Wisdom,' Ian recalls of the young talent in the Rodgers team. 'He gave Jerome Sinclair a debut in the League Cup against West Brom. I think he became Liverpool's youngest player. With Rodgers, he overachieved quite a lot very early on and then things went a bit backwards. He brought through Jon Flanagan who had come through under Dalglish, who had given Jay Spearing more chances. Spearing played in the FA Cup Final against Chelsea.

'Rodgers took them on but there weren't a lot that came through because he didn't have the time. He was only there for three and a bit years and he was trying to push on to a certain level. He forged his reputation at Chelsea, working with the youngsters. That's another example of what you see at other clubs. Watford change managers all the time but I presume the academy has got nothing to do with the first team. It's a lot easier if you're at the bigger clubs because the youngsters want to come to you!'

This has been the case since the clubs, rather than the English FA, have taken the lead on youth development. The best kids in Birmingham, for instance, may choose to sign for Aston Villa (unless they bleed blue, of course), but even Mancunians who grew up as the children of Manchester United fans have been developed at Manchester City's Etihad Campus. These include Harvey Neville, whose uncle Gary may have forgiven this since at least he didn't go Liverpool.

Had he been born in the 1990s, Harvey Neville might even have come up from Bury's youth system, given that his grandparents were involved with the club. Ian Doyle laments the paucity of players 'spotted in the lower leagues who get bumped up once they start playing full-time'.

He adds, 'Liverpool have two examples of that. Harvey Elliott played for Fulham and Kaide Gordon came from Derby County. One of them played two games, one played once and Liverpool snapped them up. Callum Scanlon is 16 now. They paid a little bit of money for him from Birmingham. I'm pretty sure they were looking at Jude Bellingham as well.

'These main academies are allowing the lower clubs to develop them to a certain point and then see they are quite good and spend a bit of money on them; £3m for a club like Liverpool is not a lot of money, and £5m for Manchester City is next to nothing. They are doing that alongside the players who have come through the Liverpool system. They put a lot of stock in spotting people pre-academy level.'

As Nigel Gibbs said earlier in the story, it is always fitting to have local lads in the first team and for fans to sing that their prodigy is 'one of our own'. The players must like it too; Wayne Rooney was a conquering hero after he scored on his Everton debut, but Ian Doyle counsels that it isn't just about where you are from.

'Jack Rodwell was at Everton. He was massively talented and could do everything. I can't remember which former player said this, but the problem is that, for a lot of players who come through the academy, almost all of them are seven out of ten over everything. It's the ones who are nine out of ten in one or two things who end up making it. They can make a difference.

'If you've got a load of sevens and eights, they are just going to blank each other out [in a game], so it's hard to elevate yourself above that. The accusation is that they could have been slightly overtrained. They've looked at that, certainly at Liverpool.

'They play the same formation and style of football all the way through [the academy system]: mostly 4-3-3, pressing football, looking for counter attacks, the high press. That is drummed into them. They will play players in different positions to find out which ones are the best ones.'

Ultimately, Ian says, it's about 'continuity' and keeping the chain of excellence going down the club. There is no better example here, in two ways, than the case of Owen Beck. Beck is a left-back from Wrexham who signed for Liverpool as a young teenager. He had once been presented with a trophy by Ian Rush, which must have been funny for both of them: Owen's grandma Carol is also Ian's aunt.

'Beck came on in an EFL Cup game having played two minutes for the first team. He slotted straight in at left-back and he knows exactly what to do because he'd spent two, three, four years doing it at the 18s and 23s,' Ian says.

So great is the team ethic at Liverpool that sometimes young lads struggle at a new employer. Ian pinpoints the struggles of Brewster at Sheffield United and Hoever at Wolverhampton Wanderers. 'You do wonder whether they are so specifically taught to play a certain way that when they go off to play somewhere else, they can't really do it.'

As a journalist who is paid to report on young players, does Ian find it fun to cover their exploits?

'Funny you should mention that,' he begins. 'In lockdown, when no fans were allowed in, I tried to get to as many home games at Kirkby because it was so much better watching those games than the first-team games in a massive stadium with no fans there. It felt more like football.

'There's a certain attachment if you spot a player at 15 or 16. It's a lot easier to do it with top clubs because LFC TV have all the 18s and 23s games on television. If not live, they show highlights so it's dead easy to see all these players. Ten, 15 years ago you'd have never heard of them. They'd pop up on the team sheet and you'd ask who they were!

'It has become a bigger deal because everybody wants to know the next thing, what the next best thing is. They want to be among the first people to spot it. I do find it more fun covering the youth games. There's less pressure on me as a journalist because they don't want as much stuff! But there's less pressure in the game itself; in the league games there's a sense that you're just trying to see who the best players are. You're not just watching Liverpool players. You keep an eye open.

'The lad at Leeds, Joe Gelhardt, played against Liverpool. I knew he was a Liverpool lad because I had spotted him at Wigan. He scored one goal from 45 yards, another goal from 35 yards and I can't remember whether he scored or missed a penalty for a hat-trick. I was getting messages on Twitter from a Leeds fan asking if he was going to make it. "Yep, he's definitely going to be in the first team soon." He got in and he doesn't look out of place. He's won a few penalties.

'There's another lad at Brighton, Evan Ferguson, Irish lad. He's going be somebody else who'll be really, really good. He's an old-school centre-forward, he's tall but he's got skills as well, good touch for a big man and all that.

'A couple of years ago I saw Manchester United play Mason Greenwood. "He's gonna make it," I thought.'

What a perfect segue into how United have been developing players in the last few years.

Nick Cox, whom we met near the opening of this story, has used experience gained at Watford and Sheffield United in one of the most wonderful jobs in English football. Away from the demands of executive vice-chairmanship, Cox works as academy manager to produce the next generation of Pogbas, Beckhams and Charltons.

However, that youth team has been overtaken by Chelsea and Liverpool in the last ten years, even as it has helped produce Greenwood, Scott McTominay and Marcus Rashford. United have been forced to buy expensive British players to augment their defence: Harry Maguire, Luke Shaw and Aaron Wan-Bissaka are today's versions of the Neville brothers and Wes Brown, except those last three cost nothing to buy.

The Europa League has been a chance for United fans to see some of the young lads in the first team. A trip to Astana in Kazakhstan had seven teenagers in the starting XI and three more brought off the bench. Thus did Ethan Laird, James Garner, Angel Gomes, Dylan Levitt, Tatith Chong and D'Mani Mellor use the lessons of their academy coaches in a first-team game in front of 29,000 people, albeit a dead rubber.

The captain for the night, and scorer in the 2-1 defeat, was Youth Cup winner Jesse Lingard. A few weeks later, he would be farmed out to West Ham United on loan, and he was rather frozen out for the 2021/22 season.

Cox's own mantra is, 'The journey is more important than the destination.' He seeks to 'help players reach their full potential … [to fall] in love with the game and continue to have a lifelong participation in sport'. What's more, 'our academy and the programme we deliver is an amazing addition to childhood years' so that, when they grow up, men can be proud of the 'positive influence' of being connected to the club.

'This is about more than just football,' he concludes, although Cox is one of the 'guardians of the culture' which stretches even beyond the days when United won the first five Youth Cups.

It must be a sadness to Cox that the Watford academy, which he was part of for 12 years, has not brought through so many youngsters to the first team. 'They were organisations of integrity,' he says of Watford and Sheffield United; the former were in administration in the early 2000s and it was essential to promote youth. Thus Cox worked at the Harefield Academy as part of 'the first full-time model in the country'. Harefield produced 60 first-team players before the Pozzo regime brought in their scouting model, as we learned about earlier. The set-up at Sheffield United, conversely, was part-time at evenings and on weekends.

Cox's words about what he does at Manchester United echo those of Tom Walley from 1982. 'We like to work with small numbers. We're not trying to produce a team here. A winning youth team is a lovely by-product of brilliant development. We want our kids to be competitive and, yes, everyone enjoys winning. We're trying to work with individuals who have a mapped-out plan.'

As for competing with Manchester City and Liverpool in trawling the local area for talent, Cox adds, 'We make sure that we remain true to ourselves at all times and we want to attract people and families to us who love the way they do things.' A sad codicil to that is the case of Harvey Neville, son of Phil, who moved across to City before turning pro at United. He now plays for Fort Lauderdale, a feeder side for Inter Miami whose first team is managed by his dad. A team-mate is Romeo Beckham, whose father David owns Inter Miami. Harvey and Romeo, of course, did not grow up with youth coach Eric Harrison, a superstar in the eyes of their fathers, but it is certain that Harrison's lessons informed their childhood by osmosis.

There is a passage in *Football – Bloody Hell!*, Patrick Barclay's biography of Alex Ferguson, where the author heeds the advice of David Pleat. 'These kids are capable of dominating

English football for ten years,' the sage said, so Barclay went to see the so-called Class of '92 for himself. The football was 'transcendental. The purity of United's passing made it so.'

Gary Neville and Keith Gillespie were on the right, Ben Thornley on the left, with 'little magician' Paul Scholes in front of Nicky Butt and David Beckham. The centre-forward was Richard Irving, who used his beginnings in a career which included flying aeroplanes and renovating property.

Barclay was enthused by Beckham, who was 'lean and upright with floppy hair'. He thought he would be a future international, as he told someone in the car park. 'He's my son,' said Ted Beckham, who agreed.

When Alex Ferguson joined Manchester United, he looked across the city at the young talent coming through City's youth ranks. They had won the Youth Cup months before Ferguson took the job in November 1986. The Scot lamented how 'even Oldham and Crewe' were doing better at converting apprentices into senior pros. Indeed, Ryan Giggs was himself poached from City, where he was known as Ryan Wilson. Ferguson famously said he wanted 'the best boy in the town or the area', not just the best one on the street.

In 1986, both Manchester clubs had excellent youth teams and the lads would socialise with one another. Yet, all the same, says another apprentice of the time, Tony Gill, 'there was nothing we felt that was extraordinary in terms of pressure', especially when compared with the team of the 1960s.

Deiniol Graham, whose career was wrecked by injury, tells Wayne Barton in his excellent survey *Fergie's Fledglings* that Ferguson would 'sometimes leave the first team to come and watch us'. When the boss was watching, says Chris Casper, one of the Fledglings who came through in the 1992 group, 'just his presence' was enough to help a player perform. 'You can't let him down,' Casper said, even if at this stage Ferguson had merely been the man who won trophies with Aberdeen and was still rebuilding Manchester United in his own image.

The boss was 'on a hiding to nothing', continues Graham, who was sold to Barnsley before the start of the 1991/92 season. 'If the kids did it for him, he [Ferguson] would be a hero. If not, he had a readymade excuse.' Perhaps Ferguson's genius was in his fearlessness, although José Mourinho didn't promote young players at Chelsea and he famously won plenty of trophies. Brian Kidd, who deserves far more credit for his work with the young players, was 'a joker who you could have a laugh with' in Graham's eyes.

Casper, whose son has followed his dad and grandfather into the game, recalled how as a 14-year-old he went to see a first-team match after training with Mark Hughes, Steve Bruce and Paul Ince that morning. Alan Tonge, meanwhile, fell under the spell of Captain Marvel, playing alongside Bryan Robson, 'a supreme player who had everything', in the reserves.

Tonge adds that the coaches 'treated you like men', and it was of course helpful that these coaches included Kidd, Nobby Stiles and Bobby Charlton. 'We hardly got any days off,' he said, thanks to Eric Harrison's regime of continual learning and assessment. This included players designing their own training schedules, with 'six-versus-eight overloads ... We were being given responsibility and taking it'. Eric Harrison had wanted the United scouting network tripled in size so as to improve the calibre of player he coached.

Casper is very good when he details the 1992 Youth Cup run. Sol Campbell, then known as Sulzeer, and Nicky Barmby were at Spurs and 'we didn't even have a video of them'. Casper and his United team-mates nonetheless won 5-1 on aggregate, helped by three early goals at Old Trafford where Ryan Giggs,

Keith Gillespie and Ben Thornley all played in front of him. Paul Scholes couldn't even make the first XI, though he had injuries throughout the season.

Karl Brown was 'one of the best midfielders in the country' but suffered a broken ankle. Proving the point made in the chapter dealing with Watford and Tottenham, Brown is back at his old employer as a coach in the academy. He left the game to enjoy 20 years as a lettings agent and property manager, but trained for his badges in 2010. He has been coach of the under-12, under-13 and under-14 sides while he also mentors players who have been released, as he says, 'to help them stay in the game or make the transition from football and finding different career pathways'.

Brown told the *New Indian Express*, 'A big part of our job is to be understanding ... I feel 80 per cent of the work is off the pitch. I think the work on the grass is the easy bit.'

The first leg of the 1992 Youth Cup Final took place a month before the second meeting. In between those fixtures, Manchester United's senior team conceded the First Division title to Leeds. Giggs had appeared in all but four league fixtures. He missed the first leg of the final, but he took the captaincy from Gary Neville for the second leg.

Jimmy Glass was the goalkeeper for Crystal Palace, who United met in the final. Casper says that Glass 'could boom the ball down the end of the pitch, so every set piece and goal kick they had we were defending in our own box'.

Glass told the official AFC Bournemouth website that he 'must have played about 200 reserve games' at Palace but was stuck behind future England international Nigel Martyn. 'I couldn't see a first-team game coming,' he said, though he was put in the reserves at Bournemouth and he realised he could have been Martyn's dependable understudy.

Glass enjoyed a peripatetic career including two years as first-choice keeper at Bournemouth, where he is now both a player liaison officer and a host of the club's matchday hospitality. In between these jobs, he drove a cab for ten years after he retired from playing at 27. Readers may remember the name because Glass scored the goal that kept Carlisle United in the Football League in 1999, after being signed as an emergency goalkeeper.

In the other goal in the 1992 final was Kevin Pilkington, who took the role briefly of being deputy to Peter Schmeichel. Casper marvels at how the keeper 'saved a shot with the back of his leg when he spun around. I'll never forget it. I don't know how he did it.'

Pilkington was also in goal when Patrick Barclay caught the youth team in 1992. 'Our digs were so close to the training facilities that we were always there,' Pilkington says, with 'we' referring to Robbie Savage ('so loud you could hear his laugh a mile away') and old friend Pat McGibbon. Pilkington joined an existing group who had come up through the under-16s together. The club had two international goalkeepers, Schmeichel and Jim Leighton, as well as the experienced Les Sealey and, coaching once a week, pioneering ex-pro Alan Hodgkinson.

Fascinatingly, Pilkington had played with his dad's Saturday team as a teenager so knew 'what you needed to hear, not talk for the sake of talking'. This prepared him well for the 'hard but fair' coaching methods of Eric Harrison.

In the words of John Curtis, a 1995 Youth Cup winner who didn't play in the final, he instilled a 'winning mentality … Everything had to be done right, and it was that kind of pressure which made people get better.' Ultimately, the progress of the 1995 team was stymied by the lads from the 1992 crop, with only Phil Neville breaking into the XI.

The star winger, Terry Cooke, had David Beckham in his way, while Curtis himself could not displace the industrious Gary Neville, though he did get a game against Arsenal in a 1-0 defeat in the Gunners' Double-winning season of 1997/98. Both Neville brothers, Beckham, Scholes and young Ben Thornley all played in the match, too.

All five men in that last sentence have won the Youth Cup. In 1995, United won on penalties, the first time the cup was decided that way, against Tottenham, who won it in 1990 and have never even appeared in the final since. For details on that victory and a full account of what it was like to be an apprentice just before the Premier League money came in, consult the fantastic recent book *Losing My Spurs* by the team's striker Anthony Potts.

A side containing two future first-team stars named Stephen, Carr and Clemence (son of Ray), went toe to toe with the next batch of Eric Harrison's pupils, pretty much all of whom had professional careers. Some of them won the European Cup, for example captain Phil Neville, who missed United's first penalty, while others were in and around the first-team squad, such as Ronnie Wallwork, who scored his.

The Spurs team captain was Kevin Maher, the Essex-born midfielder who left in 1998 after several changes in manager meant he couldn't displace the likes of David Howells and Allan Nielsen, or indeed Clemence himself. Both Maher and Clemence have completed their coaching qualifications, with the former returning to manage his old club Southend United for whom he played over 450 games.

Southend spent 2021/22 in the National League, which in its previous guise as the Vauxhall Conference had welcomed some of that 1995 Tottenham team such as Mark Arber (Barnet, Stevenage and Dartford), Simon Wormull (Dover

Athletic, Crawley Town and Lewes), and Sammy Winston (Sutton United and Kingstonian). Goalkeeper Simon Brown played for Colchester United for five seasons before moving first to Hibernian and then Brentford, who were in the fourth tier in 2007/08. 'Times have changed', to once again quote Watford coach Tom Hart.

Midfielder Peter Gain spent six happy years at Lincoln City, while Neale Fenn finally played regular first-team football at Peterborough United. He spent the rest of his career in Ireland with clubs such as Cork City, whom he also managed throughout the pandemic. Fenn told Irish website *The42.ie*, 'I didn't disgrace myself' when he lined up against Manchester United's senior team in an FA Cup third-round game in 1997.

It helped Fenn to win a five-year contract but the procession of managers, from Gerry Francis to Christian Gross to George Graham, held him back. So did the panoply of strikers in front of him, such as Teddy Sheringham before he signed for United. 'I was just waiting for someone to come and get me … Nothing was happening. It was horrible. I just sat there.' That five-year contract had become an albatross. When he finally joined Peterborough, the style was 'a little bit direct'.

It isn't fair to isolate one incident in his career but it remains the case that Fenn hit an opponent in an under-21 international against Iceland after missing a penalty. 'I had my hands on my head,' Fenn told the interviewer, 'and he was laughing in my face. So I kind of pushed him away. The ref said I headbutted him even though I didn't.' Mick McCarthy was not impressed with Fenn, and withdrew his call-up for the senior team. Fenn finished his career playing in Ireland and retired at the age of 33.

To return to Spurs' conquerors in 1995. Wayne Barton has written a whole shelf of books about Manchester United, with recent tomes on Sammy McIlroy and Wayne Rooney. He notes that, when *Fergie's Fledglings* was published, the combined appearances from that 1992 Youth Cup-winning squad was 2,400. Almost half of those were made by Ryan Giggs, who was, to Chris Casper, 'The only one who we knew for sure would go on to have a great career'.

Meanwhile, in 1992/93 those apprentices would play in front of a few hundred people for United's A team. These third-stringers were, in Casper's words, 'killing teams … We just played and played our best because that was the expectancy.' Naturally, in a workplace of young lads, 'if anyone did get above their station they soon got knocked down [and were] reminded that they were part of a team'. Remember when Terry Venables was told he would be punched in the chest unless he curbed his enthusiasm?

It is often forgotten that in September 1994 a Manchester United side beat Port Vale in the EFL Cup, with a whole host of homegrown players entertaining the Old Trafford crowd. Casper himself played at the back alongside John O'Kane and behind David Beckham; the midfield was made up of Nicky Butt, Simon Davies (not the one who played for Tottenham) and Keith Gillespie, with Paul Scholes up front. Gary Neville and Graeme Tomlinson got a game from the bench, the latter making his only appearance but becoming one of the few lads with a Watford connection (including Ashley Young and Chris Eagles) to put on a red shirt.

Barton raises the sensible point that the 'three-foreigner' rule imposed by UEFA, which was removed by the Bosman ruling, meant that a 16-man matchday squad had to include 11 English players: not British, English.

Thus the 1992 Youth Cup winners were in and around the first team for games in the 1993/94 and 1994/95 Champions

League. In fact, Nicky Butt was often preferred to Roy Keane in midfield. Chris Casper travelled too; his eyes were opened in Turkey, Sweden and Spain, which must have had a bearing on Ole Gunnar Solskjaer's decision to take young players to Europa League fixtures in recent seasons.

With Casper's progress blocked in the manner that the paths of Neville, Beckham and Butt were not, he didn't feature as often as he wanted in the 1996/97 season, although he was an unused sub in the Champions League semi-final against Borussia Dortmund. A broken leg while he was playing at Reading ended his career prematurely.

Casper's role at Salford City as director of football means he is reunited with his old team-mates, who are on the club board. He was also the coach of Team Bath, whose run in the FA Cup in 2002/03 is still remembered fondly, and was part of the team who administered the Elite Player Performance Plan in the early 2010s.

It should be noted amid all of this success that in 1997 Watford knocked out a Manchester United side who had themselves beaten a Liverpool team featuring Steven Gerrard and Michael Owen. Goalkeeper Adam Sadler made two big errors which let down team-mates including Danny Higginbotham, Wesley Brown (as he was known then) and David Healy. Watford's side included Gifton Noel-Williams, whom we met earlier in the story.

Higginbotham, whose memoir Barton co-wrote, is another Fledgling who made the first team. He signed for United at the age of nine having taken Brian Kidd's advice to shift allegiances to the Reds.

He then shifted from a winger to a full-back, and he made his senior debut in 1998. He was also lucky, after some well-documented fracas in Belgium while playing for

Royal Antwerp, that his manager offered to be a character witness for him.

Manchester United also won the Youth Cup in 2003. Phil Bardsley, Paul McShane, Chris Eagles and Kieran Richardson were in the team which beat Middlesbrough 3-1 on aggregate. As we shall discover, Boro would reach the final again in 2004 with future pros Chris Brunt, David Wheater and James Morrison. Lee Lawrence, one of the United lads, told Barton, 'We had that confidence in each other ... Sir Alex came into the dressing room before the second leg' and gave them a pep talk.

The United academy kept producing fantastic goalkeepers. Among them were Luke Steele and Tom Heaton. The former played most of his first-team games for Barnsley and Panathinaikos, and started the 2021/22 season with Notts County; Heaton moved from Burnley to Aston Villa and, as we read near the beginning of this story, back to Manchester United. At the age of 35, he made his senior competitive debut when he played 20 minutes of a Champions League dead rubber at Old Trafford against Young Boys.

As for the unlucky Ben Collett, he broke his leg a week after the Youth Cup Final and had to retire with compensation. To very little fanfare in 2021, Paul McShane returned to Manchester United as a player but also a coach whose responsibility was to the under-23s.

Conversely, the 2004 Youth Cup side who lost to Stoke City in the third round included World Cup-winner Gerard Piqué and future full internationals Jonny Evans, Darron Gibson and Giuseppe Rossi, as well as Ryan Shawcross. Bamboozled by Zlatan Ibrahimović on his only England appearance, Shawcross started 2021/22 as an Inter Miami player under the management of Phil Neville.

In 2007, Tom Cleverley and Danny Welbeck were part of the team trained by Rene Meulensteen, who emphasised the Coerver method in which touch was important. Sam Hewson, the team's midfielder, told Barton, 'Everyone played for each other and if someone else was in a better position to score they would give it to them.' The first semi-final against Arsenal had kids going in for free so almost 40,000 people saw the home side win 1-0.

Sir Alex told the media that United youngsters were better than Arsenal's and at Old Trafford the home side won 4-3 on aggregate after extra time. The prize was a final against Liverpool, a game which went to penalties after a 2-2 draw on aggregate. Hewson missed the deciding kick.

Chapter Seven

The 2000s and Assorted Teams

BEN WILKINSON started the 2021/22 season as the under-18s coach of Manchester City. Having moved across from Sheffield Wednesday in 2018, he slotted into city as assistant head coach of the under-23s and the under-16s lead coach. It thus made sense to move up with those kids as they aged up to replace the lads who had themselves completed their scholarships and were now in the Elite Development Squad.

Wilkinson told ManCity.com that his priority was to set his team up within the Guardiola style of the first team. He was also working on the players' 'individual development. In terms of 70 or 80 per cent of the squad, it's their first year of full-time football so it's about managing that transition of still being a schoolboy and being a very serious footballer.'

Oh, and 'winning is also very important' for Manchester City.

In 1997, building on his work at Leeds United, Ben's dad Howard Wilkinson used his power as technical director at the FA to reform the system. It effectively started the new era of youth football in England, because the Performance Centre at Lilleshall was to be closed. It did so in 1999.

Wilkinson's introduction to the document ends with his delight in proposing 'reasonable recommendations ... which emphasise Quality and ... Unity'. The next page includes a diagram linking Centres of Excellence to Academies to a National Football Centre, today based at St George's Park, to club competitions, the EURO tournament and the World Cup.

The Charter for Quality was a 90-page document that is available online with an introduction from Wilkinson. He convened over 100 meetings to draw up the document: there were 28 with clubs, 17 with the FA Committee chairmen and five with the PFA. There is also an appendix which notes that Ajax and Barcelona, who had both won the European Cup in the years leading up to the Charter's formation, both had a full-time director for youth development. Ajax had nine part-time staff 'employed to assist with homework, which is completed daily at the training ground', while Barcelona encouraged boys to 'stay at school until 19 years [of age]'. Over in Italy, Inter Milan had ten coaches and Parma had 22, eight of them full-time.

Point 1.3 of the introductory message to Wilkinson's document states that 'the central figure ... is the player and his or her best interests. Attempting to provide quality experiences for all young players at all levels is the overriding principle.' 'The' is in bold and underlined.

Point 1.4 deals with the elite or 'most gifted' players who need 'time' – time is also bold and underlined – to be coached and developed with 'the same sort of access that the Football Association currently has' for the lads at Lilleshall, with coaching four times a week and 'a structured match programme'. This would include a 'minimum of four weeks allocated player and coach development'.

Furthermore, 'these clubs should be encouraged' to have their own programmes, be it a Centre of Excellence or an Academy, in an era where they have more say in player development than schools. It is the parents who should have more control, too, and be 'the key individuals' in how much football their progeny should play. The FA mandated 30 games with the Charter, replacing the existing arrangements which bring 'significant problems' for 'the very gifted, 60 games in a year maximum but often exceeded'. This was in an era in which tackling from behind was, until the mid-1990s, within the rules.

Club academies would have medical staff as well as a minimum of 'six full-time staff', plus a full-time education and welfare officer. Signficantly, given what we know about historical sexual abuse of minors, there would be mandatory child protection with staff screened and trained. The FA would themselves conduct three checks a year, in a time of greater compliance and accountability.

The Charter raised the age limit for developing players from 16, where the schoolboy apprentice signed a YTS form, to 21, with a maximum of '15 players per year band'. No schoolboy could join a club which was over 60 minutes (under-9s to under-13s) or 90 minutes (under-13s to under-16s) away from their home. Effectively, Wilkinson was putting in place several mini-Lilleshalls across England which sought to develop players, at a ratio of two coaches for every 20 players.

It is a little bit of a cop-out for Wilkinson to write that 'it is hoped that conflict will be avoided' between schools and academies but, given that clubs are hoping the young player can advance to their first team, whom does Wilkinson think is going to be prioritised? It was not a case of club v country any more, as has been the case throughout the story of the FA Youth Cup, but club v school team.

A compromise was reached by noting that in 'the early part of the season, September and early October, and the late part of the season, late February and March, priority will be given to Schools' Football'. This seems farcical and, of course, would have involved lots of paperwork and registration.

It is also interesting and timely, given that Arsene Wenger was bringing sports science into elite football, that the FA had realised that the game needed to pay attention to physiology, psychology, nutrition and counselling at youth level. This would form good habits within the club and the player, which would probably benefit the football pyramid overall as players from top academies would bring those habits to the lower levels.

Indeed, this is exactly what happened to English football after the influx of top global talent: gone, at least at the top level of the game, were big sessions with the lads on days off. As Nigel Gibbs alluded to, the '24/7 footballer' was being formed.

In 1998, fully three years after Blackburn Rovers won the Premier League, the money from Jack Walker's ownership would have been combined with the payment from UEFA for Blackburn's participation in the 1995/96 Champions League. Some of this money must have filtered down to the Rovers Academy, whose products are an array of names who played in a particular era of British football and who will probably mean nothing to readers under the age of 25.

James Beattie had made his Rovers first-team debut in 1996 as a teenager but was sold to Southampton in part exchange for Kevin Davies in 1998. Damien Johnson broke through in 1997 and made over 50 international appearances for Northern Ireland; in a familiar development, he returned to his old employer in 2015 as coach, helping to bring players through from the younger age groups to the first team. Johnson is thus an employee of the Venky family, who have helped Blackburn navigate the different financial world from the one Jack Walker was involved in.

Beattie, for his part, was briefly manager at Accrington Stanley but has mostly worked on the coaching team of Garry Monk at five clubs, none of which has been Blackburn Rovers. He did take an assistant coach job at Wigan Athletic in 2021, meaning he works with captain Tendayi Darikwa.

In 1998, Blackburn Rovers had reached the final of the FA Youth Cup, losing 5-3 on aggregate to an Everton side which was spearheaded by Francis Jeffers and also numbered Tony Hibbert, Richard Dunne and Danny Cadamarteri. The losing side included hard-headed centre-back Martin Taylor and creative midfielder David Dunn, who both had heralded careers at the club and were in the Blackburn side who won the League Cup in 2002 against Tottenham Hotspur.

Gareth Stewart had by then moved to Bournemouth where he was first choice in the 2001/02 season. Back when the Cherries were struggling, that season ended in relegation to the fourth tier but Stewart happily regained his place in the starting XI for the League One season 2005/06. He is still employed by the club coaching young goalkeepers.

In 2012, Blackburn were put to the sword in the Youth Cup Final by Chelsea. After a 4-0 defeat in the first leg, Blackburn did win the second leg at Ewood Park 1-0. It was useful experience for Jack O'Connell, who has found enormous success with Sheffield United, and two players who would end up at Morecambe: defender Ryan Edwards, who captained the Blackburn team, and midfielder John O'Sullivan.

It is interesting to note that one of the Blackburn lads was from Nigeria, although Osayamen Osawe left England in 2014 for a career in Germany. Substitute Tim Payne returned to New Zealand after work permit issues prevented him from making a career in England; he nonetheless became a full international. The captain of the Chelsea side, Nathaniel Chalobah, was born in Sierra Leone and was surrounded by lads born in Sweden, Brazil, the Netherlands and Somalia.

Rovers' under-18s advanced all the way to the semi-finals of the 2019/20 tournament, which took place in October after the pandemic delayed the competition. After a 4-1 win against Arsenal, they came unstuck against Manchester City. Taylor Harwood-Bellis, Cole Palmer and Liam Delap were part of the City side which defeated a Young Rovers team with four second-half goals.

Harwood-Bellis must have impressed the Rovers hierarchy as he joined Blackburn on loan for part of the 2020/21 season, playing behind young Harvey Elliott. As of the middle of the 2021/22 season, none of that Blackburn Youth Cup side has made it into the first team, although that may be explained by the stellar first half of the Championship season. It is always tough to drop any of the senior pros when a team is on a roll.

There was more luck for the Middlesbrough lads of 2004, coached by Mark Proctor. There are highlights of both legs of the 2004 FA Youth Cup Final against Aston Villa on YouTube, which is worth watching to see a spectacular double save by Boro keeper David Knight.

Stockton lad Matthew Bates went on to make over 100 appearances for his hometown club, despite having five operations to cure cruciate ligament damage. His defensive partner David Wheater opened the scoring in a 3-0 win with a hooked shot. When I asked him via Twitter what he remembered about it, he told me it was 'a great volley!', one that went in off the post in slow motion.

James Morrison scored the other two goals in the first leg, while Hartlepool-born Andrew Taylor was also part of that team. The most famous local graduate (excluding the convicted criminal Adam Johnson) was Wheater, who had been on the losing side in the 2003 Youth Cup Final alongside goalkeeper Ross Turnbull and Chris Brunt.

Wheater told me that he 'took home approximately £0' as prize money but the medal is at his parents' house. Speaking on the *Boro Breakdown Podcast*, where he was introduced as the Redcar Rock, Wheater said he is delighted to see a lot of the same faces when he gets down to the Riverside Stadium. He was released by Oldham Athletic in 2021.

As a young Boro player, Wheater says, the team were playing 'in just a school … we were all in Manchester United and Leeds shirts'. New gaffer Bryan Robson, who took the job straight after he won the double as a United player in 1994, instantly insisted upon an academy being built, which bore fruit a decade later.

Wheater played both centre-forward ('I was taller and quicker than everyone') and centre-back. Had he stayed upfront he wouldn't have 'a broken nose like this … Strikers get all the money as well!' Everyone in the team looked up to Stuart Downing, who once gave Wheater a lift home in his Bentley – 'or maybe it was a Range Rover' – while Ugo Ehiogu and Gareth Southgate were the senior pros at the club.

In early 2022, Craig Liddle revealed how the sausages get made in conversation with the *Northern Echo*. Liddle came through at Boro and took over the reins of the Academy in 2017 after a spell as under-18s coach. There's a mixed metaphor from reporter Matty Jones that bears quoting, 'It's an eye of the needle process to pluck the ripest fruit in the north-east orchard.'

When it comes to picking up local talent, Boro compete with Newcastle United, Sunderland and Leeds United, who are all within that 90-minute distance. This, says Liddle, means that 'the eyes that we have out in and around the area on a weekend and in school games are part-time staff. They link in the three full-time staff' who work under Martin Carter. Liddle is following in the footsteps of Dave Parnaby, who brought through those 2004 Youth Cup winners.

In the 2021/22 season, the Boro first team includes former scholars Marcus Tavernier, Dael Fry and Isaiah Jones, who must be enjoying the challenges set by new gaffer Chris Wilder. Josh Coburn was introduced into the seniors by Neil Warnock and, as a centre-forward, is an outlier. Liddle explains that the club have 'produced a lot of players but not an out-and-out centre forward.

'Josh Coburn typifies what we look for in the academy, not only for a technically and tactically good player but also a fantastic young man who leads by example.'

The article mentions the Academy Productivity Rankings which the Training Ground Guru website compiles. In 2021, it was revealed that of the 83 clubs with academies, Manchester United came first once again, with Arsenal and Chelsea just behind.

Boro were ninth, ahead of Liverpool and Aston Villa; Reading, who are unable to sign new players because of financial penalties, were 12th, just behind the Crewe Alexandra conveyor belt. (The data is available for purchase for £5 via trainingground.guru.)

Just scraping into the top 20 were Norwich City. I don't want to become another one of those people who promotes the Venture Capital-backed subscription website *The Athletic*, which was bought by the *New York Times* in January 2022. Yet, as we saw with Leeds United earlier, their journalists can really tell the story of a Youth Cup-winning side.

Michael Bailey is their Norwich City reporter who, in April 2020, chose to use the pandemic stoppage to look back on the 2013 side with a 5,000-word piece which I've used to celebrate the team who broke the run of elite clubs winning England's elite youth competition.

Neil Adams was the coach who steered a team full of future first-teamers to victory, giving them options at set pieces and passing responsibility on to the players. The twins Josh and Jacob Murphy both became modern-day pros, while Harry Toffolo and captain Cameron McGeehan have had good careers with teams including Huddersfield Town and Luton Town respectively.

As seems to occur across all 70 years that the Youth Cup has been contested, team spirit was key, with 'Antenna' by Fuse ODG acting as a pre-match dance anthem. Despite losing Angus Gunn when his dad Brian left the club, they brought in Southampton youngster Will Britt on loan, who danced the worm to 'Antenna' and endeared himself to the new team-mates.

It is sad to read that Britt had to return to his parent club immediately after the final, unable to continue the celebrations. He is still the only Southampton player to win the FA Youth Cup, which seems strange given the recent success the Saints have had promoting youth (as we shall see shortly).

Britt had seen his colleagues Calum Chambers, Luke Shaw and James Ward-Prowse play in the first team while he was left with players who hadn't even signed YTS forms. He tells Bailey that there was a clique among YTS trainees who had made the first team, which perhaps made it easier to go out on loan to Norwich.

Over in East Anglia, young lads would also continue the tradition of looking after a senior player's boots and staying late after training, which Anthony Potts writes about in his book *Losing My Spurs*. One player, defender Cameron Norman, mentions how 'we were never out of each other's space ... we would do everything together', including golf and cinema trips and just socialising at one of the players' houses. At one stage, future amateur wrestler Grant Holt got physical during a snowball fight!

On the pitch, striker Carlton Morris scored three in the quarter-final match against Everton, helped by the 'unbelievable' service from the Murphy twins. After only one short appearance for the senior team and seven loan moves away from Carrow Road at five different clubs, Morris signed for Barnsley in January 2021. Nottingham Forest were dispatched in the semi-finals on penalties and the imperious Chelsea team were their opponents in the final, which gave captain McGeehan an extra incentive to win. He had been not been given a scholarship at Chelsea, so it was inevitable that he would score the penalty at the end of the first leg, which was the only goal of the game.

In front of 18,000 people at Stamford Bridge (3,000 of whom were Norwich fans), the Young Canaries held on for a 3-2 win on the night. One of their goals was another penalty which was given after a Morris dive. Since that victory, Norwich have popped out young players with stunning regularity: Max Aarons, Jamal Lewis, Todd Cantwell, Adam Idah and Andrew Omobamidele have all played for the first team.

Having already been ever-present in 2017/18 while on loan from Manchester City, Angus Gunn re-signed for Norwich for the 2021/22 season, where he filled in whenever Dutchman Tim Krul was injured. Fans chant a song for him to the tune of 'Achy Breaky Heart' by Billy Ray Cyrus, which was a hit when his dad Bryan (who gets a namecheck in the song) was in goal for the great side of the 1990s. Angus was born in 1996, so can only hear stories from dad and fans about the time Norwich beat Bayern Munich.

Stoke City knocked out Norwich City in the third round of the 2021/22 Youth Cup, in a game in which Norwich led 2-0 after 15 minutes but were 3-2 down at half-time. Stoke were rewarded with a tie against Blackburn Rovers, who beat them 3-0. Thus Stoke, in the heart of England, again failed to win a competition which they have never won.

They did get to the 1984 final but lost to that year's FA Cup winners. As for Everton's time in the Youth Cup, there is a website devoted to their history in the competition: Everton FA Youth Cup History. This means I can find out how their 1984 side won the tournament, and an 'FA double'.

It was, in fact, the second time the same side took both trophies, something Arsenal did first in 1971 and Coventry City were the third to do in 1987. Liverpool, buoyed by a performance of a lifetime by captain Steven Gerrard, would win both FA trophies in 2006. Had they beaten Manchester United in the 1996 FA Cup Final, the FA Double would have been theirs; their 2019 Youth Cup victory, of course, coincided with their UEFA Champions League triumph.

Chelsea did that double in 2012, in what was in fact a treble of FA Cup, Youth Cup and UEFA Champions League. They had won both FA trophies in 2010 and would do so again in 2018. If not for a crazy upset against Arsenal in the 2017 FA Cup Final, Chelsea would have won the FA Double again that year.

Strangely, although the Busby Babes secured a First Division/ Youth Cup double in consecutive years (1955/56 and 1956/57), Manchester United have only won the FA Youth Cup in years in which they have not won the FA Cup.

Everton won their first Youth Cup in 1965, then lost both the 1977 final and the 1983 final in a replay against Norwich City. The second leg in that game left the score at 5-5 on aggregate and thus it became only the second final after Spurs v Coventry in 1970 to go beyond its second leg.

Ian Marshall has both a losers' and winners' Youth Cup medal. He made 15 first-team appearances before playing a pivotal role in Oldham Athletic's promotion-winning team of 1990/91. Neill Rimmer, who played over 200 games for Wigan Athletic, continued the great tradition of youth products being given a sole substitute appearance for their club before being sent on their way. Indeed, this happened to Ian Bishop, who had a fulsome career after coming through Everton's ranks wearing the shirts of Carlisle United, Manchester City (twice) and West Ham United.

Stoke had beaten Arsenal 6-2 on aggregate to reach the 1984 final. Defender Steve Parkin had already made a first-team appearance during the 1982/83 season but dropped down to help his fellow apprentices in the 1983/84 tournament. He had scored both goals in the team's quarter-final win away at Chelsea. Parkin has followed near-namesake Phil Parkinson around the country. In 2021 the pair pitched up at Wrexham. Perhaps Parkin tells the club's young pros about his glory days, or educates the club's new co-owners Rob McElhenny and Ryan Reynolds about the FA Youth Cup.

Alongside Parkin in the Stoke XI was Lee Chapman's younger brother Jon, the team's striker. Both Chapman boys went into the family business following father Roy, who passed away before Jon's season as part of the Young Potters.

Lee also came through the ranks at Stoke and, after he was the team's top scorer for two successive seasons, Arsenal paid £500,000 for him. He flopped there but became a sort of teacher's pet of Howard Wilkinson, who signed him for both Sheffield Wednesday and Leeds United. Lee would win the First Division with Leeds United in 1992, but Jon's football career, sadly, faded away.

As of 2021, plenty of celebrated English football clubs have not yet won the FA Youth Cup. Given that they have not appeared in the story so far, it is only proper to mark the clubs whose players have never won a tankard.

Preston North End, the team of the 1888/89 Invincibles and the plumber/winger Sir Tom Finney, lost the 1960 final to Chelsea. Manchester United had stolen a march on other teams in Lancashire, but the immensity of talent in the county certainly spread it around. Burnley won the First Division that season and Blackburn Rovers were losing finalists in the FA Cup.

Like Finney, Preston lads were loyal to the side. Dave Wilson, Alan Spavin and George Ross were part of the losing finalists for the seniors in the 1964 FA Cup Final against West Ham United. Following in the footsteps of those Scottish players who were part of the Invincibles, Ross had moved down from Inverness to join Preston's youth system. He ended up playing almost 400 times for them.

As if to prove the point made above about the wealth of Lancastrian talent, Preston signed captain Nobby Lawton and striker Alex Dawson from Manchester United. Lawton's path to United's first team had been blocked by Paddy Crerand, who had been brought in from Glasgow Celtic; Dawson, who had scored three goals across the two legs of the 1957 FA Youth Cup Final, was impeded by the presence of David Herd, signed from Arsenal and the Robin van Persie of his day. Doug Holden had come in from Bolton Wanderers, for whom he had played in the 1958 FA Cup Final against a patched-up Manchester United side.

Peter Thompson had done so well against Liverpool in an FA Cup tie that needed two replays that Bill Shankly had poached him in 1963. He also played for England but was not taken to either the 1966 or 1970 World Cups.

Birmingham City lost the 1967 final to Sunderland with a team full of future first-teamers. The Latchford brothers, goalkeeper Dave and centre-forward Bob, were both local lads born in Kings Heath who came up through the academy. Bob was only 16 at the time and was thus in the school year where kids of his age did O-Levels. He became Britain's most expensive player when Birmingham made a profit of £350,000 when Everton signed him. They threw into the deal two players including Howard Kendall. Latchford had to wait until 1977 to win an international cap, by which point he had become a battering ram at the head of Everton's attack.

Incredibly, there were actually three Latchford brothers: Peter came through at West Bromwich Albion and was at Glasgow Celtic for 12 years, once helping the Hoops achieve victory at Celtic Park in the first leg of a famous European Cup tie against Real Madrid.

Striker Keith Bowker was stuck behind Bob Latchford during his days as a Blue. He had to move to Exeter City to play regular football. Defender Garry Pendrey was luckier: he moved up to the senior team where he played 360 times across 13 seasons, many alongside fellow Birmingham boy Dave Robinson and Wolverhampton-born right-back Ray Martin.

Pendrey spent two seasons in the late 1980s managing Birmingham when they were in the doldrums; he was powerless to stop the slide into the third tier, a floor they had never previously reached. He still made the Blues Hall of Fame and had a decent coaching career when he hitched his wagon to Gordon Strachan in the same way that James Beattie and Steve Parkin did with Garry Monk and Phil Parkinson respectively.

Cardiff City have also been beaten finalists. They earned a goalless draw at Highbury but lost 2-0 at home against the Arsenal side which won the 1971 FA Youth Cup Final. The Cardiff team was captained by John Impey, who played for Bournemouth for eight seasons after making a smattering of senior appearances for the Bluebirds.

In fact, quite a few of the team moved up to the first team, but Jimmy McInch, Alan Couch, Billy Kellock and Nigel Rees all left the club before 1975, which was the season which saw Cardiff relegated to the third tier. One player who remained at the club through those lean years was Phil Dwyer, whose 2011 memoir was called *Mr Cardiff City*. Capped ten times for Wales, he played 575 times in a Cardiff shirt before becoming a policeman, which must have been a thrill for any miscreants in south Wales.

In 2022/23, Bristol City will celebrate 50 years since they lost the final in 1973 against Ipswich Town. The Robins were promoted to the First Division in 1976 and brought in Norman Hunter, Joe Royle and Peter Cormack to add some experience to their first XI.

Plenty of local talent was in and around the squad, including centre-back Gary Collier, who graduated from the side which upset Everton in the fourth round, which I found out on that website that chronicled the Toffees in the Youth Cup. Coming through to join Collier were Chris Garland, David Rodgers, Kevin Mabbutt and Howard Pritchard, but overall those runners-up found it harder to break into the first team.

Huddersfield Town will also soon celebrate 50 years since reaching their only Youth Cup Final. The Young Terriers were narrowly beaten by Tottenham Hotspur in 1974. Spurs midfielder Neil McNab and attacker Chris Jones were the only players to go on to great things at senior level, though as we saw earlier Noel Brotherston had a good decade at Blackburn Rovers.

As for Huddersfield, they had a greater quotient of runners-up going up to the senior team, including goalkeeper Richard Taylor and defenders Alan Sweeney, Paul Garner and Martin Fowler. Lloyd Maitland was one of the wingers on that team, who in 1975 was the first black man in a senior Huddersfield XI. Bob Newton was Hartlepool United's Player of the 1980s, scoring 59 goals in 170 games after he had signed from Huddersfield (12 goals in 49 games).

So promising was Peter Hart that he made his first-team debut before he was 17. Hart became a club stalwart at Walsall, where he was captain of the side who were promoted in the first Third Division play-offs in 1988, which needed a replay whose location was decided via a penalty shoot-out. Why could the shoot-out not decide the tie? It would probably have been unfair for a 49-game season to be decided on penalties. This was 1988, after all, before football was remade for a sofa-bound audience, but that's another story which Sky will tell as it celebrates 30 years of the Premier League later in 2022.

Hart's testimonial was the final game at the old Fellows Park stadium. Along with Richard Coles, today Hart is one of Britain's most famous vicars, employed by Walsall as club chaplain.

Two seasons before they lost two domestic cup finals, Sheffield Wednesday themselves also lost the 1991 FA Youth Cup Final. The Young Owls were mauled 3-0 by Millwall in the first leg. As with Neill Rimmer, several of those players – Leroy Chambers, Brian Linighan and Simon Stewart – did make their senior debuts for Wednesday but only Ryan

Jones had any great success in a first team which was doing quite brilliantly in the top tier of English football. Wednesday finished third behind Leeds United and Manchester United in the old First Division with international players throughout their squad blocking the path for the lads to the first-team dressing room.

Finally, after chronicling the travails of some losing finalists, I must mention a side who have never reached the final. Given their two Youth Cup wins in the 1980s, Watford fans must love the fact that for 40 years they have been able to enjoy some one-upmanship against Bedfordshire rivals Luton Town.

The best the Hatters have done in recent years was in 2016, when they lost a quarter-final 1-0 at Ewood Park against Blackburn Rovers with over 30 per cent of the crowd travelling up from Bedfordshire. The Luton team included James Justin at right-back and Tyreeq Bakinson in midfield. After making over 100 appearances for Luton, Justin joined Leicester City where he impressed in the Premier League before injury struck.

Bakinson moved to Bristol City and played plenty of games in the 2020/21 season. He was frozen out under Nigel Pearson before being loaned out to Ipswich Town a few days before this book went to press. Pearson sagely told the media, 'If players don't want to be here, they can go … I'm not wasting energy on negativity.'

There was plenty of energy shown by players in the third round of the 2021/22 FA Youth Cup, which is one of the worst segues in this story.

Chapter Eight

The Third Round and the Arsenal

QUIRKILY, MOST of the second-round ties hadn't taken place when the third-round draw was made. At this point, as in the FA Cup, the elite clubs from the top two divisions enter the competition to form a 64-team knockout.

There were three shock third-round results. The holders Aston Villa were defeated by Leicester City 2-0 days before the Foxes' senior team were eliminated from the Europa League. Equally surprising was the latest batch of golden geese on the Southampton conveyor belt falling to Sheffield Wednesday, whose winning goal was scored by 16-year-old Bailey-Tye Cadamarteri (yes, Danny's son).

Joining the young Foxes (Cubs, really) and Owls (Owlets) in the last 32 were Burnley, who beat Luton Town 3-0, Blackburn Rovers (5-1 against Birmingham City), Leeds United (4-1 against Coventry City), Peterborough United (1-0 against financially strapped Derby County) and Cheltenham Town, who brought plucky Rugby Town's run to an end. Salford City, owned by some former Manchester United apprentices, were drawn away to Wolverhampton Wanderers after winning against Port Vale. Wolves won 4-1 and it took penalties to separate them from Crystal Palace in round four.

After Colchester's victory over Arsenal, which meant that 2009 remains the last time Arsenal went all the way to the final at the time of publication, round four brought a trip way up north to Newcastle, who beat West Ham 3-2. The same scoreline helped the Young Magpies advance to the last 16.

Fleetwood Town went down the west coast to Liverpool for a predictable 4-0 defeat, while it took penalties for Sheffield United to beat Millwall. Everton knocked the Young Blades out with a 2-1 win while the senior team was preparing to lose to Norwich City, a result which led to the sacking of renowned former Liverpool manager Rafael Benitez.

Everton's under-18s coach Paul Tait was born in Newcastle and was part of the equally famous Wallsend Boys Club. Set up in 1965, many old boys attended a Ruby Anniversary dinner in 2005, including Alan Shearer, Peter Beardsley, Lee Clark, Alan Thompson, Michael Carrick and Ian Bogie.

In conversation with the club's own *Bred A Blue* podcast, Tait told his story in a proper Geordie accent but with an odd Scouse affectation which meant the word 'back' sounded like 'bachhh'. Tait had come through at Everton in 1994 but, ironically, Duncan Ferguson was in his way. After scoring plenty of goals for the reserves, Tait moved on, which makes it another one of those strange football reunions that Ferguson and Tait are both, at time of writing, able to share a cuppa in the staff room at the Finch Farm training ground.

'There wasn't a great deal of support. Your name just got circulated around other clubs,' Tait remembered upon leaving Everton. 'I got a phone call from Preston. I remember playing in a practice game. I had a blinder! I was on fire.' At least until David Moyes woke up for the second half and started kicking him. Tait went to Wigan Athletic instead, making his first senior start in English football, then enjoyed time at non-league clubs like Runcorn and in league football with Crewe Alexandra, Bristol Rovers and, at the time of the Wallsend dinner, Rochdale. 'It was night and day compared to what I'd come from but I really enjoyed it.'

Tait set up a coaching school while he was still a player, then joined Everton part-time in 2007. 'Being in and out of teams, I spent time on the bench,' he said, which gave him a head start when he was coaching the under-14s, some of whom would become international footballers.

'Ross Barkley had all the attributes in all four corners. You had to challenge him because he'd run amok,' Tait said. 'Sometimes these young players are accelerated too quickly and lose the confidence. With Ross, we got it spot on. He'd play 14s on a Sunday, midweek for the 15s and sometimes play 16s on the Saturday! I'd always put him up against the best players, like Tyias Browning, or I'd ban him from using his right foot.'

As the grandson of a Cantonese chef, Browning is now a full Chinese international. 'Nobody could beat Tyias in one-on-ones. Whenever we went away to tournaments, people would be raving.'

Echoing other youth coaches whom we have met along the course of this story, Tait wants his charges 'to be well-rounded young men who are going to do well in whatever career they take. That has always been here. We want to do better. It's tough to get these boys into the Premier League so we have got to do better and work harder.'

At least Anthony Gordon has been able to impress in an injury-hit season for Everton, while Tom Davies, Jonjoe Kenny and Lewis Dobbin were all part of the senior squad for 2021/22. Dobbin signed professional terms after he did well in his scholarship and may follow his coach Ferguson and become a first-team regular.

Tait's Everton side beat Fulham 3-2 to knock out the beaten 2014 Youth Cup finalists in the third round. With news that former Spurs youth coach Kieran McKenna was about to take over as first-team manager at Ipswich Town, the two teams met at Stevenage's Lamex Stadium with Spurs coached by their academy graduate (albeit via Arsenal) Stuart Lewis. He made most of his appearances in league football for Wycombe Wanderers in the 2010s and is 13 weeks older than I am. Gaffers are getting younger these days.

Captaining the Spurs side was Alfie Devine, the aforementioned Warrington-born son of a rugby league scrum-half. Having played for Wigan's Youth Cup team in a match the previous season against Spurs, Devine was already capped at under-19 level for England, playing up a few age groups as he had just turned 17.

The Spurs line-up was full of local lads from north London, many in the first year of their scholarship. They were getting more attention than usual that evening because the men's game at Leicester City had been postponed due to Covid outbreaks. Goal updates, but not a play-by-play account, came from the club Twitter feed to their 6.6 million followers.

Spurs took the lead after five minutes and doubled it 20 minutes later through Devine. Ipswich pulled it back to 2-1 before Spurs scored again and keeper Gunter saved a penalty to keep the score at 3-1. Spurs advanced to a last-32 tie at home to West Bromwich Albion.

There were good results for south London, the famous hotbed of young talent. Crystal Palace beat Barnsley 2-1 at Oakwell while Charlton Athletic and the best of Kent's young kids demolished Northampton Town 6-0. Bromley FC, conquerors of Barnet, Lewes and Forest Green Rovers, got a home tie against Reading and rather respectably took the Young Royals to extra time, losing 3-1. Their equaliser came from a 70-yard kick up the field from the goalkeeper, which was collected and finished very well by Ben Krauhaus.

Elsewhere, the storied yet tarnished Crewe Alexandra beat Hull City 1-0, while Norwich's Young Canaries lost 3-2 to Stoke City, continuing a difficult season in East Anglia which saw the team rooted to the bottom of the Premier League.

Brighton & Hove Albion's seniors were having a better season. Their scholars beat Plymouth Argyle 2-1 to set up a home tie against the mighty Manchester City. Perhaps the Premier League money would filter down to the Young Seagulls, as had happened at City, and they would have a good run in this year's tournament.

Brighton fan and football writer Nick Szczepanik remembers watching Blackburn play an Everton team which included Francis Jeffers in the Youth Cup. It was part of a 'northern triple header' on the final weekend of the 1997/98 season, with Nick reporting on three games across a weekend for *The Times*. On the Saturday, Burnley beat Plymouth Argyle 2-1 to stay in the third tier, while Port Vale stayed in the First Division with a 4-0 win at Huddersfield Town. Nick also recalls watching Arsenal at a 'well-attended' Highbury, with Steve Sidwell and promising midfielder Jermaine Brown in their team, around the time of their 2000 Youth Cup win.

'When Manchester United played, Old Trafford would be rocking,' Nick says. 'The Youth Cup had some real history. There was a big tradition.

'It doesn't sit quite well with the actual youth structure at the moment. You have to cobble together a team out of your 18s and 23s. If Brighton can get the striking power they've got in the under-18s in the first team … They've got a very good Irish scout and the head of academy is Irish.'

Evan Ferguson was mentioned by Ian Doyle as one to watch, while Aaron Connolly had previously been one of those Irish players who moved to Brighton in 2016. Connolly was a key part of the Seagulls' side in 2019/20. Nick notes, cryptically that, 'He's a difficult child. If he can sort his personal life out and give his attention to his football … He was going out with one of the *Love Island* contestants. He was livid that she was going on to the Island!'

Graham Potter loaned him to Middlesbrough, at the opposite end of the country, for the second half of the 2021/22 season after Connolly had been limited to six appearances in the opening months. This was in a time when, happily, he and Lucinda from *Love Island* were 'Instagram official' again.

One of the players who was still eligible for Brighton's 2022 Youth Cup run was Andy Moran, who was signed from Bray Wanderers. In the 2021 edition, the Young Seagulls were unfortunate to run into eventual winners Aston Villa, with two goals from a youngster named Aaron Ramsey part of a 3-0 defeat. He will hope to follow his older brother Jacob into the Villa first team.

The aforementioned Evan Ferguson was in the Brighton team that day along with Odel Offiah, the nephew of rugby league legend Martin 'Chariots' Offiah. Odel played an hour of the 2022 FA Cup third round game against West Bromwich Albion at right wing-back, having made his senior debut earlier in the season.

Brighton screened their fourth-round tie on their YouTube channel, whereas Manchester City put it behind a paywall via their City+ service. Kick-off was at 2pm, which meant I was able to catch the first Youth Cup game during daylight hours.

The senior team were at home to Chelsea that evening and Ferguson was named as one of the substitutes, which meant Potter was keen to promote youngsters who might have been eligible for the under-18 tournament.

There was every chance that some members of that City team would train with their first team in order to take part in the game against Southampton that weekend, which meant they would go all the way back down to the south coast. The senior team's irresistible run of 12 league victories threatened to make a mockery of the Premier League season. Former Youth Cup winners James McAtee, Tommy Doyle and Cole Palmer had been in and around the first-team squad during 2021/22, following in the footsteps of Liam Delap, who was given game time the previous season.

Six City players who started the game were born in Manchester, which might support the argument that the visa system was making it harder to recruit kids from around the world. Rico Lewis broke into the under-18s at 15 and captained England's under-18s in a 1-1 draw against Wales in September 2021. Watford centre-back George Abbott, whom we will meet shortly, tried to keep Lewis and Liverpool striker Kaide Gordon quiet that day.

Interestingly, Kian Pennant, nephew of Youth Cup winner Jermaine, is also an under-18 international and is learning the art of the professional game at Leicester. By the time uncle Jermaine had turned 18, he had already played first-team football for Arsenal under Arsène Wenger and for Watford under Gianluca Vialli.

Alongside the local lads at Manchester City, the under-18s squad of 2021/22 who were working through a two-year apprenticeship included Tomas Galvez, whom Tom Hart had mentioned as being part of the Watford set-up. Galvez did not start against Brighton, but Ben Wilkinson chose to play a couple of other players who had joined the club from outside the M62 corridor.

Belgium-born Romeo Lavia was in the sitting role in the centre of midfielder. Either side of him, Glasgow-born Adedire Mebude was on the right and Portuguese player Carlos Borges whizzed by his marker throughout the game on the left. Borges was part of the Elite Development Squad (EDS), which is what City call their under-23s. He had made a senior appearance and been named EDS Player of the Season for 2020/21.

Borges was joined in that 6-1 win at the Etihad against Wycombe Wanderers by a back line that included a player whom City had brought in from Brighton at the start of secondary school. Left-back Luke Mbete-Tabu partnered Finlay Burns that night, and he would do the same in the derby against Manchester United the weekend before the Brighton game.

With Mikki van Sas behind them in goal, Lavia, Breckin, McAtee and fellow Youth Cup winner Joshua Wilson-Esbrand – who followed Mbete-Tate up to Manchester, this time from West Ham United – also played for the EDS that night. Two of them, McAtee and Wilson-Esbrand, were non-playing substitutes in the 1-1 Premier League draw against Southampton which was mentioned earlier. All these talented young lads were playing below their level when they stepped down to help the under-18 team in Brighton.

The home side spent the first 13 minutes 'defending for their lives', according to the in-game commentary, much as you would expect senior defender Lewis Dunk to do had he been able to play. Wide midfielder Joshua Duffus threw his body across for a sliding tackle, which proves that they do still teach the art form at apprentice level. This was rather undone when he conceded a foul in the next passage of play.

For all the pressure and possession, there were few shots to test Brighton goalkeeper Tommy Reid, who on the day he could legally go out for a driving lesson mixed short restarts with long balls to striker Zak Emmerson's head. The number nine spent the first half pressing the City defenders, who were comfortable on the ball, or saving his energy.

Reid did make two excellent saves, one from a Nico O'Reilly free kick, a few minutes before half-time. The teams went in goalless at the interval.

One to watch for Brighton was Samy Chouchane (pronounced like 'choo-train'), who was born in Paris to Tunisian parents and joined the club at the height of the pandemic, during the summer of 2020. At one point in the first half, Marcus Ifill carried the ball 60 yards down the right-hand side but nothing came of it. He went close midway through the second half when he found a half-yard of space in the City penalty area but his shot was deflected and the pace was taken off the ball.

Halfway through the first half, City had a free kick right on the edge of the Brighton penalty area, which was taken by Kian Breckin. He is described on the City website as a 'cultured attacking midfielder', and newspapers salivated when Barcelona were rumoured to be interested in him before their financial implosion. Why would any kid, though, want to leave the best-funded youth development scheme in England? City's players travelled with the first team around Europe to play in tournaments including the UEFA Youth League. In 2021/22 they lost the two big games at home, 5-3 against Club Brugge and 3-1 against PSG. They did, as consolation, thrash Red Bull Leipzig 5-1 with two McAtee goals.

Remember I said that Zak Emmerson was saving his energy? Well, it worked. Fifteen minutes from time, City twice lost possession in the space of five seconds 25 yards from their own goal. Emmerson seized the ball, flicked it behind him and turned. With the goal in sight, he hit a swerving shot as hard as he could, as he had probably been taught to do from an early age.

In the sort of clip that you hope does not go around the world, Mikki van Sas thought he had it under control but he misjudged the flight of the ball. It slipped off the tips of his gloves, flew behind him and into the net for 1-0. Tommy Reid ran 80 yards to celebrate with Emmerson and his team-mates. The commentator shouted 'City stunned!' Youth football – bloody hell.

Brighton's defenders spent the last 15 minutes competing in a Lewis Dunk impersonation contest. My prize went to Leigh Kavanagh, one of those Irishmen about whom Nick Szczepanik told me, though Northern Irishman Ruairi McConville was highly commended. The Young Seagulls held on for a famous victory. Let us hope City don't wave a chequebook at the kids and tempt them up to their EDS, the production line that brought you Phil Foden and Liam Delap. Indeed, if you are a Brighton player, why would you not be tempted by this set-up?

Brighton would learn their opponents in the last 16 that evening. Accrington Stanley welcomed Charlton Athletic to the north-west. Stanley had been pegged back from 3-0 up to 3-3 after normal time in their extra-time triumph over Wigan Athletic. They then beat Bolton Wanderers 2-1 in the second round and saw off Swansea City at home in the third after extra time.

To owner Andy Holt's delight, they held on to win 1-0. In a tweet, he quoted the opening line of 'The Greatest Love Of All', 'I believe that children are the future.' He applauded the young lads and commended Accrington itself for 'getting behind them. [It] isn't far off some of the crowds not many years ago. First class from everyone.'

This is all part of Holt's plan to invest in youth. It is bearing fruit as, he wrote, 'Seven players that played against Bolton were under 23.' Indeed, Accrington's senior team had beaten Charlton 3-2 in October with youth product Toby Savin proving that nominative determinism is alive and well (he's a goalkeeper, you see). The right-back, Yeboah Amankwah, had been brought in on loan from Manchester City.

Suitably for a man who played for Stanley for three years, John Miles is now in charge of the youth team. He came through the Liverpool academy in the late 1990s but never made an appearance; giving a post-match interview, he revealed the same accent that Walton-born Paul McCartney had. (At this point, a true writer would quote a Beatles lyric but in this ever-changing world in which we're living, I think that's unnecessary.)

The team Miles picked for the game, which was screened live on CharltonTV, contained players named Gough, Pickles, Monk, Trickett and Harper, which makes me think that every club has had Youth Cup XIs full of these names. In an interview for the club website, local lad Connor O'Brien said it was 'magical' to captain the under-18s. The Youth Cup 'is the big competition for us. It's all about winning. It's not about the performances, it's about results.'

The away side, meanwhile, were captained by Karoy Anderson. Wingers Tolu Ladapo and Mack Reilly played either side of Daniel Kanu, a striker in form, but could he do it on a Tuesday night at Accy? He could, as it happens, and he scored the game's first goal after 14 minutes.

Brilliantly, on the half-hour, Accy equalised through a Leslie Adekoya header. The striker had started the season in what is known in football writing as scintillating form, with 11 goals in five autumn games. In the last four of those, his team scored 20, which goes some way to explaining why they had advanced to the last 32 of the Youth Cup.

Born in Salford, Adekoya joined Accrington as a 15-year-old. In advance of the Bolton game he told the club website, 'All of the coaches are brilliant. They really pinpoint what they want us to do and how they want us to play. Everyone knows their jobs and roles in the team.'

Unfortunately, Charlton scored a second goal right on half-time through their captain Jason Adigun. If you really have a sensational memory, you may recall that he scored against AFC Wimbledon in the second round. According to the Accy Twitter feed, nothing at all happened in the opening 18 minutes of the second half. Young Aaron Pickles had a goal ruled out for offside after 63 minutes – and yes, a wag named Stuart Chilmad knew his World Cup trivia and hoped 'he found the World Cup there' – before Harley Lawton was brought on for Calvin Harper. It was Lawton who, aged 15, scored the winner against Wigan in the first round back in October, after replacing Adekoya, who had scored twice.

Meanwhile, Liverpool's rearranged game against Burnley was happening at the Kirkby academy. Unsurprisingly, given the talent available to Liverpool, they were coasting, in spite of the presence of young Michael Mellon, the son of Tranmere Rovers manager Micky, in the Burnley side.

With updates from Ian Doyle of the *Liverpool Echo*, Melkamu Frauendorf scored in the third minute then Mateusz Musialowski scored in the 11th minute. After half-time the famous Oakley Cannonier, who could already have scored twice, added to his CV with a goal, and Musialowski banged in another on the hour after Burnley pulled one back.

'Complacency may be the only issue,' was Ian's ominous summary of the first half.

In the second half at the Wham Stadium, Henderson came on for Gough. Just look at those last paragraphs again and you can see the gulf between an elite club, where youngsters come in from Germany and Poland, and a League One side, whose young players do not. It was fourth time unlucky for Stanley and Charlton advanced to play Brighton in the last 16.

The game at Kirkby finished 4-1 and the tie of the fifth round had to be Liverpool v Chelsea. They were joined by Nottingham Forest, who beat Peterborough United 2-1, and Sheffield Wednesday, who beat Preston North End 1-0 with a goal direct from a Leojo Davidson corner. I think that makes three appearances for the lost art of a goal from a corner in this story. Wednesday would go to Blackburn in the next round, while Forest would travel to Cambridge United, who beat 1993 winners Leeds United 2-0 and continued a fine month for the Us.

Every proper football fan knows about the miracles performed by John Coleman at Accrington Stanley on a barely fourth-tier budget to keep a true community club in the third tier. In his 2021 book *Whose Game Is It Anyway*, Michael Calvin remembered exactly why he loved football when he went to watch a game at the Wham.

Yes, he would agree, Liverpool play in some of the top stadia in the world and have top talent managed by a top gaffer, but Accrington have a charm that someone will have to put into words in a full book. I am sure owner Andy Holt can write his own book without assistance, but should he need some help, I will offer my services. Up the Stanley, I say.

Accrington's under-18 manager John Miles is a local lad who played almost 100 times for Stanley in the 2000s. Arsenal recruited their academy manager Per Mertesacker from abroad. After time as first-team and club captain, in which he also collected the dressing room fines, as of the start of the 2021/22 season Mertesacker oversees the age groups at London Colney.

The under-18s are run by Dan Micciche, who previously worked with the under-15s and under-16s in the three years prior to taking over as the boss of promising scholars. This is smart from Arsenal as it means these teenagers have a familiar face as they try to break into the senior squad. Many of them, including Bukayo Saka and Emile Smith Rowe, have a fighting chance of a seat on the plane for the 2022 World Cup. Saka, by the way, was part of the 2019 Arsenal under-18s team who fell at the last-16 hurdle to West Bromwich Albion. He scored the equalising goal but West Brom went through thanks to a winner from Finn Azaz, who moved across the Midlands to Aston Villa in 2021. Having spent 2020/21 gaining first-team experience at Cheltenham Town, Villa loaned him out to Newport County, for whom he has been a regular.

Micciche brings experience to his job at Arsenal from his time as the technical lead coach of kids from under-12 to under-16 levels at the National Football Centre at St George's Park. This was the replacement for Lilleshall and is non-residential. It has all modern conveniences to help England's seniors reach the last four in consecutive international tournaments. Perhaps Howard Wilkinson deserves even more credit even than being the last English manager to win the top division of English football.

At MK Dons, Micciche had a hand in developing the young Dele Alli, who may have abandoned all hope of a seat on the plane to the Middle East. Emile Smith Rowe has therefore benefitted from Micciche's help, since he has been given the same chances to shine in the Arsenal first team that Dele was given at Spurs.

Jonathan Northcroft wrote a piece for the *Sunday Times* in January 2022 which describes Dele as 'a haunted young man … It is hard to think of a comparable dip in status involving a British player.' One assist in two years of football, plus 'only 14 successful passes into the box since the start of 2020/21', is bewildering for one of the most mercurial English talents of the Premier League era.

Dele made his England debut in 2015 and was given a £5m-a-year deal by Spurs at the start of the 2018/19 season. He started the 2019 Champions League Final against Liverpool but, after Mauricio Pochettino left the club, the appointments of José Mourinho and Antonio Conte have stalled his development.

Northcroft suggests that the problem with Dele is a matter of tactics. 'Leading sides these days rarely play with second strikers … Compared to classic number tens, [Dele] is not an especially creative passer … He seems to be a talent without definition or direction.' Not even the best youth talents are assured a path to being champions. Yes, I have chosen not to include 'so why did he sign for Spurs then?' in that last sentence.

Talking to the *Training Ground Guru* podcast, Micciche says of his new boss Mertesacker, 'He's been fantastic to work for. He's extremely humble and practices what he preaches in terms of the values that he wants for the academy. He does remind me a lot of my time working with Gareth Southgate at the FA. You only find out about his experiences by chance or if you probe him.'

The 'Big Effing German' is part of the 'strong spine' at the club including football director Edu and manager Mikel Arteta.

The youth coaches do four player reviews per season, Micciche says, with players creating their own clip packages and taking ownership of their career, with coaches as facilitators. The term used for this is '360 feedback'. In addition, four players form a regular leadership group which revolves every few months and there are set-piece leaders given particular defensive and attacking roles.

Mertesacker preaches personal responsibility and likewise Micciche says that the academy's philosophy is 'to create strong young Gunners by creating the most caring and challenging Academy in the world', on and off the pitch.

Micciche says his job as coach of the scholars is 'to give them ideas and make them believe what they might perceive is impossible is possible, to give them the confidence and belief'. He talks about various tournaments aside from the Youth Cup, and how one player walked off the pitch in disgust with himself when he took a shot with his right foot instead of working on his left foot as his targets dictated. Micciche adds that, if these improvements were not made under controlled conditions, it was 'just a piece of paper'. Elite players, after all, need challenges, as Paul Tait noted when training Ross Barkley.

In the 2020/21 iteration of the Youth Cup, Arsenal advanced to the quarter-finals where they were defeated 3-1 by Liverpool. Charlie Patino was missing with injury, but Miguel Azeez scored the consolation for Young Gunners. Born to a Nigerian dad and a Spanish mum, Azeez has worked his way through the ranks at Arsenal and England. He made a ten-minute Europa League cameo in 2020 then spent 2021/22 on loan at Portsmouth, where he learned valuable lessons from the likes of John Marquis and Manchester United graduate Ryan Tunnicliffe.

In January 2022 came a third-round shock at the JobServe Community Stadium in Colchester, as an Arsenal side captained by Charlie Patino lost 3-0 to a team which had beaten Swindon Town in round two. Patino would score on his senior debut in the EFL Cup victory over Sunderland, after which Paul Merson said on TV, 'Who knows, it could be the next five, six, seven years, the next Man United.'

Perhaps Merson just forgot the loss to Colchester the week beforehand in his joy at Arsenal reaching the last four of a domestic competition. He was, after all, part of the 1986 lot of lads who became champions of domestic trophies in the 1990s, before any of these kids were born.

When Merson was a baby, in 1971, Arsenal had completed a treble of sorts when the seniors won the First Division and FA Cup. They won the 'FA Double' when the youngsters beat Cardiff City in the Youth Cup. Brendon Batson was playing in defence for that side and, in the half-century since picking up his medal, he has seen black players be picked for and captain England and Arsenal. Batson will always be Arsenal's first black player, but his first-team appearances were limited by the ever-present Pat Rice, who would become Arsène Wenger's assistant coach in 1996.

The club had still happier times in the 1980s. We already discovered how good they were in 1986, when Merson and his team-mates were only penalty kicks away from advancing to the Youth Cup Final.

They did take that last step in 1988 and, what's more, came home with the trophy. Readers who haven't jumped straight to this section will know that it was Doncaster Rovers who were pummelled 5-0 in the first leg, although they put up a better fight in the second leg when they were playing for pride and earned a 1-1 draw.

As Nick Hornby chronicled in his book *Fever Pitch*, the Gunners' senior team were about to win the First Division in the final minute of the final match of the 1988/89 season. In the youth ranks were three players who would be in the matchday squad when Arsenal won the 1994 European Cup Winners' Cup against Parma. Alan Miller, who passed away in 2021, was David Seaman's understudy that season, while Steve Morrow recovered from the broken arm he sustained when Tony Adams dropped him during the celebrations after winning the 1993 League Cup – the first leg of their Wembley double, as the Gunners also went on to win the FA Cup that season. Kevin Campbell was never capped by England despite scoring consistently at Everton and Nottingham Forest after his five years at Arsenal.

David Hillier captained the 1988 side and added to the contents of his cabinet when he helped the senior team win the First Division in 1991. Two years later he was wretchedly unfortunate that injury ruled him out of both of those 1993 domestic cup finals. 'My job was to win the ball and give it to Anders Limpar,' Hillier modestly told *The Guardian* while talking about his second career as a firefighter based in Bristol. 'We get cows stuck in mud. I've even had a cat stuck in a window!'

Neil Heaney was on the wing for that 1988 team. His time at Arsenal was less heralded than that of Hillier, but he did go on to play for both Southampton and Manchester City. Today, Neil is the chief executive of Judicare, a law firm which formed a partnership in 2021 with Player4Player to assist ex-pros with their legal needs, especially when dealing with property outside the British Isles.

Neil can count his chat with me in early January 2022 as pro bono work rather than billable hours.

'Remind me again, when did we win it?' he asks. 'I believe, at that time, I was the youngest player to ever win the FA Youth Cup.

'I was just over 16, technically a schoolboy, so I was travelling down [from Middlesbrough] every holiday, every half-term to play in Pat Rice's youth team.'

Some of the lads in the first team had played in that 1986 side but Neil was mostly training away from the seniors, 'I was aware of the lads in the first team as that's what we aspired to.

'Sometimes you would be called over to train maybe once or twice, but in those days you really had to earn your stripes. You had to be doing it week in, week out with the reserves to be asked over. That's not to say there was a them-and-us mentality because George Graham wasn't of that thinking.'

Even in 1988, says Neil, 'It was very different to now, training methods, diet and everything ... Pat was a big character and an immense manager for lots of reasons. He was very strict, but he had a huge amount of respect. He could be one of the guys. He was just a fantastic person to have looking after us at that stage. He was a legend at the club. The methods were the methods in those days – things evolve, don't they? – but Pat wasn't one to put the balls away and say, "Let's run around the pitch for 40 minutes." He definitely wanted the lads to get on the ball.'

How does Neil use the lessons of his Arsenal career – or, we agree, career with 'the Arsenal' – as a CEO?

'The qualities that Pat Rice instilled have stayed with me. He used to have a saying, "Remember who you are, where you are and who you represent." You are an ambassador and you must set certain standards for yourself and everyone around you. If you don't meet those standards, you're out the door.'

In 2022, there is a coterie of academy graduates in and around the Arsenal squad. 'If you're brought up at the club from a very young age and you come through the ranks, it's strange but it doesn't mean more,' says Neil.

'You've started the dream and you've gone all the way through and realised it. They clearly have all of the attributes and skills necessary to represent the Arsenal.'

As is the case with Swansea City and Liverpool today, back in the late 1980s the youth team played in the same way the first team did, 'And I believe it would be the same today, with the same thought process,' Neil says. 'Ultimately one day the reserve-team and youth team players would have to step in. If they played in the same manner every week, it's a much easier transition for them to play as the manager wants you to play.'

Would this mean, therefore, that the under-18s at Arsenal would have their defenders roped together and learn to stick their hands up in unison for offsides? Neil laughs politely.

'I think that's an urban myth! I never saw that, even the first team. That back four, five, six and seven almost, were incredibly talented individuals who could play in that unit. It may have happened but we certainly were never tied together!'

In 1986, Middlesbrough had been wound up, with the Ayresome Park gates padlocked. They were rescued by Steve Gibson, who is still the club's owner today. Gibson is thus to be credited with helping the young Boro lads in the same way as Elton John has a share in Watford's youth players of the 1980s. Coaches like Dave Parnaby and Tom Walley used the resources supplied by benevolent owners, then helped the young lads transition to the senior side where Gibson and Sir Elton saved a lot of money filling a squad with players.

Young Heaney may well have ended up as one of those Boro players had Gibson come in a few years before he did, 'I was attending the Boro academy as well. I don't know whether or not I would have signed for Middlesbrough but I suppose when Arsenal come calling it's very difficult not to want to go there. It was extremely exciting times there. It would have been very hard to not go after being asked to go there.'

Indeed, as we saw earlier, a lad from the north-east would not have been allowed to move to Arsenal because of the 90-minute rule. In the late 1980s, Neil was able to meet up with players from around the country when he played for an England under-21 team under Lawrie McMenemy with Andy Cole, Ian Walker, Jamie Redknapp, Chris Sutton, Ugo Ehiogu and Steve McManaman, 'We had a fantastic bunch of lads coming from Derby, from Chesterfield. It wasn't just that if you weren't at one of the big clubs you wouldn't get in.'

At clubs like Arsenal it was 'British kids, homegrown talent' such as Hillier and Campbell, who both went through the under-21s set-up too. I ask Neil to remember those players with whom he shared a dressing room as a teenager for club and country.

'David was an incredible passer of the ball, a very tough south London lad, very strict with the rest of the lads, always demanding good standards,' he replies.

'Kevin was a centre-forward, just destroying every record in the junior leagues. He was a phenomenon for his size, his pace, his finishing. At that age group he was virtually unplayable. In the final [of the 1988 Youth Cup], he scored a hat-trick in the first 20 minutes and the game was over. He had a fantastic career.'

Hillier and Campbell did what Neil could not do and became first-team regulars. I ask whether it was more about attitude than talent to do so.

'There's a lot of luck involved as well, being in the right place in the right time, your form being good in the reserves. When a chance in the first team comes, you've got to be able to grab it because you might only get one chance. Talent in any form of life will only get you so far.

'The majority of the guys are all talented or they wouldn't be there. You've got to be dedicated and I think that's what separates the greats from the others.'

Neil did wear the Arsenal shirt before moving away to Southampton. He adds, 'George Graham was very fair to me when Alan Ball came calling. He said, "Look, if you stayed her your chances would be limited so I think you should take this opportunity to play first-team football." Obviously I loved my time at Arsenal but it was time for me to move on.

'It was a life-changing experience to be a professional footballer at that time. I was on the fringes and in and out, but as a winger it was extremely difficult to get in George Graham's side. There was Merse [Paul Merson], David Rocastle, Anders Limpar, Martin Hayes. All of those players were ahead of me. There were lots of things that had to happen for me to be a regular.

'Even now, all of the years after, my team is still Arsenal. I played in some veterans football a few years ago but that chapter in my life is over now. It would be great to go back and see the guys and have a beer.'

While he was still contracted to Arsenal, Neil was loaned to Cambridge. Managed by the idiosyncratic John Beck, the Cambridge team included Dion Dublin and Steve Claridge, while Neil played on the opposite wing to Gary Rowett. 'Beck had, shall we say, different ideas of how the game should be played! But he was also a very astute coach. You can only get so far with gimmicks,' he explains.

'It was a great experience for me, a very different attitude in the dressing room. When you walk into Arsenal's, you have to be spoken to before you speak, there was that much respect. At Cambridge, it was slightly different. I couldn't be silent or a shrinking violet as that wasn't the kind of person John Beck wanted. He wanted combative people who were up for a bit of a fight. They were two very different dressing rooms but equally important for me.'

Currently working for the Chilean Football Federation, Francis Cagigao was born in London to immigrant parents who came from Galicia. As profiled by Sid Lowe in *The Guardian* on his departure from the club, he 'went to his first game aged four' and played for Deportivo Galicia, a team his father had set up in London. As a player he was 'engulfed by the values, tradition and class' of Arsenal but moved to Barcelona as a young professional.

Cagigao would probably be a pointless answer on *Pointless* if the category was 'Arsenal staff in the Arsène Wenger era'. Monsieur Wenger appointed him as a scout for the Iberian region when he was 26, which was useful for finding the likes of Cesc Fàbregas, José Antonio Reyes, Nacho Monreal and Santi Cazorla.

As the head of international scouting, Cagigao helped bring a host of foreign talent to north London, stretching back all the way to the Invincibles' right-back, Lauren.

Neil saw 'Franny' and the other Youth Cup winners when they were paraded on the Emirates pitch at half-time a few seasons ago, 'We were all invited to a game and we went out with Pat and with Terry Murphy, who was one of the scouts and a very influential person. It was the first time I'd seen Kevin, Alan, Dave Hillier and Franny for 20 or 30 years. I'd spoken to them on the phone from time to time.

'I didn't realise how high Franny had climbed within the coaching structure of the Arsenal. It was good to catch up with him and spend some time with him. He's a very amiable, likeable guy.'

Regardless of whether the Arsenal can repeat their league titles of the last 30 years, they will always produce good young talent, as we saw earlier in the story when we met the conquerors of Millwall in the 1994 Youth Cup Final.

But let the record state that Adrian Clarke, who came through the Arsenal ranks in the early 1990s, played no part in that win.

'It's always been on my write-ups but that never came from me!' he told me politely with some bemusement.

'The confusion lies in A. CLARKE. The A stands for Albert who was a young striker at the time.' The information, probably purloined from a well-known online encyclopaedia, has now been edited.

Ironically, Arsenal loaned two academy products out in January 2022. Ainsley Maitland-Niles went to AS Roma to join Tammy Abraham, and Folarin Balogun headed up to Middlesbrough to join Aaron Connolly, the Brighton player who needed some calm in his private life.

Given that some players were competing in the African Cup of Nations, or they were afflicted by injuries, serving suspensions or had tested positive for Covid-19, Arsenal were left with only 13 fit outfield players. Bizarrely, the Premier League granted their request to delay the match away at Tottenham Hotspur.

Jonathan Northcroft, writing in the *Sunday Times*, placed an exasperated groan next to his piece on the fall of Dele Alli. 'The Premier League's lack of belief in its own youth system' was one of three things being exposed, along with the 'disdain for fans' who may have 'taken time off work or organised family life around fixtures'.

'What is the point of academies and the under-23 league,' asks Northcroft, 'if none of the young players involved is considered adequate enough to, in emergency, help a team fulfil a fixture?' Bear in mind especially that Arsenal had already been knocked out of the 2021/22 FA Youth Cup.

In the shadow of Chelsea's imperial period, Fulham have quietly produced several talented young players since the injection of money from first Mohamed Al-Fayed and then Shahid Khan. This was the club which paid a footballer £100 a week back in 1961 and brought through England internationals Alan Mullery and George Cohen, who spent his entire career at Craven Cottage.

In their 1997/98 season in the third tier, Rufus Brevett was one of 20 signings who were brought in to play for Fulham after they achieved promotion. Sean Davis had made his debut in 1996 as a 17-year-old academy graduate and must have been impressed at the investment made by al-Fayed so that the squad could compete at the new level.

It worked, with Fulham gaining promotion to the First Division (now the Championship) at the second attempt. Employing Kevin Keegan, who left at the end of the 1998/99 season to take the national team job, also didn't hurt the club's prospects.

In 2000, there were at last some youth players making matchday squads. Mark Hudson would go on to Crystal Palace and Charlton Athletic before heading to Cardiff and Huddersfield to earn his living. Along with the presence of Calum Willock and Elvis Hammond, Fulham were producing their own talent who could play a role in the club's first stint in the Premier League, which began in 2001.

Dean Leacock, Darren Pratley, Zesh Rehman and Malik Buari also made first-team appearances in the following seasons. Famously, left-back Matthew Briggs became the youngest Premier League player two months after he turned 16. His career petered out domestically, although he did play a small role in Watford's failed promotion push in 2012/13. His true success came for Guyana, whom Briggs captained after he switched allegiances.

John Murtough was in charge of youth development at Fulham. He was later brought in alongside David Moyes by Manchester United in 2013, becoming their football director in 2021. Fulham's technical director in the early 2000s was the famous Les Reed, who had led Wealdstone to FA Trophy success in 1985. Reed was headhunted by the FA to work at Lilleshall and he eventually succeeded Howard Wilkinson in the role of technical director.

His greatest success, however, came with Southampton, where Reed spent eight years revamping the club's football operations and helping them clamber back up to the Premier League. Talented teenagers were sold before they could become club legends, although they have done well to hold on to James Ward-Prowse after he made his England debut.

Think how menacing Southampton would have been if they had kept Luke Shaw, Gareth Bale, Adam Lallana and Theo Walcott until their prime. Famously, Walcott re-signed for Saints in 2020, fully 14 years after he had left as a wonderkid.

Along with Walcott, Bale and Lallana, several more of the 2005 side who were losing finalists against Ipswich Town went on to have senior careers. Future Finland captain Tim Sparv, strikers Leon Best and David McGoldrick, and future Premier League winner Nathan Dyer all played in that team. Lloyd James played in the squad relegated from the Championship in

2008/09. His team-mates included Lallana, McGoldrick and Dyer as well as Morgan Schneiderlin and fellow youth team graduate Andrew Surman.

Continuing the work Les Reed did at Fulham two decades ago is Huw Jennings, whose career has followed a similar path to that of Reed. Jennings worked at Southampton in the early 2000s and was also persuaded to join a bigger organisation, in his case the Premier League. In 2008, he joined Fulham in the era in which they reached the Europa League Final thanks to the managerial expertise of current Watford manager (at the time of writing) Roy Hodgson.

By 2014, young talent was once more banging on the first-team dressing room door at Craven Cottage. That year, the kids reached the FA Youth Cup Final where they ran into their neighbours Chelsea. A first-leg victory was overturned as Chelsea won 5-3 at Stamford Bridge to take the tie 7-6. Dominic Solanke scored the winner for Chelsea to prevent the game going to extra time.

Many of the Class of 2014 would graduate to the senior team. Goalkeeper Marek Rodak was Fulham's short-lived number one for the 2020/21 Premier League season having helped his club gain promotion and his country of Slovakia qualify for Euro 2020. Defender Cameron Burgess was sold to Ipswich Town in 2021 after an impressive season at Accrington Stanley, while midfielder Emerson Hyndman is currently back in his homeland of the United States playing for Atlanta United. Winger George Williams returned to his hometown of Milton Keynes before settling for a few years at Forest Green Rovers.

The pair of Moussa Dembélé and Patrick Roberts starred in the white shirt before wearing green and white hoops. Celtic poached the former, who has also played for Lyon and Atlético Madrid, and were loaned the latter by Manchester

City. Roberts, who was born in Kingston upon Thames just down the river from Craven Cottage, made his professional debut aged 17 against the club who would sign him. City had him under contract for seven years, loaning him out to Girona of La Liga, Norwich City, Middlesbrough, Derby County (where he played under manager Wayne Rooney) and Troyes.

When I decided to tell the Youth Cup story in the middle of 2021, both Roberts and Lewis Baker of Chelsea were still contracted to elite clubs. When I delivered the manuscript, both had moved on. In the January 2022 transfer window, with Roberts aged 25, Sunderland took him on a six-month deal which left the player's options open. Baker headed to Stoke City on a deal which will last until the middle of 2024.

From kids to being associated with a team of champions, Roberts and Baker eventually gave up the quest of forcing their way into the plans of their first-team manager. It is the best for both parties to let the player play, but what a waste of two talents who are going into the prime years of careers which promised so much more. We should watch their progress carefully over the coming years.

Huw Jennings gave an interview to Gerald Lami's podcast and YouTube channel in April 2021 where Lami asked, 'What does it take to become a football academy director?' I settled down with a cup of tea on a cold Sunday afternoon to watch it, keeping an eye on Liverpool's game against Brentford to see if any other west London lads were playing Premier League football that day. Brentford's XI contained players who had come through at Oxford United (Shandon Baptiste), Walsall (Rico Henry), Dulwich Hamlet (Ethan Pinnock), Northampton Town (Ivan Toney) and Troyes (Brian Mbuemo had left by the time Patrick Roberts arrived).

On the bench was Finley Stevens, a Brighton-born Wales under-21 international who had been released by Arsenal at 16 and who moved to Brentford via Worthing. He had been a non-playing substitute in the 2021 Championship play-off final. On the same day as Liverpool v Brentford, West Ham conceded three goals at home to Leeds, all scored by Jack Harrison, who left Manchester City for first-team football. In another era he would have stayed at Manchester United but chose to attend high school in the USA from the age of 14.

Handily for whatever Jennings was about to say, his old employers had destroyed Bristol City 6-2 the day before, with Nathaniel Chalobah coming off the bench for Fulham. With just over half the season gone, Fulham were on top of the Championship.

'All I have tried to do throughout my career is work as hard as I can to try and help young players help themselves to be the best they can be,' Jennings tells Lami of his 35 years in youth development. 'It's been a fantastic journey. There have been downs, inevitably, yet the privilege to be able to do what started off as my hobby is still a strong emotion.'

When he was young, Jennings attended a rugby-playing school on the border of Buckinghamshire and Northamptonshire. There was 'no organised football outside schools' but Jennings would not have excelled anyway as he was not a good enough player. 'I had a capacity to read the game, understand and appreciate it. I had an opportunity to study the game. It was incredibly limited: you had one live game a year, the [FA] Cup Final.'

Having qualified as a teacher and found a job in Oxford, Jennings 'rapidly realised that coaching was much more a vocation than playing'. He volunteered to be part of the coaching programme at school, then worked in the district, the county and then at Oxford United, working part-time. 'I absolutely loved it,' he says. 'It served as my apprenticeship.'

When asked about the challenges in those days, Jennings focussed on the 'infrastructure'. He explains, 'I was driving the minibus, making the phone calls, putting nets up, pulling the dog crap off the pitch!

'Resources were very limited. It was pioneering stuff for the professional game to get into coaching young players in the 1980s. It started with 15–16, then 12–16 then under-nine to under-18 when the academy movement came in'.

Jennings finally decided to abandon the classroom and worked at the training ground full-time. In the absence of a professional career as a footballer, he had to build his credibility.

'I was starting off a long way back and I had no issue with that. I was open to learning, experimenting and trying to always think about what worked for the young people. Not for it to be about me as a coach but for them as players.' He made mistakes (there was 'a lot of command-style coaching in the early days') but he had ironed them out by the time he was bringing lads through at Southampton.

Several local boys, including Wayne Bridge, had come through before Jennings got his teeth stuck into the project, where, 'Two things came together: the commitment from board level down, and the recruitment of the talent.

'They were one of the last to make the commitment. Southampton weren't really sure if they had the resources or the ability that was required to launch the academy. I found good people but probably a lack of organisation and real clarity of purpose.'

The three Wallace brothers and Alan Shearer had developed there but they were born well north of the south coast. The club, to Jennings, didn't look after the local kids. 'Darren

Anderton was from Southampton and went to Portsmouth!'
he almost spits out.

'In the early days, we noticed that we had to up the standard
of recruits. Over time, we brought in Malcolm Elias and we
were well supported by [owner] Rupert Lowe. He really invested
in the academy, not just resources but the personal investment
in believing that the model was one that he wanted to back.

'Andrew Surman might have fallen by the wayside had he
not had a good standard of player around him. We attracted
talent, "Come to be part of our programme!" We made
some statement signings, like Leon Best, Dexter Blackstock,
David McGoldrick. They were a different profile to what
Southampton had. They were big personalities who fill a room
when they come into it. They gave such momentum to the
work we were doing. We built from the front.'

Gerald Lami asks about the kind of character Jennings
wants his scholars to have. 'What we wanted were players who
had inner drive, a desire to succeed and a level of resilience
that set them apart,' comes the response. This is all displayed
by players such as Bale, Walcott – whose Southampton
debut was Jennings's favourite football moment – Lallana
and Oxlade-Chamberlain who have all fought back from
injury at some point in their careers, which have all included
international caps.

'We didn't have all those slogans plastered around the
corridors!' Jennings says. 'But we worked very closely: me,
Malcolm, Steve Wigley, coach George Prost … The Academy
Lodge, which was a den of iniquity(!), played a huge part.'

As often happens to a club on a downward slide, problems
in the boardroom impacted the playing staff, especially after
relegation to the second tier. Southampton was a PLC in the
mid-2000s, so, 'The finances took a massive hit. The club

didn't have the resources to be able to continue to operate at the Premier League level. I could see what was coming.'

Jennings jumped before he was pushed and used his expertise to help put the foundations of youth development into place at national level, while experiencing 'a lot of frustration' thanks to the poor performance of the national team who failed to qualify for Euro 2008.

'Steve McClaren was during my era. I'd worked with him at Oxford when he was a youth coach. The [England men's] team was really struggling but there was a lot of talent coming through the academies. The top end of the game was not working out,' and the Elite Player Performance Programme (EPPP), helmed by Ged Roddy, 'took that baton forward'.

In 2017, all this investment paid off. Under the management of Steve Cooper, who spent 2021/22 remaking Nottingham Forest in his own image, England's under-17s won the World Cup with a squad which included Player of the Tournament Phil Foden and future Manchester United player Jadon Sancho. Five lads from Chelsea were picked, including Conor Gallagher, Callum Hudson-Odoi and Marc Guéhi, while Rhian Brewster and Angel Gomes put club rivalries aside. Both have since moved on from Liverpool and Manchester United respectfully.

Manchester City goalkeeper Curtis Anderson played in the final and later earned a move to Wycombe Wanderers. He has since been loaned out to non-league clubs such as Eastbourne Borough. Joel Latibeaudiere, as we learned earlier in the story, joined Cooper at Swansea City, while a few players went abroad: Danny Loader to Porto and Jonathan Panzo to Monaco after he won a 2018 Youth Cup medal with Chelsea.

The EPPP had helped these players become some of the world's best talent at their age group. Foden and Hudson-Odoi were champions for their country as kids and, a few years later, added some international caps and club trophies to their cabinets.

'Their journey through the academy movement was one in which they were supported by an increased level of investment from the clubs,' says Jennings. 'It's to the clubs' credit and the [Premier] League's credit. There was a lot of scepticism about the underachievement [of the national side]. If you have the backing from the top of the organisation, you have a good chance to succeed.'

At Fulham, Shahid Khan was used to recruiting playing staff from the college system as the owner of NFL franchise Jacksonville Jaguars. College football is entirely amateur, so Jennings had to explain the academy movement to Khan and his family. Happily, he says, 'They immediately got it. They saw its value and they have backed us fantastically.'

Late developers are the next topic of discussion, with mention of one player who made his senior debut for Liverpool after an impressive season on loan at Blackburn Rovers.

Fulham have the best record in England at bringing players through the ranks and into a professional career across the pyramid after their scholarship. One example is Elijah Adebayo, who departed Craven Cottage for Walsall and then joined Luton in the January 2021 transfer window, where he scored on his first start and kept scoring into the 2021/22 season. That gives Jennings and his staff at Fulham 'a lot of pleasure. You need lots of those players to help that diamond come through and reach the pinnacle.

'Some of the best work is done between the ages of seven and 11. Youngsters cannot register until they are in the under-nines but many attend pre-academies. It's an early specialisation sport and a lot of research says that the fundamental skills are acquired in that early phase.

'Harvey Elliott had been with us at pre-academy level but he decided to go to QPR. We kept watching him and he was fantastic in a small-sided game on the Cottage. We approached him and the family agreed. Size was never a factor. His qualities were there for everyone to see.'

Jennings stays motivated to succeed, he tells Lami, because his love of the game has never changed. He quotes Gareth Southgate's famous words, 'I love the game but I hate the industry.' Jennings also adds that 'there are dark forces at work' within the game. All the same, he has established a credo which the players work towards regardless of these outside forces.

'We have the three Hs: Honesty, Hard Work and Humility. To live those values is not easy at times. The longer I get into my dotage, the more I am drawn towards watching younger players in the foundation phase. There is a freedom, an expressionism amongst the players.' This is helped by superb coaches like Les Reed or Huw Jennings who help them blossom.

Across town from Fulham, West Ham were enjoying a superb season under the management of David Moyes. The current boss of the under-18 side is Kevin Keen, who played over 200 times across a decade at the Hammers having joined them from Wycombe Wanderers as a teenager.

He followed his father into football; his dad Mike was the Watford manager who was fired by Elton John in 1977 after the Hornets found themselves bottom of the Fourth Division. In fact, it was Mike who gave Kevin his debut at Wycombe as a 15-year-old.

After Kevin finished his playing career, he joined the coaching staff at the West Ham academy in 2002 before moving up to the reserves when Alan Pardew and Alan Curbishley were managers. He has also worked with Steve Clarke and Chris

Powell as their assistant coach, as well as briefly managing Colchester United for 24 games in the 2015/16 season. He won only five of those matches.

After being knocked out of the Youth Cup by Arsenal in the last 16 in 2020/21, which was at least a change from the seven consecutive defeats the team had suffered at the first hurdle, the 2021/22 tournament matched them with Newcastle United in the third round.

Many of the same lads who had played in the under-18s the previous season moved into the second year of their scholarship. Their team captain at the time of publication was Northern Irish centre-back Michael Forbes. Several players had been in matchday squads for the senior team's Europa League run, with Jamal Baptiste, Sonny Perkins and Freddie Potts (son of former Hammer Steve) among those who played against Dinamo Zagreb at the London Stadium.

Michael Carrick was one of seven players in England's 2010 World Cup squad who had been partially or wholly developed at West Ham's so-called 'Academy of Football'. The others included Frank Lampard and Rio Ferdinand, runners-up in 1996 to Liverpool, as well as Joe Cole, Jermain Defoe, Glen Johnson and, before he went to Chelsea, John Terry.

The key figure at West Ham was Tony Carr whose 'old school training', Carrick writes in his memoir *Between The Lines*, doubled as a fitness tool and mental tool, while the 'third man run' was a big part of the ball work.

Carr presented his own life story in the spring of 2022, with assistance from many famous faces he turned from kids to champions, including Carrick himself. Carr broke his leg as an academy prospect at West Ham; aged 23, he became director of youth football at the club, remaining there until 2016 and coaching under 12 managers.

Carrick notes correctly that this group were 'the last breed before the academies started ... You had to suffer a little to reap the rewards,' and that suffering included old staples of apprentice life. Boots needed cleaning, terraces needed sweeping, lost balls needed finding, slips needed putting in the skip and, worst of all, the 'big heavy goals for the first team before and after training' needed moving.

Respect and hard work were still part of the life of a young trainee. When Tony Adams nodded to the lads, who had cleaned the away changing room after a match, he transferred stardust to Carrick and his mates. He was also in awe of Manchester United's players, from whom he tried 'to pick up tips on how to be a top pro just like them'. At West Ham, the first-year pros had a dummy fight with the second-years because 'the players' code demanded we go through with it', Carrick explained.

Having earned a princely £42.50 per week as an apprentice ('Craig David or Usher CDs' were his luxury purchases), Carrick signed a contract on his 17th birthday for the sum of an initial £400 per week, with incentives if he made the first team. For the Youth Cup, it was an accumulating scale of payments starting at £10 for a first-round win, rising to £100 for each leg of the final.

The FA Youth Cup 'obsessed everyone' at West Ham. Perhaps they knew that in 1981 the Young Irons had beaten the young Spurs 2-1 on aggregate. The goal they conceded in the second leg was only the third they had let in across the tournament. Paul Allen, who would later play for the Spurs' senior team, had been part of the West Ham side which won the 1980 FA Cup, and he brought that experience to a side which contained young Bobby Barnes, who would make his first-term debut at the Bernabéu against Real Madrid Castilla, and fellow first-teamer Alan Dickens, later of Chelsea. Sadly, youth team captain Everald La Ronde only played seven times for the Irons and had to retire very early into his career.

The 1996 final, whose home leg Carrick attended and saw Lampard versus Carragher and Owen against Rio Ferdinand, 'was all people talked about around the club'. For the second leg of the 1999 final, Upton Park was 'heaving. They only opened three stands and left one closed ... Kick-off had to be delayed' to let the punters in and so fans were 'around the pitch, four or five deep' because the turnstiles were closed.

The Class of '99, Carr's latest batch of kids, faced Coventry City. Carrick wrote, 'We weren't just team-mates, we were real mates. We played with a smile on our faces, having the time of our lives, all on the same wavelength ... We were almost just messing around on the pitch.' In that second leg, they added six to the aggregate score and won 9-0 over the two legs, which led to a fun moment when Ian Wright celebrated with them back at the training ground. 'He went mental, singing and shouting,' said Carrick.

Two months later, Carrick adds, instead of watching him practicse his finishing, the pair were training together.

It is quite incredible that, with the departure of his friend Ole Gunnar Solskjaer, Carrick was caretaker manager of Manchester United in November 2021. The man Carrick had replaced in the United team was Nicky Butt, who grew up idolising Bryan Robson. Nick Cox notes that Robson took Butt under his wing and 'made sure that as he broke into the team that he was there for him and had his back'. Butt would do the same for the next generation.

Butt left Old Trafford six months before Solksjaer and Carrick in May 2021, amid reports of an argument about his role at the club. Sadly for fans of local talent, he told *The*

Athletic's Andy Mitten, 'We have to keep buying the best players.' José Mourinho asked for Mason Greenwood to train with the first team even though he was 15 and rules forbade it because he was still at school. Scott McTominay had no such issues and has become a mainstay of the men's squad and his national team. Butt is humble, telling Mitten how he 'just carried the baton for the next generation'.

In January 2022, Anthony Elanga scored for Manchester United against Brentford. To quote Huw Jennings, the baton has been passed and the relay continues.

Chapter Nine

The Fourth Round and Watford v Chelsea

VISION 2030 is the new project for Chelsea to keep the conveyor belt pumping out talent, and the driving force behind it is Neil Bath. Academy manager from 2004 and now head of youth development, Neil is a local lad born in Battersea who got his start running leisure centres.

As such, it was imperative that I got along to Norbiton, south-west London, to see Chelsea's kids play Leyton Orient at noon on Sunday, 12 December in the third round of the 2021/22 FA Youth Cup.

I had been to Kingsmeadow previously to watch AFC Wimbledon and Chelsea's women's team, so I completed the hat-trick on a mild afternoon. Ominously for Orient, Chelsea had beaten Brighton 6-1 in November 2021, although Brighton led for 15 minutes of the first half.

In the introduction of this book, I noted the homegrown presence in the 2020/21 UEFA Champions League winners. Six months later, three of them were on the scoresheet against Juventus at Stamford Bridge: Trevoh Chalobah, Reece James and Callum Hudson-Odoi all started and scored, while

Ruben Loftus-Cheek and Mason Mount came on from the bench.

Before their Youth Cup tie against Leyton Orient kicked off, three things stood out. There was the 'Five In A Row' banner behind one of the goals. There was the familiar pre-match earworm 'Liquidator', the ska piece which is played just before the teams come out at Stamford Bridge.

Most impressively, to remind the spectators who were playing, the video screen at Kingsmeadow showed footage of James, Hudson-Odoi and Mount playing as kids and as champions. There is, thankfully, a pathway to the first team as part of Vision 2030, not just a route on loan to Vitesse Arnhem, where Lewis Baker spent two years as part of his development.

Chelsea hit the upright in the first minute and showed their elite status all over the pitch. The Young Blues had won the game by half-time and were three goals up and cruising. Orient would at least draw the second half 1-1, after a rare mistake in possession at the back for Chelsea, to make it 4-1 at full time.

I was torn between two players when trying to name a man of the match: Lewis Hall, wearing number six, made the second Chelsea goal with a 50-yard one-two that literally got me out of my seat applauding. My favourite moment of the game was when Orient's tall defender was muscling him at a set piece; there was a foot in height between them.

At one stage, Hall won the ball back from an Orient attacker, retained possession, nutmegged his opponent by the corner flag and gave it to a team-mate with ebullience. It doesn't hurt that he looks like a figure from an old *Roy of the Rovers* comic, with a chiselled jawline and a stocky build. Claude Makélélé is available at the club as a mentor, and I am positive that Hall has gone to him for lessons on playing in the hole between defence and midfield.

It is no surprise that Hall has represented his country at youth level, having been with Chelsea since he was a child. It was no surprise, to me at least, that Hall started for the senior team, albeit as part of a back three, at Stamford Bridge in the FA Cup game against Chesterfield. His biggest contribution was to pull the ball back for Romelu Lukaku to score Chelsea's third goal. Forgotten man Baker, aged 26, came on as a substitute almost eight years to the day after his debut for the club in 2014. As we discovered in the last chapter, ten days later he was sold to Stoke City, ending his time as a Blue.

If not Hall, then Silko Thomas was my pick for stardom. Thomas has also come up through the age groups, playing across the front mainly, but he was wearing number two against Orient. His heroes, he told the club website, are Ronaldinho because of his 'confidence' and Cristiano Ronaldo for his 'mentality'.

The Chelsea tactic seemed to be to get it out wide to Thomas on the right so he could stand it up for an attacker, although silky Swede Edwin Andersson put in the cross for the first goal. Thomas himself smashed in Chelsea's third after playing a one-two with the overlapping centre-back, showing the team ethic and the confidence that an elite academy athlete can possess. They may have grown up playing in a different position when they were 12 or 13 to when they turned 16.

The current under-18 coach at Chelsea is a former youth team captain. Ed Brand was released by the club in 2005 and, speaking at the time, he felt he was 'moved [around] in several different positions'. He was able to thank the club for developing his skills in words which he must repeat to the Young Blues today: 'If you have the belief in yourself, in your own abilities and you're willing to work hard then hopefully you'll be rewarded for something.'

As Nigel Gibbs did before him, Brand became a holder of a UEFA Pro Licence in the summer of 2021 alongside former Arsenal trainee Ryan Garry, ex-Manchester United winger Quinton Fortune and the former Chelsea and England 'captain, leader, legend' John Terry.

Still chasing the story, Henry Winter of *The Times* got hold of Jody Morris, the former Chelsea midfielder who worked in the academy alongside Brand before stepping up to become Frank Lampard's first-team assistant. He was pictured next to Lampard as the young lads made their debut for the first team after the year-long transfer embargo was imposed in 2019.

In the 2017 FA Youth Cup Final against Manchester City, Reece James had to look after Jadon Sancho. 'Jadon never got a kick,' says Morris. 'Reece was outstanding. He was the right side of a back three.' Conor Gallagher came off the bench in the first leg of that 2017 final. 'I remember him as a 16-year-old and questions being asked, "Is he one of the better ones?"' Morris continues.

'The minute he went full time [as a pro], all of a sudden he was just overtaking people because of the type of character he was. He has personality ... It's not often nowadays you get a holding midfielder and attacking midfielder in one. He does both. He's hungry.' It can only help Gallagher's development that Patrick Vieira was his coach when he spent 2021/22 on loan across town at Crystal Palace. It was his fourth loan move following time spent at Charlton Athletic, Swansea City and West Bromwich Albion.

The Academy Player of the Year in 2018/19, Gallagher became a full England international in November 2021. He made his debut against San Marino and, in a crowded departure lounge, Gallagher may well find himself on the plane to Qatar for the 2022 World Cup alongside fellow Blues

Mount and James. Both of those players won the Academy Player of the Year award in 2016/17 and 2017/18 respectively and also benefitted from loan moves. Mount played under Frank Lampard at Derby County, while James was part of a Wigan Athletic side alongside FA Youth Cup winner Darron Gibson and Watford academy graduate Gavin Massey. The system works.

Morris went up to Glasgow to watch Billy Gilmour, who spent 2021/22 at Norwich City having become a full Scotland international. The youngster was sent off after going in for a tackle with someone who had 'whacked him a few minutes before'. Morris left the ground and winked at Gilmour, explaining, 'I'll take that attitude all day long over someone who shies away from it. I preferred my players to train like that as well so you've got competition, whatever level you're working … They are all pushing themselves.'

Perhaps with the knowledge that Chelsea wanted to fund a new stadium, which would impact transfer fees, the best way to save money seems to be to do what elite clubs have done in the modern era. Finding young players would be a reversal of their former policy which impeded, for example, the Chelsea careers of Lewis Baker, Dominic Solanke and Nathaniel Chalobah.

Watford fans still salivate over Chalobah's first touch on his debut for the club against Wolverhampton Wanderers. He was 17 and in his first spell at Vicarage Road in 2012 where he was a key part of the promotion push under the management, ironically, of Chelsea treasure Gianfranco Zola. Chalobah showed his precocity when he received the ball from the goalkeeper, dropped his left shoulder and took it on his right foot, sending the attacker the wrong way.

Weeks later, Chalobah became an England under-21 international, going on to play 40 times in total, and made his senior debut in 2018 as a Watford player. He followed in the footsteps of Luther Blissett and John Barnes, which is truly esteemed company.

Later in the season, live on Sky Sports, he banged in a 30-yard thunderbolt against Leicester City. In May 2013 he was on the pitch when Watford beat the Foxes with the last kick of the game, known as the Deeney Goal, but he was powerless to stop Crystal Palace winning at Wembley in the play-off final a fortnight later.

Chalobah was at that time still only 18 years old. He went on to enjoy five more loan spells in the next three years while battling injuries. He wore the shirts of Nottingham Forest, Middlesbrough, Burnley, Reading and Napoli. In 2017, Watford fan and *Guardian* writer Simon Burnton wrote a piece surrounding Chalobah's permanent move to Watford at the age of 22.

Chelsea, Burnton remembered, 'had spotted Chalobah as a ten-year-old and nurtured his talent through 12 years … culminating in him making one start and nine substitute appearances for them in the Premier League. And then they lost him.' Chelsea then signed Tiemoué Bakayoko for £40m.

I was at a Watford–Chelsea game in early 2018; it was the first home game of the Javi Gracia era. Bakayoko was sent off in the first half and it was as if Chelsea were trying to get manager Antonio Conte fired. Watford galloped to a 4-1 victory. Days later, Bakayoko had been turfed out to AC Milan, where he returned in 2021 after loan spells at Monaco and Napoli.

Six months before that disgraceful red card at Vicarage Road, Burnton wrote that the Bakayoko deal was a 'dismal failure' by Chelsea, given that Watford only paid £5m for Chalobah. Chalobah then signed for Fulham in 2021 for an undisclosed fee after being relegated and promoted with

Watford, so nobody knows if Watford made a profit apart from their accountants. Bracketing Chalobah with Michael Keane, who had also been 'owned and disowned' by a top team (in his case Manchester United), Burnton argued, 'Logically the aim must be to catch the best young players on the first rungs of the ladder, before they make their names and inflate their values.'

Bakayoko, and indeed Eric Bailly at Manchester United, seemed to appeal to their international fanbase who would be 'particularly appreciative of the teams most crammed with expensively assembled headline players ... Spending more money leads directly to earning even more money.' Burnton even compared this young talent to how the crown jewels could have been decorated with sparkly diamonds from the Isle of Man and Cornwall, but Britain 'plundered the most splendid gemstones from across the globe'.

Thus, at the time Chalobah finished his scholarship and signed professional terms with Chelsea, British football loved foreign talent which 'used to be somebody else's'. This is persuasive and points also to how the likes of Lucas Piazon and Mario Pašalić were purloined and then boomeranged around the world as part of the Chelsea loan system. As this book was being written, Piazon has regular first-team football at long last as a Braga player while Pašalić is starring in this season's hottest hipster team, Atalanta.

Chalobah's brother Trevoh, who also won the Youth Cup with Chelsea, is in and around the first-team squad at Stamford Bridge, and even scored a famous goal against Crystal Palace where, according to the club's official website, 'He succumbed to the emotions and sunk to his knees in tears.'

When Watford met Chelsea at Vicarage Road on 13 January 2022, the draw for round five of the FA Youth Cup had already been made. The winners would travel to Liverpool or Burnley in what would probably be the tie of the round, although the winners of Crystal Palace v Wolves were drawn at home against the winner of Tottenham v West Brom and Manchester United would face Everton if those sides were to beat Reading and Sheffield United respectively.

Regardless of what the players achieve domestically or at international level, whether they have a good few years in the professional game or hang up their boots early, they will forever be immortalised in print. Nobody can tell whether injuries or, increasingly, personal issues will impede their progress. They are frozen in time, playing at a Premier League stadium under floodlights, doing a job they are paid to do for their employer.

In my report on the game, I will use the vivid present tense because it's better that way.

I reach the ground at 6.30pm, having walked down Vicarage Road as I had done many times before to watch the senior team. Tonight, there are no road closures around the ground and traffic is still able to drive down towards west Watford and the hospital where I was born, which sits next to the ground.

Players on both sides are limbering up with the full range of stretches and ten-yard sprints. Watford's side, many of who are unknown to some of the crowd, are encouraged by their conditioning coach who claps his hands rapidly. I spot Dave Messenger, the lifelong Watford fan who gets paid to work on behalf of the club in a disability access officer role. Seven buzzwords are written along the stand named after Graham Taylor, including 'Together', 'Diversity' and 'Inclusion'.

The under-18 game thus offers the club a chance to put this into practice. A parade of kids in grey Watford training jackets lean on to the advertising hoardings that line the pitch. Coach

Tom Hart does a bit of chinwagging with the younger Hornets, who must be under-12s or, at a stretch, under-14s.

Sundry Chelsea fans, who have made a simple trip by car or on a Southern Rail service from Clapham Junction, do the same the other side of the halfway line. The Young Blues are training, tapping the ball about to one another in a rondo exercise in a grid that looks 15 yards long and five yards wide.

Some of the lads who played in the third round are present and correct, including captain Alfie Gilchrist and the midfield pair of Lewis Hall and Charlie Webster. Silko Thomas and Edwin Andersson are absent; perhaps they have been moved up to the under-23s.

The goalkeepers are getting in some shot-stopping practice, with the Chelsea keeper Prince Adegoke tipping balls over the crossbar. He will hope he has more to do today than he did against Leyton Orient in the third round.

The seating, by the way, is not segregated, so Chelsea fans and Watford fans can mix together. After they are patted down at the entrance to the Sir Elton John Stand, they are met by a mural which features blown-up pictures of the eponymous rock star. There is one terrific photo of Elton John kneeling among young fans from the days when he was chairman in his late 20s or early 30s. His well-known passion for football is only rivalled by those fans who have spent years traipsing up and down the country and the divisions with Watford, with no world tour to take them away from their beloved team. I see the odd two or three of these old-timers in the stand throughout the evening.

The floodlights are on full beam and it occurs to me that I will be sitting in a stand which did not exist in 2012 when I watched Watford beat Burnley thanks to Troy Deeney's winner off the bench in a mid-table Championship game. Only if the club needed a fourth stand would it be built, replacing the old, demolished stand which had once contained the Family Enclosure where Dave Messenger once sat watching Watford in the happy days of the 1980s. This was the era when Elton John, Graham Taylor and Tom Walley were all key figures in the team's rise to three Youth Cup finals.

As I clamber up the concrete steps, I recall too that this stand would have been swept by the apprentices whom Walley was bringing through to Taylor's first team, which was bankrolled by Elton's money. I do not imagine the under-18 lads either at Watford or Chelsea would be doing this sort of manual labour today, because it has been replaced by gym work and nutritional lessons so that these club employees can bring out a return on their initial investment. Some of the players I will watch this evening will be released at the end of the 2021/22 season or given a full-time professional contract.

Some might be snapped up by bigger fish, as I discover on social media. Days before the fourth-round game, a Watford lad had moved to Chelsea before he could even sign youth terms as a Young Hornet. Centre-back Travis Akomeah moved down to Cobham in a deal reported on by Watford fan Fabrizio Romano, who also made a living breaking news about Chelsea's latest signings.

The Blues beat at least four other teams including Arsenal and Liverpool to sign Akomeah. It may well be that, when someone reads this story in 2032, he will have made a fabulous start to his career. Such are the unknown unknowns of being a teenager signing a scholarship with any club, let alone one who won the biggest European trophy the year before.

A few of these lads have, since the third round, entered the first-team dressing room as a member of a matchday squad. For Chelsea, Lewis Hall and Charlie Webster both remained unused on the bench in the EFL Cup quarter-final against Brentford. They watched their mate Harvey Vale make his senior debut off the bench that night, after Jude Soonsup-Bell (who had been the number nine against Leyton Orient) had played the first half. All four players would start the game at Vicarage Road.

For Watford, Shaqai 'Shaq' Forde had been thrown on at the end of their 4-1 FA Cup third round defeat at Leicester City. He was not even 18 years old and already had a shirt number (47) from his debut. His strike partner Emmanuel 'Tobi' Adeyemo has the build of a professional athlete but is not even 17. Nor are George Abbott, who is starting with the tall Will Hall at centre-back, or left-back Hamzat Balogun. Like Adeyemo, they are first-year pros and cannot legally pass their driving theory test yet. Vale and Soonsup-Bell, meanwhile, have represented Chelsea and also England under-19s.

I wonder if Dave Messenger has met Reg 'Skilly' Williams, who starred for Watford as an amateur and Chelsea as a professional before retiring at 29. His great-grandson Jack Grieves is up against Webster and Hall tonight, an unenviable task. While Jack gets some shooting practice in on the far side, the defensive four do a drill of their own. With Hall opening his arms wide in a pose familiar to any defender looking for the line with which to spring an offside trap, the four yellow shirts practice attacking the ball from a standing start.

I take my seat in Row K, six rows from the back of the stand and a few paces away to the right of the halfway line. Looking up and backwards, I spot two cameras which, it turns out, are there for coaching reasons. In the middle of the opposite stand, another camera is operating a live feed which is relaying the game on to YouTube for the benefit of those in St Albans or St Lucia who fancy watching the game.

There is no rain. A cloudless, black sky is overhead. The PA plays a worship song with an emphatic beat that endorses the Lord's greatness and the sanctuary which He provides. A gentleman wearing a jacket with the Three Lions and the letters 'FA' upon it finds a seat at the back of the stand. He will be assessing to ensure the fixture abides by the laws of the game.

Three seats to my left, a father calls out to his son who, as he disappears to change into his shin pads and blue kit, sticks his thumb up. The owner of the thumb is Charlie Webster, whose dad is watching him at work. How would any other teenager cope if Dad showed up to watch his son or daughter earn a living while also trying to impress his employers into giving him another deal after his initial two-year scholarship?

Fans have clustered in the seats near the halfway line all the way up the stand. Among them are small groups of teenagers who, as I saw at Barnet and Wimbledon, are supporting their mates. They can look out over three stands which are bare except for ball boys who have been employed to retrieve any wayward shots. Below in the away team dugout, a member of the Chelsea staff has his laptop out, crunching some numbers. To his right, two tabard-wearing stewards hand out A4 sheets upon which the line-ups have been printed in lieu of a match programme.

Moments later, the theme to the TV show *Z Cars* starts up and we stand to applaud the teams as they emerge from the tunnel. They have numbers on their backs and resolve on their faces. Watford's shirts lack the logo of an offshore gambling site because it would look awful for kids under the age of 18 to be advertising such an activity. There's enough chance involved in just getting to the stage they have reached, as Charlie Webster's dad would tell me if I dared to distract him from cheering on his son.

There is no pre-match handshake because over 300 people have died that day of a Covid-19 variant. After the game, I would be incredulous to read a Conservative-leaning newspaper break a story of parties which occurred the day before Her Majesty The Queen saw her husband buried. Football is a game; politics is not.

The teams are read out in the gruff voice which belongs to the club's communications manager Richard Walker, himself a Watford fanatic. The noticeable thing is that small pockets of fans cheer individual names, with the loudest coming from a family ten seats to my right and up a bit. They are here to support Watford's number 11, Adrian Blake, who looks like the youngest and skinniest player on the field. If you blew on him, he'd fall to the floor. Wingers, as from the dawn of association football, are still 'wiry'.

Blake, his team-mates and his opponents kneel in solidarity with the fight against racism. Chelsea keeper Adegoke raises his right fist in the air. He had not played the game until he was 11 and joined Chelsea soon afterwards to play alongside lads who had started very young.

In a strange habit that I have never noticed before, the referee counts the players on the pitch to make sure there are 22 of them. He gets an all-clear from both assistants and goalkeepers and the game kicks off. Watford defend the goal at the Rookery End which means, as the senior team do when the stadium is full, they will attack that end in the second half.

With wearisome predictability, Chelsea lead after ten minutes. The Chelsea Youth Twitter feed sends news to its 221,000 followers: 'Malik Mothersille cuts the Watford defence open and Harvey Vale applies the finish inside the box. A bit too easy, that.' They don't mention that Mothersille has been left wide open between the lines, with no player within what might be three yards of him. Vale is as clinical as you would expect a second-year scholar at Chelsea to be, letting the ball run across him and then scoring with his left foot right into the corner of the Watford goal. 1-0.

A couple of minutes later Watford's defender Abbott nods wide and then Adegoke is forced into his first save which reminds me that it was prudent for him to practice tipping the ball over the bar. Luke Badley-Morgan has to change his shirt due to a blood injury, so will now be numberless for the remainder of the game. I wonder if they had spare shirts knocking about in Tom Walley's day.

Mothersille adds a second after 23 minutes. It is an incredible goal but not for the usual reason. Watford take a corner which is cleared. When the ball is kicked upfield, three Chelsea players are ahead of Watford's last man. Who is still in the Chelsea half. I groan loudly.

With no offside, Watford goalkeeper Alfie Marriott has to run towards Jude Soonsup-Bell, who skips around him halfway inside the Watford half. A defender rushes back to the goal-line and watches Watford defender Balogun scythe the Chelsea player down, much as Terry Fenwick did Maradona in 1986.

Mothersille ensures he stays onside and taps the ball into an unguarded goal for 2-0. Watford have conceded from their own corner kick, although Chelsea got lucky with the bounce of the ball as they cleared it. When Manchester United did this in the Champions League, they were laughed at.

At one stage George Abbott falls over with the ball on the edge of his own penalty area and recovers just in time. At any level of the game, it is about fine margins and knowing what to do with the ball when you have it: give and go, boot it out, pass it back. Play the game, not the opponent. Play again, fail better, as Samuel Beckett would surely counsel.

Five minutes later, just as I am commending Watford's general play and lack of nerves despite being 2-0 down, left-back Balogun slips after cutting out a crossfield pass from Lewis Hall. Chelsea right-back Brodi Hughes, who has taken lessons from Silko Thomas in attacking his opposing full-back, can't test Marriott. Five minutes after that, Mothersille should bury the game but he gets too far underneath the header after a Soonsup-Bell cross and Watford survive.

I spend the end of the first half being entertained by a babbling toddler whose eyes have been taken off the game by my own shouts, usually imploring Shaq Forde to get into the game. He's a bystander and has hardly had a touch until he drops back into midfield and even into the middle of his own half.

I am also very keen to show Charlie Webster's dad that I recognise his son's talent, so I clap when he gives the ball to a team-mate and shout 'Look up!' when he's got his head down. Chelsea's one-touch play sometimes dazzles, while Prince Adegoke makes a good save from Grieves. The game is open in spite of Chelsea having much of the ball.

Proving that he is human, the squat and muscular Lewis Hall mis-kicks a free kick and audibly yells. This is not what a Chelsea first-team player does. There's plenty of time to learn, though, either at Vitesse in the Netherlands or any number of English clubs who work with Chelsea's loan managers to nurture their blue-shirted assets. He might go to Stoke to play alongside Lewis Baker or to Sunderland to play with Patrick Roberts.

Meanwhile, Tobi Adeyemo's frustration shows when he goes in late on a Chelsea defender. It's hard being a lone frontman when there are three centre-backs waiting to take the ball off you. No wonder Manchester City have pioneered the formation with no number nine.

The end of the first half is as bizarre as Chelsea's second goal was strange. The referee gives a throw-in to Watford which displeases Ed Brand in the Chelsea technical area. After some bickering, the throw is taken. It has more height than breadth and, just as it is about to head out of play, it lands on a Watford hand. Play stops and the referee gives a handball.

Moments later, under no pressure whatsoever as he keeps the ball alive, Chelsea keeper Adegoke controls a pass back to him. He knocks it forward but mis-kicks it, leaving the ball loose. Having been taught to anticipate this, Adeyemo sprints ten yards on to the loose ball and rolls it into the net. I stand up and cheer, as any football fan does whenever their team scores; 2-1.

Adeyemo has scored at Vicarage Road from absolutely nothing at all. As with the handling error made by Manchester City goalkeeper Mikki van Sas against Brighton, Adegoke's mistake will live online forever and I hope it doesn't cost him a pro deal at Chelsea. Watford fans start with that familiar noise which immediately follows a goalkeeping error, 'ooooohhhhh' is how I transcribe it here without the second brutal summary of the quality of the goalkeeper.

The third strange moment comes before half-time. The referee is keen to play the full duration of the one added minute of injury time but Watford winger Kyreece Lisbie goes down with an ankle problem. The players all head to the touchline to refuel. Rather than ending the half a few seconds early, the referee allows Lisbie to be treated, calls the players back to their positions with a 'Gents, let's go', drops the ball for the Chelsea player and blows for half-time.

A more experienced referee would have blown early, but perhaps the news from the African Cup of Nations that another ref had blown well before the end of the game has convinced this official, named on the A4 sheet as Andrew Humphries, to play it extremely safe.

The chances and possession have mostly gone to the away side, but there have been flashes of wizardry from the Watford midfield, especially young Grieves and the yellow-booted Lisbie (coach Tom Hart was right about the boots, by the way). My eye is also drawn to right-back Ryan Andrews, the son of Wayne, who knows the art of the tackle and was committed in several duels. He will do well in the lower levels of the professional game where players can still make this sort of challenge.

Chelsea, who conceded just before half-time and should be at least 4-0 up, must have had a robust team talk from coach Ed Brand. I remember that Ed and Tom Hart were FA coaching buddies and also how excited Tom was to match Ed. They treat each other with respect on the touchline, knowing that their role is to help their young charges do their best, rather than making it all about them. The pair give advice to their players or ask them to take up particular positions.

Tom takes a bit longer in the dressing room than Ed, meaning the blue shirts fill the pitch a few minutes before we see yellow ones. The game recommences, at 2-1 to the away side, who have won the competition nine times to Watford's two.

In fact, the Youth Cups are about the only trophies Watford have won in their history, discounting county tournaments and play-off victories. Playing in front of a home crowd will help them in the second half; in addition, the players get given free tickets to watch the men's team and many of them will have been ball boys in a Premier League fixture. They know where the goal is, so to speak.

Shaq Forde so badly wants to be involved in the game that he concedes a corner when he is back defending. Alfie Marriott turns a shot around the post and Chelsea keep up the attack at the start of the half. Their other winger Zain Silcott-Duberry (whose name will one day, but not tonight, be sung to the tune of 'Seven Nation Army') runs across the width of the pitch pursued by Andrews, who plays the role of the cat to Silcott-Duberry's mouse.

Central midfielder Adian Manning, wearing number four for Watford, looks like a young Étienne Capoue, with the same gait and haircut. He dances around Lewis Hall in the middle of the pitch as if in tribute to Capoue, whom Watford fans agree has been one of the most naturally gifted footballers to play for the senior team in the Pozzo era. I do not see Gino Pozzo or chairman Scott Duxbury. They might both be watching from home on the live stream or perhaps sat in the posh seats in the opposite stand.

On the stream, by the way, the commentator says that Manning is outnumbered in the centre of midfield, 'up against two players ... that's why Chelsea are getting success being a bit more directional'. By that he means 'long ball', a charge famously aimed at Watford in those glory days of the 1980s.

The man with no number on his back, Chelsea's Badley-Morgan, moves his arms down in the well-known 'calm down!' gesture as the ball goes dead and, for the second time in the game Watford right-back Andrews goes down. Chelsea are 2-1 up and need to take control of the match.

As the play pauses, a caricature of a football agent, in a coat that looks expensive and chic, chats to the blokes in the row in front. It turns out that some of the players on the pitch are on his books but 'these games don't mean so much'.

Not to someone who gets a cut of any transfer fee, I bet. The agent also names a well-known Premier League player whom he wants to see at Wembley playing in the EFL Cup Final.

A few moments later, Hall and Forde crash into one another. It's like when the two Spidermans face each other in that meme, except here one is wearing blue and the other yellow. It's a foul by Hall on Forde, after he slips while clearing the ball, but both are up within 15 seconds to continue the game and give each other a quick hug. The referee, recognising the collision was accidental, restarts with a drop ball to Chelsea.

The next action in play is a save by Marriott from Hall, who grabs himself a yard of space in the penalty area but scuffs his shot a little bit. As he had done against Leyton Orient, Hall is running this game, while centre-back Alfie Gilchrist is scrapping with Watford scorer Adeyemo just behind him. By this point, the little girl in front of me is focussed on bright blues and yellows on a screen, not on the pitch.

Adrian Blake has his hands on his young head, having been put through by Forde. Gilchrist nips back and, in the style of John Terry, comes across to divert the ball out for a corner. Chelsea's first change is a straight swap on the wing: Soonsup-Bell off, Leo Castledine on. Perhaps he knows Quaine Bartley and Morgan Williams because he was poached from AFC Wimbledon. Born in Kingston upon Thames, Castledine has been involved at under-15 and under-16 level for England.

Four minutes later, with 15 minutes left of the game, Watford equalise. A foul by Castledine puts Manning on the floor and the free kick comes to Andrews on the right. He knocks it forward to Grieves on the edge of the Chelsea area. Grieves does brilliantly to sneak in behind Charlie Webster, who is focussed on cutting out the pass but doesn't guess the path of the ball correctly. Grieves controls it with his right foot with Badley-Morgan at his heels. The Chelsea defender dare not make a tackle because he's in the penalty area.

Grieves heads towards the byline, now with his opposite number Hall in pursuit. After a ricochet off his right shin, he is able to cut the ball across the corridor of uncertainty, where three Chelsea defenders fail to get a foot on the ball. Right-back Brodi Hughes has raced to the goal-line, leaving a man unmarked at the back post.

Adrian Blake cannot miss. He puts his right foot through the ball and it hits the roof of the net. It's 2-2.

The Watford fans explode. The home team's substitutes race down to the corner flag where Blake has slid on his knees to celebrate. I hear loud cheers above me and look back to see his mum dancing and his dad holding his fists in the air, as if he himself has scored. He looks, in football parlance, over the moon to see his son score, from about four yards, at Vicarage Road.

Blake adjusts his headband as he heads back for the restart. Watford fans start some chants of 'olé!' as passes find yellow shirts. Manning makes a strong, fair challenge on Webster, like the sort you used to get in 1982. There is always a chance that the underdogs will vanquish the favourites, which summarises the power of spectator sport. I gave Watford a two per cent chance of winning the game before kick-off. It may nudge five per cent now.

Harvey Vale is the player who is most likely to score a Chelsea winner. In a move started when Webster wins the ball and chips it forward 40 yards, Vale receives possession on the right-side touchline, the one nearest to the Sir Elton John Stand. He moves the ball to his left and beats two men on the edge of the penalty area. The ball moves from Hughes to Hall and back to Vale, who creates space for himself and shrugs off the attention of a defender. Level with the penalty spot, he curls the ball with his left foot.

It beats Alfie Marriott. It strikes the inside of his right-hand post. An inch to the right and the ball was in. Which ghost of the Vic has kept that ball out?! Seconds later, Marriott is possessed by one of those ghosts, stopping a shot by Hughes with his fists with a save that proves he has worked on his instincts and intuition. Ryan Andrews goes down, and Adian Manning gives Adrian Blake a hug. I wonder if Blake's heart is still racing after the goal and the ensuing celebration. The Young Hornets are still in the game, with ten minutes of it left.

Of course, if they keep it at 2-2, they will need to somehow keep the lactic acid away enough to endure a full 30 minutes of extra time. Watford players take on some fluids as the attendance of 1,147 people is announced. Andrews gets up and, for a third time, tries to continue playing.

Charlie Webster blazes a shot over the bar from 25 yards out. His dad has relocated, possibly to be closer to the Watford goal over which his son has just shot. Eight minutes until extra time, but there will be time added on. What is Tom Hart thinking? His boys have an equaliser and momentum. He directs his players with bellows and exhortation.

Two to go. Watford win a corner from nothing after Lisbie puts pressure on Badley-Morgan on the byline. Chelsea have every blue shirt in the penalty area, doing something they do not usually do: prevent a last-minute winner.

Watford take as long as they legally can getting the ball into the box, with Grieves and Forde standing on the goalkeeper's toes. Adegoke does excellently to fist the ball towards the near touchline, where Watford repeat the charade to win another corner, where they repeat the charade for a third time. Adrian Blake puts the ball down and walks forward, as if inviting somebody else to take the corner. The ball is cleared eventually and Webster knocks it to Vale.

With a jetpack on his back that makes a mockery of the 87 minutes he has already played, Vale plays it short to Webster who shoots over the bar once again. Coach Ed Brand has his head in his hands.

A Watford fan nearby shouts 'Time for a winner!' with blind enthusiasm. There is light, nervous chatter in the crowd, who have accepted another 30 minutes of a wonderful game under the Vicarage Road floodlights.

Four minutes go up on the board held aloft by the fourth official. Webster is booked for persistent fouling. Lisbie, who has hardly been in the game this half, is booked for delaying the game at a Chelsea free kick. His shirt, socks and boots are yellow, and moments later he wants a penalty when a cross hits Badley-Morgan's naturally positioned arm from eight nanometres away. Play continues. Manning goes down with cramp, easing his way up from the turf like a giraffe. I wonder if he or any of his team-mates had thought they would be taking Chelsea to extra time.

Brand gets his players in a circle and tells them what they need to do in the next 15 minutes, gesticulating emphatically, bashing his hands together. His glare is piercing and menacing. I imagine 'score a goal' is high on his list of priorities. So far, his team's results have included a 5-2 win at home to ten-men West Brom, a 7-2 trouncing at Tottenham and a 4-1 victory against Arsenal. They have also beaten Crystal Palace 4-3 and drawn 4-4 at Fulham. You will notice that no sheets have been kept clean in any of those matches.

Strangely, over on Twitter, Chelsea Youth indulge in some petty banter at the news that Granit Xhaka has been sent off in the first half of the EFL Cup semi-final against Liverpool. They post a quote from the midfielder which draws over 800 likes. The announcements of both Chelsea goals in this game had a combined 450. It's as if bantz trumps goals, which is entirely in line with what following football is about for a certain type of fan today.

The Watford FC Academy social media team send out a picture of the team in a huddle at full-time, to their 3,000 followers. They choose not to tweet an image of four players on their back next to the dugout trying to get some oxygen into their legs to clear the lactic acid that is the worst enemy of an unfit player. Those grey-jacketed kids rush to the hoardings to peer over at them and shout words of encouragement.

Interestingly, Chelsea's media team do mention this, with particular attention paid to Ryan Andrews 'who is obviously playing through the pain barrier'. They also remark on how the 'underdog carrying the momentum ... noticeably slowed things down' as Watford saw out the second half.

After a blast of 'Firestarter' by The Prodigy, a UK number one before any of these players were born, extra time begins. I reposition myself next to Adrian Blake's parents just in case he scores again. I am directly in front of two men, and behind another one, who are so clichéd that any reader must think I have used some artistic licence and added them to the narrative for more colour. 'I don't understand why professional footballers aren't fit enough,' one of the men says. 'It's a big test for them.'

The third man moves up a row to sit beside me and asks his friend to 'keep the ticket' after the Newcastle–Watford game that Saturday. 'They know me at the ticket office!' The three men are more interested in marvelling at how many games one of them has been to already that season. 'My most ever! Thirty-five new grounds!'

On the pitch, George Abbott hesitates at the back for Watford, letting in substitute Tudor Mendel-Idowu who, on another day on a different ground, would have taken his chance. His shot from ten yards comes off the crossbar.

Tudor's father is a pastor who has written books on theology and religion. Born in Slough, Tudor is currently at Eton College, where he is a King's Scholar. Other famous people to win that award include Aldous Huxley, who wrote *Brave New World*; John Maynard Keynes, who was the greatest economist of his age; punk/folk songwriter Frank Turner; and three former prime ministers, Harold Macmillan, Robert Walpole and Alexander Boris Johnson, back in the days when people called him Al.

Tudor has been called 'the genius in Chelsea's academy' because he appeared on the TV show *Child Genius*, finishing in second place. He also won a language challenge, the prize for which was a trip to Malawi. 'My favourite language this time was Mandarin, because I enjoyed the way it related to other languages I'd learnt before,' young Tudor told GetReading. co.uk, which refers to the Berkshire town but is a pun I am sure he would appreciate. (You see, not all Etonians are rule-breaking party-goers.)

Tudor's LinkedIn page includes a mention of being in 'England Men U15' with international caps against Ireland and Turkey jostling for place with prizes for German, Classics and History amid his accomplishments. He is 'looking to connect with other intelligent minds and further enrich the school through the invitation of authoritative speakers'. While he was showing off his knowledge in competitions, Tudor was training with Chelsea's younger age groups, so he has grown up with some of the lads in this youth team.

Having sprinted back to cover, Watford left-back Balogun falls on to his back and is treated for cramp. He spends the next five minutes running it off, while Ben Smith replaces Jack

Grieves. Moments later, Tudor is in the Watford penalty area looking for a foul. He had whistled past two Watford players and it looked like there might have been contact from Will Hall who 'looks a bit nervous' according to the commentator on the stream. 'He looks guilty doesn't he? I think it's a penalty.' Referee Humphries had caught up with the play and must have judged that the ball was not in Tudor's control.

I am sure the same three letters would have popped into the mind of every Chelsea fan in the ground, and indeed the reader's, but there is no video referee available at under-18 level. Yet.

Tudor looks disappointed not to get the penalty. Around me, the three old football blokes continue their football chatter. Then comes a goal.

After Chelsea spread the ball around the pitch, with the Watford press tiring, Castledine turns Abbott who steps to the right while the Chelsea player goes left. His shot is saved by Marriott but the ball pops out to Harvey Vale, who has been called up to the Chelsea senior team for precisely this reason. Right place, right time, excellent team goal; 3-2 with 20 minutes of extra time to go. In fairness to the Chelsea fans who were more interested in Xhaka than their under-18s, over 500 of them click the like button on news of Chelsea's goal.

Prince Adegoke runs 100 yards to join the dogpile on top of Vale, who looks a little like the comedian Ed Gamble but with the physique of Hakim Ziyech. Balogun's night is done, and Freddie Moriarty replaces him. 'Heads up, Watford!' is the shout from Adrian Blake's dad, and the first half of extra time dribbles to its conclusion. I move back to my original seat away from the Blake clan and the trio of groundhoppers. The little girl is still glued to the phone screen and is sitting on her mum's lap.

To my left is a man in a blue hat with a stopwatch around his neck and a long-suffering friend, or perhaps spouse, beside him. He holds a pen and has a printed grid into which he has written in the attendance and the team. He places crosses and marks next to the players' names too. I mistakenly think for a minute that '1,147' is the number of Chelsea games he has seen in his life.

Young Louis Flower comes on for the final quarter of an hour, with Malik Mothersille having run non-stop for 105 minutes. Shaq Forde is still looking to impose himself on the match. He runs 50 yards and passes it forward to Ademayo, whose progress is halted bravely – as a goalkeeper's intervention at a striker's feet is always called in football reporting – by Adegoke. He stays down on his back and the physios run on to the pitch to provide treatment for the injury, which resulted from Ademayo's stray boot. There is a spare keeper on the bench but he is not called upon. Time will be added on at the end of the game, which has ten minutes to go.

Kyreece Lisbie has a chance for Watford after Brodi Hughes switches off at left-back but his shot is weak and is cleared away. It has turned into a cup final, not an opportunity to advance into the last 16, and Watford take off Will Hall and leave only Abbott at the back. A wild shot from 35 yards by Ryan Andrews clears the crossbar. Five minutes remain. Lewis Hall trots off the pitch too.

A Forde shot from a long way out takes a nick and Watford have a corner. I spot Alfie Marriott wanting to join the attack and he gets an OK from Tom Hart. Every player on the pitch apart from the corner taker is in the penalty area. The ball lands on Marriott's head on the back post but his header lacks power and Adegoke saves it while Marriott picks himself off the floor. He has left an open goal but fortunately for him, Tom

Hart and the Young Hornets, nothing comes of the attack. Four minutes remain, and a thousand voices raise themselves up to try to rouse their team.

Poor Ben Smith, who receives a terrific crossfield ball from Andrews, is left alone on the right-hand side. 'Help him. Please!' I cry, hearing someone behind me mimic the last word. Possession goes to Chelsea and suddenly, with Forde (unbelievably!) tackling back as the last man in defence, Flower races towards the ball. So does Alfie Marriott, who coolly passes to his nearest yellow shirt.

A minute later, under no pressure, Chelsea again concede a corner as the ball dribbles over the byline. Marriott canters up the field again as Richard Walker announces four minutes of added time thanks to Adegoke's injury. The keeper punches the corner clear and the ball is thwacked over on the volley by Blake. Now it is Chelsea who try to run the clock down, with Flower taking a booking for knocking the ball away after an offside.

Then an extraordinary moment. Moriarty is wide open at the back post, ten yards out, and volleys just over. It was an astonishing ball into the box by Ben Smith and a really composed volley which had beaten Adegoke but unfortunately cleared the crossbar too. At the other end, Castledine looks clean through but Watford's sub Christos Batzelis makes a superb covering tackle to knock the ball back to Marriott.

The Chelsea fanatic to my left is shouting. Both offside flags have been raised in succession and he is perplexed, to put it mildly, that the game wasn't stopped even as Chelsea emerged with the ball. Watford get a decision after the referee played the advantage, with Tudor being booked. 'Offside! Unbelievable!' complains the blue-hatted man. One phase of play remains.

Marriott's hail Mary is headed clear by Hughes. Ryan Andrews nods it back into the area. Adrian Blake knocks it to Watford sub Enoch Muwonge who finds an iota of space in a crowded penalty area. He gets a shot in eight yards out. The ground takes a breath in.

Harvey Vale, whose goal put Chelsea ahead, extends his long left leg and makes an impeccable block. It is 'as good as a goal' according to the summariser on the stream. He is correct. Right place, right time. Again. Prince Adegoke gives Vale a bearhug. The full-time whistle goes.

Watford are out of the 2021/22 FA Youth Cup. Captain Will Hall collapses to his knees. His namesake Lewis Hall gives him a pat on the head. Vale does the same with Kyreece Lisbie, then gives the officials fist bumps. 'My word, they have had to work for this!' says the commentator. I spot the guy in an FA anorak putting away his tablet PC. It turns out he is a referee's assessor. 'He did great tonight,' he says, agreeing with me.

Some of the Watford lads head over to the hoarding to speak to friends and family before going for a post-match shower and debrief. Tobi Adeyemo looks wiser than his 16 years, while Shaq Forde looks ready for a loan spell at a League Two club.

The loveliest sight of the evening is seeing the Blake family pose with their boy Adrian at the hoardings, with the Graham Taylor Stand in the background and the floodlights beaming on to the playing surface. I catch Blake just before he poses and wish him well for his career. Not many teenagers get to play on a Premier League pitch, seldom fewer score, and I wonder how hard it will be to readjust to longer, muddier grass.

In conversation with the club media, coach Tom Hart says he is 'heartbroken'. He adds, 'They gave us everything and worked their absolute socks off. They created enough chances to probably win it. A lot of other teams could have crumbled.

'[Academy director] Richard Johnson just came in and said how everyone is so proud of them. It's a reminder of what they are capable of doing. They need to show that more often. It will hurt right now but I am sure they will remember it.'

Tobi Adeyemo thanks God, his family and the supporters. 'It was a lovely game. The boys dug very deep. We knew we had to work hard and stick with each other. I am delighted with my goal.

'Tom Hart told me, "You can get the boys going," so I took it under my wing. I had belief in the team, belief in myself. Under the lights of Vicarage Road you couldn't ask for anything more. I'm going to make sure that I'll keep the same standard into the next game and the next game.'

Just over 36 hours later, while Chelsea's under-18s were playing against Brighton, the senior team started a game at the Etihad Stadium against Manchester City by fielding not a single British, let alone English, player. City began with a front three of Raheem Sterling, Jack Grealish and Phil Foden, the most famous product of the Etihad Campus.

Admittedly, Mason Mount and Callum Hudson-Odoi came off the bench seconds before Chelsea let in the only goal of the game. It was scored by former Blue Kevin de Bruyne, who did not even come through the academy to find that he had no place in the Chelsea team.

Nonetheless, it is the 199th game in a row that Chelsea have had a graduate in the matchday squad. Lewis Hall was included in the 200th game alongside Ruben Loftus-Cheek, Mason Mount and Callum Hudson-Odoi.

Chelsea celebrate a run of 200 games, which is creditable. The Manchester United streak is now above 4,100. Seven decades after first winning the FA Youth Cup, the club are still turning kids into champions.

Conclusion

A Youth Cup All-Time XI

THAT'S THE story of the FA Youth Cup. Or at least *a* story.
The aim of this book is also to attract you to this
competition. The Youth Cup may not be held in the same
esteem as the EFL Cup or even the EFL Trophy, and the quality
of the teams is dependent on which players under the age of 18
are available on the night.

I have set out what the FA Youth Cup seeks to do, starting
the path from kids to champions over the last 70 years of
English football. I have spoken to players from the 1960s
(George Scott), 1980s (Neil Heaney), the post-Bosman Era
(Lee Fowler) and what I call the post-modern football era (Rio
Campbell). Watford coach Tom Hart talked about the role the
academy system plays, while Rocco Dean and Merv Payne gave
a fan's-eye view. Nick Szczepanik was paid to report on football
matches, something Ian Doyle still does on Merseyside.

Starting in the preliminary rounds, I headed to Canons
Park to watch Barnet, Norbiton to watch Chelsea and Plough
Lane to watch AFC Wimbledon. I did my best impression
of a *When Saturday Comes* match review by wandering up to
Vicarage Road to watch the FA Youth Cup fourth-round tie

between Watford and Chelsea, which was a much better game than I thought it was going to be. It just proves that energy matters as much as quality.

I delivered this book in January 2022 so it could be published in late spring, which means I couldn't chronicle the final rounds of the tournament or finish with a report on how one team of kids became Youth Cup champions. The quarter-final draw was made just before the book was delivered to Pitch, with all 16 teams from round five in the pot.

Blackburn Rovers or Sheffield Wednesday v Cambridge United or Nottingham Forest

Wolverhampton Wanderers or Tottenham Hotspur v Charlton Athletic or Brighton & Hove Albion

Manchester United or Everton v AFC Bournemouth or Leicester City

Liverpool or Chelsea v Blackpool or Newcastle United

You can write a history of English football through these 16 clubs, from the early triumphs of Blackburn in the 1890s, to the First Division wins by Forest, Wolves and Spurs. The struggles of Charlton and Brighton read as tragicomedies in parts, while Leicester were the 5,000/1 shot that won the 2016 Premier League. Plus, of course, there are the combined 39 titles of Manchester United and Liverpool, which will be detailed in a forthcoming book by Phil McNulty and Jim White.

The tie of the round was played on 29 January 2022 at Kirkby on the Liverpool academy pitch. Throughout the story, as you have read, I was keen to point out that Liverpool and Chelsea had both included scholars in their line-ups throughout the 2021/22 season. Many of them featured in the fifth-round game: Kaide Gordon and Melkamu Frauendorf for Liverpool; Harvey Vale, Charlie Webster and Lewis Hall for Chelsea.

In decades past you could only find out the starting XIs if you were inside the stadium or via BBC local radio or TV if they were by chance covering the game. The home line-up was posted to Liverpool's 19 million Twitter followers; although the @ChelseaYouth feed did post it, Chelsea's account chose not to do so, instead posting a photo of Chelsea flags holding a banner with the captain KTBFFH, 'Keep the blue flag flying high'. As an interesting experiment with which to conclude this story, I thought I would keep two tabs open, one with the Chelsea Youth account and the other with the Liverpool account open. I will revert, as in the last chapter, to the vivid present.

Just above a post promoting a pre-match interview with Liverpool under-18s coach Marc Bridge-Wilkinson, a procession of first-team players wishes Chinese fans well over the Lunar New Year in a 15-second video clip. I wonder how many of those fans know about Liverpool's four Youth Cup wins, and indeed the story of George Scott from the Shankly days.

Depressingly, under the post announcing kick-off, several fans want the club to 'announce Díaz', a winger with whom Liverpool are linked. The match is played two days before the closing of the January transfer window, in which Liverpool have made no new signings.

Five minutes in, and the four-time winners lead the nine-time champions. 'WHAT A START!!!!' reads the @LFC feed. 'Luke Chambers drives down the left and smashes the ball across the keeper to put the Reds ahead.' They also put the 'flex' emoji. I learn a new word, 'transfersexuals', in a reply to this news, which has no connection to Chambers's brilliant strike.

Chelsea announce the goal event with a mistyped tweet, which reads as follows, 'Chelsea luke Luke Chambers run forward unchallenged from left-back and that affords him the time to lash past Adegoke into the far corner.' In the first reply to this, someone calls it 'terrible defending'. Well, as anyone following Chelsea's scholars know, it has been very tough for them to keep clean sheets.

Liverpool's feed puts up footage of the goal and, for me, it is an avoidable goal. The left-back, who joined the club's pre-academy at the age of six, is captain of the side. He picks the ball up on the halfway line and, tapping it forwards, his momentum carries him towards goal. He has so much space to run into that by the time he reaches the Chelsea area, he probably thinks he may as well have a shot, considering the game has just started and he has the energy to sprint back to his position. The ball flies into the opposite corner and I don't think Prince Adegoke has a chance. He has been let down by his defenders, though.

After another Liverpool chance, the Chelsea feed notes that the team 'haven't found their footing in this one yet'. They soon do, with a Soonsup-Bell cross 'that ended up more of a shot' and another 'great move' that is cleared by Liverpool. All in all, however, this is 'a lacklustre first half an hour'.

On 38 minutes, Liverpool double their score, 'Real trouble for Chelsea. Balagizi surges through a wide open midfield, plays in Gordon and he beats Adegoke.' Liverpool's feed reports that Balazigi 'skips past' the defender and Gordon 'places the ball into the back of the net' with an added 'hands in prayer' emoji.

That is Kaide Gordon, signed from Derby County in 2021. He had been a Ram from the age of eight, working through the age groups with his much older brother Kellan, who dropped down to League Two and played for Swindon Town, Lincoln City and Mansfield Town. As Kaide prepared for the Liverpool-Chelsea game, Kellan was helping the Stags beat Leyton Orient to move to sixth in League Two. One of the goals was scored by Jordan Bowery, who had been released from Derby before signing a scholarship with nearby Chesterfield. Since then, his career has taken him to Aston Villa, Rotherham United and, believe it or not, Orient themselves.

At half-time Chelsea make a double change, bringing on Silko Thomas and Malik Mothersille, but they have to wait for the restart due to one of the officials picking up an injury. Chelsea's Twitter feed is adding more criticism and commentary than Liverpool's, including a shot on goal by Thomas.

Thus the third Liverpool goal, 'a superb counter-attack ... finished off in style by Oakley Cannonier' on the hour, comes as a surprise to Liverpool fans. Chelsea fans will despair as the goal comes 'on a break from the corner and those huge moments matter'. One Liverpool fan quite correctly calls the scorer 'the goat [greatest] of all ball boys'.

With 20 minutes to go in the game, good old Charlie Webster 'smashes one in from 25 yards out'. I saw him try at least two of those against Watford but nothing went right, so it proves that if you keep practising, one of them will go in at some point, hopefully when it matters. The shot takes a deflection off Liverpool defender Lee Jonas, who switched sides from Everton after choosing to sign for Liverpool's under-12s. Thus he would not work with Paul Tait.

Liverpool's account is rather slower to update fans, who still thought it was 3-0 when Chelsea scored again to peg back the deficit to one. Jude Soonsup-Bell got his head on the end of a Lewis Hall 'hanging cross and it's game on'. I was impressed by the forward both times I saw him even though Thomas, Vale and Hall upstaged him. It is moments like this, however, 3-0 down away from home in a Youth Cup tie, that will really show whether these young technicians have the talent and mentality to show themselves as future professionals.

Upset that Liverpool's feed is so lax, I focus on the Chelsea feed, which does not have people demanding that the club signs another winger, probably because Soonsup-Bell has already played for the first team. As I was hoping for, Etonian scholar Tudor Mendel-Idowu comes on for Chelsea's third change. Lewis Hall has missed an attempt at goal after good work from Soonsup-Bell and Vale.

At this point, it feels like I am following the bar at the bottom of a match simulation on *Football Manager*. On 87 minutes, Chelsea equalise and in my head I see the bar flashing blue. 'A Liverpool clearance rebounds off Mothersille and flies into the back of the net!'

I cannot believe that Chelsea have come from behind but, as I saw in both the third and fourth rounds, this team is the cream of Cobham, a set of elite young lads who know that they are capable of adding their names to the club's roll of honour.

The Athletic's Chelsea reporter Simon Johnson turned the stream off at 3-0 down, ironically adding, 'Now 3-3. Didn't miss much.' He was able to see Soonsup-Bell narrowly miss a chance to win the match. Chelsea fans would have to watch the game on the club website or, if they were in the UK, via the 5th Stand app. As for Liverpool fans watching on LFC TV or online, their evenings have become a little less comfortable.

The next update simply reads 'GOAL 4-3 CHELSEA MENDEL IDOWU'. Utterly incredible. The Etonian has come good, getting on the end of a Silko Thomas cross, 'Mendel-Idowu throws himself at it and gets just enough on it to get it over the line (90+5).' If his dad used his prayers that day, then God has blessed Chelsea with a comeback.

As the people who run the Chelsea Youth Twitter calm themselves, I patiently wait for confirmation of the result, which is announced as 'one of the most improbable and memorable Youth Cup comebacks ever'. I wonder if the referee was tempted to blow the whistle straight away, as Pierluigi Collina did in the 1999 UEFA Champions League Final.

For Chelsea, the spoils of victory; for Liverpool, a harsh lesson in how to fail to see out a game. The @LFC feed eventually pipes up with news of 'a second-half comeback from Chelsea', which does not please the thumb warriors.

It would not surprise me at all if, by the time this book reaches you, Chelsea have won a tenth FA Youth Cup. The final of the 2021/22 edition took place on April 30, just as copies of this book were being sent to various warehouses or bookshelves. If your curiosity has been piqued by any reports on the final, thank you for coming to this book to learn more.

I am sure many readers used to doodle football XIs in the back of exercise books. I certainly did. I think this would be an apt way with which to end the story.

You are welcome to send your teams to the Pitch Twitter account @pitchpublishing and I'll see if my team can beat yours.

Goalkeeper: Kevin O'Callaghan
Keen-eyed readers will know that Cally was a successful winger and penalty taker for Millwall and Ipswich Town, but Merv Payne chortled and gave me his blessing when I told him I was going to put Cally in goal. He's on film, too, albeit in *Escape to Victory* in which he kept goal for the Allies.

Full-backs: Steve Perryman and Nigel Gibbs
Two men who came through the ranks to represent their team and only their team; they might as well be Mr Spurs and Mr Watford (with apologies to Luther Blissett). They both remained in the game after they retired from playing, showing

their dedication to the sport that extended from kids to another generation of kids.

Centre-backs: Paul Lake and Everald La Ronde
Lake's memoir *I'm Not Really Here* is a proper football story, which began as a star of the 1986 Manchester City team. La Ronde's name deserves to be better known but the 1980s was a less than ideal time for a black footballer to advance in the professional game.

Central midfielders: Nathaniel Chalobah and Robert 'Bobby' Charlton
Given that I saw a teenage Chalobah play his first full season in men's football at Watford, I have to put him in as a defensive midfielder. He would get the ball to Bobby, the World Cup winner who survived the Munich air disaster to become a hero to millions.

Wide midfielders: George Best and Joe Cole
There have been plenty of books written about Bestie, so there's little point emphasising how he kicked football into the celebrity era, primarily because he was very good at his job. Cole was so good at his age that Alex Ferguson invited him on to the team bus for an FA Cup Final in order to tempt him to sign for Manchester United. Though Ferguson managed to secure Rio Ferdinand (via Leeds), he could not do the same with Cole, who lit up the Chelsea team just as he had done so with West Ham.

Attacking midfielder: Paul Gascoigne
In a floating role in front of the midfield two, the man who became Gazza can bring his street-fighting skills to this side. Anthony Potts has included some fine anecdotes in his book *Losing My Spurs*, which shows the competitive nature and generosity of the man he calls 'the last of the mavericks'.

Centre-forward: Jimmy Greaves

No contest whatsoever. He scored on his debut for every club he played for, and he's also the subject of a book in 2022 by Norman Giller, Jim's partner in sobriety.

Substitutes

Peter Bonetti

Bonetti was unfairly blamed for England's loss against West Germany at the 1970 FIFA World Cup. The Chelsea keeper was known as 'The Cat' because of his agility.

Duncan Edwards

Bobby Charlton has often praised Edwards, whose life was claimed by the Munich tragedy which spared Charlton and his manager Matt Busby. Of all the Babes, Edwards was the one with the most promising future, thanks to his versatility and enormous calf muscles.

George Scott

A mainstay of Liverpool's reserve team in the 1960s, he will forever lament the chance he missed in the first leg of the FA Youth Cup Final against West Ham United. His memoir is worth a read.

Lee Fowler

The Coventry City kid who was close to the Wales senior squad ended up travelling around England in search of a dressing room. His memoir, should he choose to write one, will be a superb, smart read.

Neil Heaney

The lad from the Boro played on the wing for the Arsenal youth team. After a respectable career, Neil retired early to go into an office job where the lessons he learned from Pat Rice are put into use.

Bibliography

Barclay, Patrick, *Football – Bloody Hell!: The Biography of Alex Ferguson* (Yellow Jersey, 2010)

Barton, Wayne, *Fergie's Fledglings* (Vertical Editions, 2014)

Birnie, Lionel, *Enjoy The Game: Watford Football Club, The Story of the Eighties* (Peloton Publishing, 2010)

Bishop, John, *How To Grow Old* (Ebury, 2019)

Calvin, Michael, *Family: Life, Death and Football* (Integr8, 2011)

Calvin, Michael, *Whose Game Is It Anyway? Football, Life, Love & Loss* (Pitch, 2021)

Carragher, Jamie, *Carra* (Transworld, 2008)

Carrick, Michael, *Between The Lines* (Bonnier Books, 2019)

Gatenby, Phill and Waldon, Andrew, *Teenage Kicks: The Story of Manchester City's 1986 FA Youth Cup Team* (Empire Publications, 2013)

Hilaire, Vince, *Vince – The Autobiography* (Biteback, 2018)

Lake, Paul, *I'm Not Really Here: A Life of Two Halves* (Arrow, 2011)

McGuire, Brendan, *Growing Up with the Trinity* (Pitch, 2019)

Payne, Merv, *Ordinary Boys: The Class of '79* (independently published, 2020)

Potts, Anthony, *Losing My Spurs: Gazza, The Grief and The Glory* (Pitch, 2022)

Redknapp, Harry, *Always Managing* (Ebury, 2013)

Schindler, Colin, *George Best and 21 Others* (Headline, 2004)

Scott, George, *The Lost Shankly Boy* (Pitch, 2020)

Souness, Graham, *Football: My Life, My Passion* (Headline, 2017)

Vardy, Jamie, *From Nowhere, My Story* (Ebury, 2016)

Venables, Terry, *The Autobiography* (Michael Joseph, 1994)

Walters, Mark, *Wingin It* (Pitch, 2018)

Wilkinson, Howard, *Charter For Quality*, accessed via sportspath.typepad.com/files/charter-for-quality.pdf

Podcasts

Coach Gerald Lami

Kickback with Nedum

The Official Everton Podcast

Training Ground Guru

News Sources

The Athletic

The Guardian

The Times

Website Articles

Glanvill, Rick, 'Future Blues: A History of the Founding of Chelsea Juniors'. https://www.chelseafc.com/en/news/2020/05/31/long-read--future-blues---a-history-of-the-founding-of-chelsea-j

Also available at all good book stores

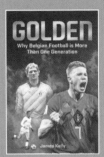

9781801501057

9781801501323

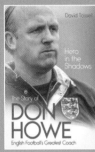

9781801500876

9781801500753

9781801500739

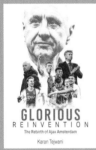

9781801500692

9781801500586

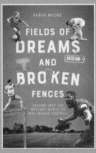

9781801501002

9781801500470